More Advance Praise for *This Nonviolent Stuff'll Get You Killed*

"What most of us think we know about the central role of nonviolence in the long freedom struggle in the South is not so much wrong as blinkered. Or so Charles Cobb says in this passionate, intellectually disciplined reordering of the conventional narrative to include armed self-defense as a central component of the black movement's success. Read it and be reminded that history is not a record etched in stone by journalists and academics, but a living stream, fed and redirected by the bottom-up witness of its participants."—Hodding Carter III, Professor of Public Policy, University of North Carolina at Chapel Hill

"Popular culture washes the complexity out of so many things. Charles Cobb works mightily against that torrent. *This Nonviolent Stuff'll Get You Killed* shows that the simplistic popular understanding of the black Freedom Movement obscures a far richer story. Cobb defies the popular narrative with accounts of the grit and courage of armed stalwarts of the modern movement who invoked the ancient right of self-defense under circumstances where we should expect nothing less. This book is an important contribution to a story that is becoming increasingly difficult to ignore."—Nicholas Johnson, Professor of Law, Fordham Law School, and author of *Negroes and the Gun: The Black Tradition of Arms*

"*This Nonviolent Stuff'll Get You Killed* is the most important movement book in many years. Charles Cobb uses long-standing confusion over the distinction between violence and nonviolence as an entrée to rethinking many fundamental misconceptions about what the civil rights movement was and why it was so powerful. This level of nuance requires a disciplined observer, an engaged participant, and a lyrical writer. Cobb is all these."—Charles M. Payne, author of *I've Got the Light of Freedom: The Organizing Tradition and the Mississippi Freedom Struggle*

"Any book that has as its central thesis that armed self-defense was essential both to the existence and the success of the civil rights movement is bound to stir up controversy. But Charles Cobb, combining the rigor of a scholar with the experience (and passion) of a community organizer, has made his case. This book is a major contribution to the historiography of the black freedom struggle. More than that, it adds a new chapter to the story of the local people who, often armed, protected the organizers and their communities during the turbulent civil rights years."
—John Dittmer, author of *Local People: The Struggle for Civil Rights in Mississippi*

"Charles Cobb's *This Nonviolent Stuff'll Get You Killed* is a marvelous contribution to our understanding of the modern black freedom struggle. With wonderful storytelling skills and drawing on his unparalleled access to movement participants, he situates armed self-defense in the context of a complex movement and in conversation with both nonviolence *and* community organizing. Cobb writes from personal experience on the frontlines of SNCC's voter registration work while also using the skills of a journalist, historian, and teacher. The result is a compelling and wonderfully nuanced book that will appeal to specialists and, more importantly, anyone interested in human rights and the freedom struggle." —Emilye Crosby, author of *A Little Taste of Freedom: The Black Freedom Struggle in Claiborne County, Mississippi* and editor of *Civil Rights History from the Ground Up*

"This long overdue book revises the image of black people in the South as docile and frightened. It tells *our* story, demonstrating that black people have always been willing to stand their ground and do whatever was necessary to free themselves from bondage and to defend their families and communities. This is a must-read for understanding the southern Freedom Movement."—David Dennis, former Mississippi Director, the Congress of Racial Equality (CORE) and Director, Southern Initiative of the Algebra Project

THIS NONVIOLENT STUFF'LL GET YOU KILLED

THIS
NONVIOLENT
STUFF'LL
GET YOU
KILLED

How Guns Made the Civil Rights Movement Possible

CHARLES E. COBB JR.

BASIC BOOKS

A Member of the Perseus Books Group

New York

Books published by Basic Books are available at special discounts for bulk purchases

in the United States by corporations, institutions, and other organizations. For more information,

please contact the Special Markets Department at the Perseus Books Group, 2300 Chestnut Street,

Suite 200, Philadelphia, PA 19103, or call (800) 810-4145, ext. 5000,

or e-mail special.markets@perseusbooks.com.

Library of Congress Cataloging-in-Publication Data

Cobb, Charles E., Jr.

This nonviolent stuff'll get you killed : how guns made the civil rights movement possible /

Charles E. Cobb.

pages cm

ISBN 978-0-465-03310-2 (hardback) — ISBN 978-0-465-08095-3 (ebook)

1. African Americans—Civil rights—History—20th century. 2. Civil rights movements—United

States—History—20th century. 3. Self-defense—United States—History—20th century.

4. Firearms—Law and legislation—United States—History—20th century. 5. Gun control—United

States—History—20th century. I. Title.

E185.61.C633 2014

323.1196'073—dc23

2013045809

1 3 5 7 9 10 8 6 4 2

This book is dedicated to

Ella Baker, Herbert Lee, Medgar Evers, Amzie Moore, Fannie Lou Hamer, Annie Devine, Victoria Gray Adams, Aaron Henry, Hartman Turnbow, C. O. Chinn, Hazel Palmer, Vernon Dahmer, Laura McGhee, Robert Burns, Cleveland Jordan, Joe and Rebecca McDonald, Janie Brewer, Henry Sias, E. W. Steptoe, Alyene Quin, Curtis Conway "C. C." Bryant, Webb "Super Cool Daddy" Owens, George Metcalfe, Wharlest Jackson, Joseph Mallisham, Harry T. and Harriet Moore, Henry J. Kirksey, Annie "Mama Dolly" Raines, Ernest "Chilly Willy" Thomas, Frederick Douglass Kirkpatrick, Robert Hicks, Charles Sims, A. Z. Young, Vernon Johns, Golden Frinks, Annie Lee Cooper, Amelia Boynton, John Hulett, Reverend Fred Shuttlesworth, Septima Clark, Reverend Samuel Wells, Robert Williams, Jim Forman, Ann Braden, Myles Horton, and all the other strong elders who kept a-comin' on, kept us safe, taught us much, and made us better.

**It is also dedicated to the memory of
these freedom fighters of my generation:**

Cynthia Washington, Ed Brown, Ruby Doris Smith Robinson, Stokely Carmichael, Bob Mants, George Raymond, Lawrence Guyot, Sam Block, John Wilson, Ralph Featherstone, Prathia Hall, Richard Haley, Oretha Castle Haley, Sammy Younge, Endesha Ida Mae Holland, Fay Bellamy, Mimi Shaw Hayes, Mendy Samstein, Hellen O'Neal McCray, Willie McCray, Cordell Reagon, James Orange, Jimmy Travis, Annelle Ponder, John Buffington, Matthew Jones, June Johnson, George Ware, Amanda Bowens Perdew, Jim Bevel, Billy Stafford, James Peacock, Randy Battle, Lafayette Surney, Mario Savio, Ralph Allen, Michael "Mickey" Schwerner, James "J. E." Chaney, Andrew Goodman, Bill "Winky" Hall, Patricia Stevens Due, L. C. Dorsey, Sam Shirah, Frank Cieciorka, and Butch Conn.

Their life force remains with us, strengthening us. *Ashe!*

I never was a true believer in nonviolence, but was willing to go along [with it] for the sake of the strategy and goals. [However] we heard that James Chaney had been beaten to death before they shot him. The thought of being beat up, jailed, even being shot, was one kinda thing. The thought of being beaten to death without being able to fight back put the fear of God in me. Also, I was my mother's only child with some responsibility to go home in relatively one piece and I decided that it would be an unforgivable sin to willingly let someone kill my mother's only child without a fight. [So] I acquired an automatic handgun to sit in the top of that outstanding black patent and tan leather handbag that I carried. I don't think that I ever had to fire it; I never shot anyone, but the potential was there. And I still would hurt anyone if necessary to protect my son and grandson and his wife.

—Cynthia Washington, former field secretary of the Student Nonviolent Coordinating Committee

CONTENTS

Illustrations begin following page 148.

AUTHOR'S NOTE

One of the crucial but mostly ignored aspects of the freedom struggle of the 1950s and '60s is how near we were in time and collective historical memory to slavery and the post–Civil War Reconstruction era. Each generation of black people carries a memory of the struggles taken on by the generations that preceded it, and that memory settles in the collective soul and becomes the foundation for the struggles of one's own generation. To borrow words from author and professor Jan Carew, we are haunted by "ghosts in our blood."

I was born in 1943, just eighty years after President Abraham Lincoln signed the Emancipation Proclamation—a nanosecond in historical time. I was told stories of my family's enslavement by my great aunt Hattie Kendrick, who was told them by her father and other relatives who had been born into slavery. My grandmother Ruby Moyse Kendrick, whose mother was born into slavery, was a publicist for the National Association of Colored Women's Clubs founded by Mary Church Terrell, who was born the year Lincoln signed the Emancipation Proclamation. In 1950—when I was seven and she was eighty-six—Mrs. Terrell was leading sit-ins and pickets protesting segregation and employment discrimination in Washington, D.C.

These stories represent but tiny drops in the great pool of black historical memory, yet they greatly affected people who, like me, joined the Freedom Movement with the winds of history at our backs. Indeed, most of the adults we worked with in the South were only two or three generations removed from slavery or its immediate aftermath. For example, the grandparents of Fannie Lou Hamer were born into slavery. Others we worked with were children during the violent horrors that followed the destruction of Reconstruction governments and the "redemption" of white supremacy, an era that spilled over into the early years of the twentieth century. Yet these men and women could also remember that even during this time of terror, there were pockets where black authority lingered. They could point to instances of courage, rebellion, and resistance as well as to moments of brutal oppression.

This book, although analytical and carefully researched, is not "objective" in the strictest sense of that word; rather, it is a fleshing out and contextualizing of the stories I began hearing in childhood, continued to hear as a young Freedom Movement activist in the South, and have been reflecting on all my adult life. Importantly, this book is also more than a collection of stories and personal reminiscences about the southern Freedom Movement of the 1950s and '60s. It is an effort to think carefully about the past and to understand its lessons, recognizing that, as William Faulkner once put it, "The past is never dead. It's not even past." My goal has been to help us understand ourselves as a nation, cutting through platitudes and romance about the southern Freedom Movement as well as persistent stereotypes about black people. I have wished to demonstrate in an unexpected way how black people and their responses to white-supremacist oppression continue and advance the struggle that was articulated as a constitutional ideal in the formation of the United States: "to form a more perfect union."

I draw on and embed in this story reflections and analyses rooted in my experiences as a Student Nonviolent Coordinating Committee (SNCC) field secretary from 1962 to 1967. This book is neither a memoir nor an autobiography, yet in some respects it is my story. SNCC was unusual in placing its field secretaries in rural southern communities to work from the bottom up instead of from the top down. Living among the downtrodden but resilient black men and women of the Deep South, I underwent a subtle conversion. The principles and illusions I had brought with me—of nonviolence, of the uniformity of the southern black experience—were reshaped by the men and women I encountered there.

Especially important among these life-changing adults was Ella Josephine Baker, a name that should be much better known, for we young people in the Freedom Movement were and are in many ways her political children. Of all the adults we encountered, she did the most to steer us into grassroots organizing. We in SNCC were radicalized by working with people in their homes and communities much more than by ideology. Dimensions of black culture and black community experience opened up and became clearer to us. The real story of the southern Freedom Movement lies with this work, and neither what took place in the South nor what the United States is today can be fully comprehended without it.

THIS NONVIOLENT STUFF'LL GET YOU KILLED

INTRODUCTION

The struggle of black people in America for freedom, justice, and self-definition stretches from the colonial and antebellum slaveholding eras to the twenty-first century, but its intensity has varied from one period to the next. One of the most intense periods occurred in the 1950s and '60s, when the struggle was usually associated with the tactical and strategic use of nonviolence. Scores of Afro-Americans, many of them still too young to vote, took to the streets to peacefully assert their rights as citizens. In retaliation, men, women, and children were surrounded by raging mobs or assaulted by helmeted white policemen wielding batons and fire hoses. The photographs and film footage of these events shocked the American public and rallied popular support for such historic legislation as the Civil Rights Act of 1964 and the Voting Rights Act of 1965, laws that to varying degrees continue to protect Americans of every color and creed.

But although nonviolence was crucial to the gains made by the freedom struggle of the 1950s and '60s, those gains could not have been achieved without the complementary and still underappreciated practice of armed self-defense. The claim that armed self-defense was a necessary aspect of the civil rights movement is still controversial. However, wielding weapons, especially firearms, let both participants in nonviolent struggle and their sympathizers protect themselves and others under terrorist attack for their civil rights activities. This willingness to use deadly force ensured the survival not only of countless brave men and women but also of the freedom struggle itself.

This was nothing new. Armed self-defense (or, to use a term preferred by some, "armed resistance") as part of black struggle began not in the 1960s with angry "militant" and "radical" young Afro-Americans, but in the earliest years of the United States as one of African people's responses to oppression. This tradition, which culminates with the civil rights struggles and achievements of the mid-1960s, cannot be understood independently or outside its broader historical context. In every decade of the nation's history, brave and determined black men and women picked up guns to defend themselves and their communities.

Thus the tradition of armed self-defense in Afro-American history cannot be disconnected from the successes of what today is called the nonviolent civil rights movement. Participants in that movement always saw themselves as part of a centuries-long history of black life and struggle. Guns in no way contradicted the lessons of that history. Indeed, the idea of nonviolent struggle was newer in the black community, and it was protected in many ways by gunfire and the threat of gunfire. Simply put: because nonviolence worked so well as a tactic for effecting change and was demonstrably improving their lives, some black people chose to use weapons to defend the nonviolent Freedom Movement. Although it is counterintuitive, any discussion of guns in the movement must therefore also include substantial discussion of nonviolence, and vice versa. This book does that.

I should note that although I sometimes seem to use "civil rights movement" and "Freedom Movement" interchangeably, they in fact have two quite separate though closely related meanings. By "civil rights movement" I mean the efforts to secure equal rights under the law, as with the passage of the 1965 Voting Rights Act. The "Freedom Movement" is a larger idea whose goal is the achievement of civil rights, civil liberties, and the liberated consciousness of self and community. It recognizes that law alone cannot uproot white supremacy, ever creative and insidious in its forms and practices, and that civil rights law alone cannot create a new liberated sense of self and human capacity. In my thinking on the differences between the "civil rights movement" and the "Freedom Movement," I have been greatly influenced by the "freedom rights" postulation laid out by historian Hasan Kwame Jeffries:

> Framing the civil rights movement as a fight for freedom rights
> acknowledges the centrality of slavery and emancipation to con-

ceptualizations of freedom; incorporates the long history of black protest dating back to the daybreak of freedom and extending beyond the Black Power era; recognizes the African Americans' civil and human rights objectives; and captures the universality of these goals. Moreover, it allows for regional and temporal differentiation, moments of ideological radicalization and periods of social movement formation.

The southern Freedom Movement of the 1960s was broad in its objectives and its strategies, which helps explain the seemingly paradoxical coexistence of guns and nonviolence within it. As noted in 1964 by Robert P. "Bob" Moses, director of the Mississippi project of the Student Nonviolent Coordinating Committee (SNCC): "It's not contradictory for a farmer to say he's nonviolent and also pledge to shoot a marauder's head off." A story Stokely Carmichael liked to tell was of bringing an elderly woman to vote in Lowndes County, Alabama: "She had to be 80 years old and going to vote for the first time in her life. . . . That ol' lady came up to us, went into her bag, and produced this enormous, rusty Civil War–looking old pistol. 'Best you hol' this for me, son. I'ma go cast my vote now.'"

The 1955–1956 bus boycott in Montgomery, Alabama, the student sit-in movement that began in 1960, and the Freedom Rides of 1961 all persuasively demonstrated that nonviolent resistance was an effective way of fighting for civil rights. These were not acts of hate or brutality toward white people, who were themselves ignorant of their imprisonment by a system that led them to believe in white supremacy. They were, instead, aggressive confrontations that challenged the *system*, and recognizing this refutes the notion that nonviolence was a passive tactic. Nevertheless, it was startling to see the willingness of southern civil rights activists to put themselves in harm's way and their refusal to respond with violence when assaulted. Almost immediately nonviolent resistance was criticized as dangerous foolishness that reflected weakness, even cowardly submission. Writing in 1957 about the Montgomery bus boycott, W. E. B. Du Bois expressed great skepticism about nonviolence: "No normal human being of trained intelligence is going to fight the man who will not fight back . . . but suppose they are wild beasts or wild men? To yield to the rush of the tiger is death, nothing less." Six years later Malcolm X, then a leader of the Nation of Islam, showed greater hostility and less restraint than Du Bois: he denounced Martin Luther King Jr. as a modern Uncle Tom subsidized by whites "to teach the Negroes to be defenseless."

Their reactions suggest that neither Dr. Du Bois nor Malcolm X could grasp the fact that nonviolence—although risky, as any challenge to oppression always is—was not passive, that it provided an effective means of directly challenging white supremacy with more than just rhetoric. Acts of nonviolent resistance contributed mightily to ending the mental paralysis that had long kept many black people trapped in fear and subservient to white supremacy, reluctant to even try to take control over their own lives despite the fact that slavery had ended roughly a century earlier. The principled, militant dignity of nonviolent resistance also won nationwide sympathy for the idea of extending civil rights to black people.

Early proponents of nonviolence—such as Bayard Rustin, Pauli Murray, or James Farmer, founder of the Congress of Racial Equality (CORE)—embraced its dynamism and militancy. By the 1960s others also embraced it for these reasons, especially students attending historically black colleges and universities, giving the southern Freedom Movement new force. Former SNCC chairman Stokely Carmichael, because of his 1966 Black Power speech, is not usually associated with pacifism or nonviolence. Yet in his autobiography, he credits nonviolent activism for marking the path he followed from Howard University into political engagement: "[It] gave our generation—particularly in the South—the means by which to confront an entrenched and violent racism. It offered a way for *large* numbers of [African Americans] to join the struggle. Nothing passive in that." Extending this thought, historian Vincent G. Harding, who worked closely with Martin Luther King Jr. and the Southern Christian Leadership Conference (SCLC) he founded, emphasizes,

> Our struggle was not just against something, but was trying to bring something into being. Always at the heart of nonviolent struggle was, and still is, a vision of a new society. Nonviolence enabled people to see something in themselves and others of *what could be*; they had been captured by the possibility of what could be.

Few involved with the southern Freedom Movement would deny that non-violence was a creative and proactive way of challenging the status quo, or that it succeeded in doing so even if every problem was not solved.

By no means, however, were most in the black community committed to nonviolence as a way of life. To be sure, in a significant portion of the southern black community, nonviolent resistance tapped deeply into a vein of righteousness that was rooted in Afro-Christian values and provided moral guidance in a political struggle where hate and anger could easily blind and become overwhelming. But an idealized acceptance of the kind of redemptive love and suffering expressed in the New Testament is the closest black people have come to embracing the philosophy of nonvio-lence en masse. Black Christians, however, have also readily embraced the Old Testament, with all its furies and violence. A pre–Civil War black spir-itual that has always been sung hopefully, even exuberantly, in black churches and by black gospel groups vividly illustrates this:

> If I could I surely would
> Stand on the rock where Moses stood.
> Pharaoh's army got drown-ded.
> Oh Mary don't you weep.

It is not difficult to understand Afro-Americans' skepticism. The courage and discipline required for a total commitment to nonviolence was and still is alien to U.S. culture—a culture created as much by black people as by white people, and one driven by the principle that might makes right. And although black people (like Native American peoples) have often suffered as a result of this principle, they have never had much moral objection to the idea of armed self-defense. Indeed, self-defense was a crucial part of life for many black Americans, especially in the South. The prevailing system of white supremacy in the South was enforced by violence, and black people sometimes used the threat of an armed response to survive. Nonviolent organizers had to come to terms with this reality when they attempted to make inroads with southern black communities in the 1950s and '60s. There was always resistance to the idea of nonviolence, even though it won some acceptance as a sometimes useful tactic. Bob Moses in 1964 expressed the futility of expecting black communities to surrender their right to protect themselves from terrorists: "Self-defense is so deeply ingrained in rural southern America that we as a small group can't affect it."

Willingness to engage in armed self-defense played an important role in the southern Freedom Movement, for without it, terrorists would have killed far more people in the movement. "I'm alive today because of the Second Amendment and the natural right to keep and bear arms," recalled activist John R. "Hunter Bear" Salter in 1994. In the early 1960s, Salter, of Native American descent, was a professor at historically black Tougaloo Southern Christian College in Mississippi and adviser to students nonviolently sitting in at segregated lunch counters and other public facilities in downtown Jackson. But he always "traveled armed," said Salter. "The knowledge that I had these weapons and was willing to use them kept enemies at bay." And the knowledge that guns would be used to defend his Tougaloo campus, well-known as a launching pad for civil rights protest and thus always a target of terrorists, also helped deter assaults against it, although it could not prevent them completely. In one campus attack, Salter remembers a bullet narrowly missing his daughter. Yet neither the local nor the federal government offered help to people targeted by this sort of terrorism, so, says Salter, "we guarded our campus—faculty and students together. . . . We let this be known. The racist attacks slackened considerably. Night-riders are cowardly people—in any time and place—and they take advantage of fear and weakness."

It cannot be emphasized enough that by asserting their right to defend themselves when attacked, the students and staff of Tougaloo were laying claim to a tradition that has safeguarded and sustained generations of black people in the United States. Yet this tradition is almost completely absent from the conventional narrative of southern civil rights struggle. The fact that individuals and organized groups across the South were willing to provide armed protection to nonviolent activists and organizers as well as to black communities targeted by terrorists is barely discussed, although organized self-defense in black communities goes back to the aftermath of the Civil War, and white fear of rebellion and weapons in black hands dates to colonial America. Guns were an integral part of southern life, especially in rural communities, and—as Moses noted in 1964—nonviolence never had a chance of usurping the traditional role of firearms in black rural life; although many rural blacks respected protesters' use of nonviolence, they also mistrusted it. Hartman Turnbow, a black Mississippi farmer and community leader, was a case in point. Turnbow welcomed the presence of movement organizers in Holmes County and even invited organizers to the area himself, but like Salter, Turnbow also "traveled armed." With tragic foresight, Turnbow bluntly warned Martin Luther King Jr. in 1964, "This nonviolent stuff ain't no good. It'll get ya killed."

Reverend King knew the risks. In fact, after the January 30, 1956, bombing of his home in Montgomery, he himself—a man of the South, after all—applied at the sheriff's office for a permit to carry a concealed weapon. He was denied the permit, but this did not stop him from having firearms in his house (although it is not clear whether or not he owned them). Journalist William Worthy learned as much on his first visit to the King parsonage in Montgomery. Worthy began to sink into an armchair, almost sitting on two pistols. "Bill, wait, wait! Couple of guns on that chair!" warned the nonviolent activist Bayard Rustin, who had accompanied Worthy to the King home. "You don't want to shoot yourself." When Rustin asked about the weapons, King responded, "Just for self-defense." They apparently were not the only weapons King kept around the house for such a purpose; Glenn Smiley of the Fellowship of Reconciliation, who during the Montgomery bus boycott advised King on techniques of nonviolent protest, described his home as "an arsenal."

The fact that guns were present inside King's home and were carried by the neighbors who took turns guarding his family and property should not be surprising. The easiest way to understand this is to begin with the basic fact that black people are human beings, so black people's responses to terrorist attacks are the same as anyone else's. As the civil rights struggle intensified in the 1950s, and with it attempts at lethal attacks, most black people did whatever they could to keep themselves and their friends and families safe and alive, and guns were never ruled out—reflecting a propensity for self-defense with weapons that has been basic to human beings since the first person stood upright and walked on the earth.

Indeed, there were few black leaders who did *not* seek and receive armed protection from within the black community. They needed it because both local law enforcement and the federal government refused to provide it. Daisy Bates, publisher of the *Arkansas State Press* newspaper and mentor to the Little Rock Nine (who in 1957 enrolled in Little Rock's Central High School, desegregating it), recalled that after the Ku Klux Klan burned a cross on her lawn and fired gunshots into her home, her husband Lucious Christopher "L. C." Bates began staying up to guard their house with a .45-caliber pistol. Friends also organized an armed volunteer patrol to protect the Bates home and the surrounding neighborhood. Daisy Bates herself sometimes carried a .32-caliber pistol in her handbag. Canton, Mississippi, businessman and movement supporter C. O. Chinn (who usually carried a pistol in his pants pocket and sometimes wore one holstered in plain sight on his hip) went a step further: he instructed friends and family members to chaperone CORE organizers wherever they went in the rural areas of the county and sometimes even in town. Like Chinn, these chaperones routinely armed themselves. Recalled former CORE field secretary Mateo "Flukie" Suarez, they "watched over us like babies. I mean, it was like having your own bodyguards."

Some black leaders were committed to nonviolence as a way of life. Borrowing from Mohandas Gandhi's concept of "soul force," they rejected the idea of harming another person even when their own lives might be at stake in civil rights struggle. King is perhaps the most prominent of these figures, although he came to this outlook slowly. Another is Reverend James M. Lawson, the mentor of the student movement in Nashville, Tennessee. The Nashville movement was a springboard for a small corps of young activists (including former SNCC chairman John Lewis, now a Georgia congressman) who were also firmly and philosophically committed to nonviolence as a way of life and who would find their way into leadership positions in SNCC and SCLC.

For most activists, however, nonviolence was simply a useful tactic, one that did not preclude self-defense whenever it was considered necessary and possible. Even King, his commitment to nonviolence as a way of life notwithstanding, acknowledged the legitimacy of self-defense and sometimes blurred the line between nonviolence and self-defense. "The first public expression of disenchantment with nonviolence arose around the question of 'self-defense,'" he wrote. "In a sense this is a false issue, for the right to defend one's home and one's person when attacked has been guaranteed through the ages by common law." Ironically, on this point blacks and whites in the South tended to be in unexpressed general agreement. It was not uncommon for black adults to teach young whites how to use a weapon for hunting, and incidents of gunplay inside black communities were frequently ignored by white authority. Although many whites were uncomfortable with the idea of blacks owning guns—especially in the 1960s—the South's powerful gun culture and weak gun control laws enabled black people to acquire and keep weapons and ammunition with relative ease.

Because guns are so common a part of southern culture, there was far less controversy about their use in the nonviolent Freedom Movement than one might imagine. Indeed, the characterizations that have so often pigeonholed movement activists and activity—"militant," "nonviolent," "radical," "left-wing," "moderate"—really only apply to a very thin layer of leadership. Ordinary people, the local folk who made up the force that really shaped southern civil rights struggle, did not use such labels for themselves. They saw themselves and spoke of themselves as being "in" the movement. The categorizations so convenient to the media and to scholarship were not part of the natural language of their community, even when these expressions seeped into their speech. In one widely circulated movement story— usually repeated with laughter and almost certainly apocryphal—an older woman active in the movement in Mississippi (or Louisiana or Alabama or Georgia or somewhere in the South, depending on who is telling the story) responds to radio, television, or newspaper denunciation of some movement activity as a communist plot by saying to a movement worker, "I'm sure glad you Communists came in here." Labels aside, it was what people encountered in everyday life that had the greatest impact on their thinking, and southern black people had a powerful incentive to arm themselves. Because the federal government was unwilling to protect southern freedom fighters, local law enforcement officers—many of them also members of the Ku Klux Klan—ignored their duty and frequently joined in terrorist acts themselves. People in black communities were willing to do what was necessary to protect fellow blacks who were risking their lives by speaking out against and actively challenging the status quo; the willingness of some to take armed defensive action enabled the civil rights movement to sustain itself during the mid-twentieth century.

Despite its importance to the southern Freedom Movement, the relationship between nonviolence and armed self-defense has been consistently overlooked and misunderstood. The dichotomy between violence and nonviolence so often imposed by historians and other analysts is not very helpful for understanding either the use of guns in local black communities or contemporaneous movement discussion and debate about self-defense. The use of guns for self-defense was not the opposite of nonviolence, as is commonly thought. Something more complicated but absolutely normal was at play. Hartman Turnbow precisely illustrates what when explaining why, without hesitation, he used his rifle to drive away night riders attacking his home: "I had a wife and I had a daughter and I loved my wife just like the white man loves his'n and a white man will die for his'n and I say I'll die for mine."

How we interpret the role guns have played in the history of the United States and the ways they are woven into the fabric of life in this country—North and South—depends on when and where we look. "Violence is as American as cherry pie," declared SNCC's fifth chairman, Hubert "Rap" Brown (now the Imam Jamil Abdullah Al-Amin), in 1967. Brown, like many other Afro-Americans before and since, recognized that violence has shaped much of U.S. life and culture; the Civil War is one good example, as is the highly romanticized westward expansion of the nineteenth century. Indeed, gunplay and the "taming of the West" (meaning the conquest of Native Americans through armed force and the seizure of their lands) have long been celebrated in that most influential segment of the U.S. media, Hollywood films. On the other hand, black rebellions—often poorly armed attempts to throw off the bonds of chattel slavery and escape to freedom in some other place—are largely ignored and are sometimes denounced when presented as a legitimate part of the black freedom struggle. There is no Spartacus in the romanticization of U.S. history.

All of this is to say that how we understand violence, its use, and its place in United States history depends on what sort of violence is being described and who is describing it. My view of slave revolts, for instance, is certainly colored by the fact that I am a descendant of Africans who were enslaved. And my specific view of the place of slave revolts in the continuum of the black freedom struggle is affected by my own awareness and understanding of my forebears' desire for freedom.

This is not a book about black guerrilla warfare, retaliatory violence, or "revolutionary" armed struggle in the South, and I make no attempt to argue that such actions were either necessary or possible. In fact, I consider these notions political fantasy. Nor is this a book about nonviolence. Rather, it is about the people—especially the young people—who participated in a nonviolent movement without having much commitment to nonviolence beyond agreeing to use it as a tactic. As their involvement in the movement and with rural communities deepened, however, they found themselves in situations where they, their colleagues, and the people they were working with could get killed for even trying to exercise the ordinary rights of citizenship. What, then, would they do? This was in part a question of ethics and morality: Could you really kill someone? And at the same time it was also a question of responsibility: What obligations do you have to the people who are supporting you and whose lives are endangered because of it? But at its core, of course, it was also very much a question of practicality: What do you need to do to stay alive?

This book explores the choices movement activists and organizers made when confronted with these questions, and the circumstances underlying those choices. I try to look beyond some of the widely held assumptions in analyzing and reaching conclusions about these choices. For instance, I emphatically do not subscribe to the view that a black man established his manhood by picking up a gun. The notion that "real men" fight back and that "fight" only means responding to offense with violence is deeply embedded in U.S. culture (and in world culture, for that matter). Psychiatrist Frantz Fanon wrote extensively about the mentally liberating effect on men who picked up guns and rebelled against French colonialism in Algeria, and he was widely read by movement activists. Colonialism was overthrown in Algeria in 1962, but that nation's history since does not show much liberated thought. Guns get you only so far. Genuine political resistance, to be effective, has to be more creative than simply using lethal weapons. Movement men, their homes, and their communities were under attack because they were challenging white supremacy, and were thus acting like "men" in the first place. Picking up guns was only one of a range of possible choices that were always determined by the realities on the ground.

Many black women also kept guns within easy reach. But it is important to mention that women and their use of guns present the historian of the southern Freedom Movement with a particular problem. Many of the women from this era (like the men) have passed away and cannot be interviewed. And although a few of the men have written or been extensively interviewed about their role in self-defense, the women have publicly left little record and have generally been ignored in the discussion and debate over armed self-defense. Some of the male leaders of Louisiana's Deacons for Defense and Justice were widely interviewed, and Robert Williams, a leader of the National Association for the Advancement of Colored People (NAACP) in Monroe, North Carolina, wrote prolifically about armed self-defense and even guerrilla-like retaliation against Ku Klux Klan marauders. For the most part, however, we do not know what many women who were active in the movement were thinking, or whether and how they organized for self-defense. Historians are therefore dependent on males for portrayals and interpretations of women's thoughts and actions. This disparity in the historical record weakens this book.

———

The narrative that follows does not move strictly chronologically. I prefer instead to examine the complex of time and events across the history of the southern freedom struggle, although some chronological order is necessary for coherence. Many of the ideas that informed the Freedom Movement emerge, then seem to disappear, and then reemerge with greater intensity or in more elaborate form. Therefore some flexibility with respect to chronology is needed in approaching the ideas embedded in black struggle, and this costs scholarship nothing.

My account ends in 1966, with the arguments over whether or not the Deacons for Defense and Justice should protect the James Meredith March against Fear in Mississippi. The period after that (more precisely, the period following Stokely Carmichael's call during the march for Black Power) initiates a different dynamic of black struggle, much of it made possible by the events discussed in this book but set against a political and cultural backdrop involving the evolution of Stokely's call for Black Power, the emergence of a national black politics as the number of black elected officials grew, the Black Arts movement, Pan Africanism, and various strands of black nationalism. The epilogue briefly discusses these developments and suggests that, notwithstanding the vital role of guns and self-defense in the civil rights movement, in today's violently tumultuous world, nonviolence may be the movement legacy most worth looking at again.

A final caveat: in some respects, this book is a way to introduce readers to people and political currents that have never been particularly visible in the history of the civil rights movement. Although their attitudes toward self-defense were certainly important, the larger story, even more ignored in the conventional narrative than are guns and self-defense, is the story of black communities organizing and fighting for change, unwilling to live under white supremacy any longer. This is the story of lives and people at the grassroots. The story of guns in their hands simply commands your attention.

———————

The history of the southern Freedom Movement is rooted in community organizing, an approach to struggle that began long before the mass demonstrations and public protests associated with the 1960s. Enslaved Africans were not marching on auction blocks or conducting sit-ins to secure a seat at the plantation manor dining-room table. Rather, they were organizing surreptitiously, out of sight of white people. They planned sabotage, escapes, rebellions, or, most often, the simple ways and means of survival in a new and hostile land. Still, their efforts and those of the movement participants of the 1950s and '60s exist on the same continuum, and the struggles of black people and communities during the mid-twentieth century were certainly shaped by the centuries of oppressive history that preceded them.

Chapter 1, accordingly, is dedicated to the pre-twentieth-century history of black struggle and its significance to the southern Freedom Movement of the 1950s and '60s. I begin with a discussion of the fear of slave rebellions and insurrections that accompanied the birth of the United States and that underlay almost all gun laws in colonial America. I also briefly examine some of the founding hypocrisies and contradictions of the United States, along with the social construction of race in the country's earliest days. This first chapter also focuses on the post–Civil War era of Radical Reconstruction, when emancipated black people were poised at freedom's threshold before savage violence beat them back and "redeemed" white supremacy.

This great injustice begins what historian Vincent Harding has called "the Great Tradition of black protest," which sought rights that were newly promised by law and constitutional amendment but were betrayed at every level of government. Free at least from chattel slavery, African Americans began agitating for fulfillment of the promised freedoms. During Reconstruction, black Union Army veterans politicized by the Civil War and galvanized by their newfound freedoms aggressively pursued full citizenship, even though white America remained generally uncertain about how much black political power it would support. Meanwhile, the defeated Confederacy, using terrible violence, including lynching and mass murder, waged a ruthless, relentless, and ultimately successful campaign to restore white supremacy. Blacks resisted, however, and one unprecedented development after the Civil War was the formation of black militias, some integrated into the state militias of Reconstruction governments, and all of them striving to protect political activity aimed at securing the new promise of freedom. In this and subsequent community-organizing efforts, many black Union Army veterans took the lead (just as black veterans would do in the next century). As in every phase in the evolution toward greater democracy in the United States, however, their efforts were complicated and compromised by national irresolution over the status of people of color and by often hostile reaction to their struggles to secure freedom and justice.

The book's remaining chapters extend the story of resistance and community organizing to the mid-twentieth-century southern Freedom Movement, beginning with the important role played by black veterans of World Wars I and II. Having fought overseas under the banner of democracy, they were determined to fight for democracy at home. If any single group within the black community should be highlighted for their importance to the Freedom Movement, it is these veterans. Although they cannot be defined entirely, or even mostly, in terms of armed self-defense, many were willing to resist terrorism with guns.

In my examination of the role guns played protecting the southern Freedom Movement, I focus on Mississippi, widely considered the most violently racist state in the South. As a SNCC field secretary, I spent most of my time in that state. The stories that have emerged from Mississippi introduce a set of extraordinary heroes and heroines who need to be better known: small farmers, sharecroppers, day laborers, craftsmen, entrepreneurs, and church leaders. Many of these men and women, chafing under white supremacist rule, chose to fight back. Like Salter and Turnbow, they often "traveled armed," and they kept their homes organized for defense as well. Much of their story is set in rural communities and reveals an unexpected form of "black power" that was grounded in a collective determination to defeat white supremacy, manifested well before that term was popularized by Carmichael in 1966. Like the veterans who returned from Europe determined to fight for their rights, these ordinary people were attracted to the nonviolent movement because of its militancy. The movement in its turn welcomed and needed them because of their strength.

I devote considerable discussion to two formally organized self-defense groups that bear mentioning for the leading role they played in defending the southern Freedom Movement at its most vital yet vulnerable moments: the Deacons for Defense and Justice, formed in Jonesboro, Louisiana, and Robert Williams's branch of the NAACP in Monroe and surrounding Union County, North Carolina. The Deacons protected nonviolent CORE workers under attack by the Ku Klux Klan; the Monroe NAACP, largely led by World War II veterans, also protected the black community from Klan attacks. I also examine the veterans organized in Tuscaloosa, Alabama, by Joseph Mallisham, an unnamed group less well-known than either the Deacons or Williams's NAACP. Their 1964 protection of the nonviolent Tuscaloosa Citizens for Action Committee (TCAC), an SCLC affiliate, played an important role in bringing about the unexpectedly rapid elimination of segregation in the city's public accommodations.

It is particularly interesting that nonviolent CORE organizers in Louisiana chose to integrate their efforts with the well-organized Deacons for Defense and Justice. This cooperation successfully reduced antiblack terrorism, but it also contrasted sharply with choices made by SNCC and CORE in Mississippi and Southwest Georgia. It was often stated at the time that organized self-defense groups who confronted police authority with weapons would endanger the movement by triggering a murderous response from the state. In Louisiana, this did not always, or even mostly, prove true.

These organized groups, of course, are hierarchical in structure, so it is easy to fall into the trap of defining them by using the top-down analysis that has dominated so much scholarship of the Freedom Movement. This analysis emphasizes prominent, visible leaders, seeing them as the key to understanding events. I present these organizations as organic parts of the community-organizing tradition, as entities that are incomprehensible if they are isolated from the broad dynamic of community life. In this context, I consider the question of how the attitudes and behavior of young organizers who emerged from the nonviolent student protest movement fit the older, more deeply rooted tradition of self-defense into their grassroots organizing work. I also trace the various ways that nonviolent activism, particularly in the form of sit-ins, marches, and other direct action protests, converged with grassroots community organizing.

Significantly, it was most often the relatively conservative adults involved with the movement, rather than the radical young "militants," who organized armed self-defense in southern black communities. But in the latter part of the 1960s, guns were less important to political struggle in the South because for the most part whites had learned that antiblack violence was ineffective and counterproductive in stopping black political momentum. The conservative men and women who had kept movement organizers alive were in no way raising the banner of revolutionary change, even though the desegregation and voting rights they had fought for were radical ideas at the time. In Memphis, Tennessee, during the 1968 sanitation workers strike, King and his associates felt pressure from the Black Organizing Project (BOP) to sanction retaliatory violence. But generally in the South, despite some continuation of white violence, such as the Orangeburg massacre and the assault at Jackson State College (now University), the need for organized self-defense seemed to decrease after the early 1960s. By 1968 even the Deacons for Defense and Justice had disbanded. The rhetoric of revolution, violence, and retaliation (even covertly advocating the assassination of "conservative" black leaders) was more often heard above the Mason–Dixon Line. Breakthroughs won by movement struggle had also brought new forces, both local and national, into play in the South. Grassroots organizing for political change diminished as poverty-program money began pulling activists and many of their local supporters away. Furthermore, the tenor of movement protests became distinctly different when some leaders used threats and even guns to enforce boycotts. The presence of genuinely radical figures like Mrs. Fannie Lou Hamer of Sunflower County, Mississippi—and they were few—led a political process that had heretofore excluded black people to worry that the southern movement was too "radical"; sharecroppers, day workers, and the like were insisting on being part of the political process. The opening up of the Democratic Party in the South following the flight of Dixiecrats to the Republican Party triggered a scramble among some black leaders to gain influence in the new political climate. This, of course, is not a gun story of the South; rather, ironically and perhaps unfortunately, it is a "success" story.

PROLOGUE

"I Come to Get My Gun"

The late-summer sun was broiling the already sunbaked floodplains of the Mississippi Delta on August 31, 1962, when Mrs. Fannie Lou Hamer and seventeen other men and women boarded an old school bus in front of the Williams Chapel Missionary Baptist Church in the little town of Ruleville. The bus was normally used to haul day laborers to the cotton fields, but today it was headed for the Sunflower County courthouse twenty-six miles away in Indianola. The seat of Sunflower County, Indianola was also the birthplace of the Citizens' Council—the white-collar, white-supremacist organization of prominent planters, businessmen, and politicians who professed to disdain the hooded garb and violence of the Ku Klux Klan.

At the courthouse, Mrs. Hamer and the others intended to register to vote, a radical and dangerous action for black people in Mississippi at the time, especially in this river-washed fertile cotton plantation land of northwest Mississippi known as the Delta. Here, black people formed an overwhelming majority of the population. If they gained voting rights, there was a very real possibility that black power could displace white power in local government. Local whites had proven themselves willing to fight that possibility in every way they could. In the 1950s and '60s, white-supremacist terror besieged black communities in Mississippi and across the South. Black leaders had been assassinated or driven from the state; new laws were put in place both to maintain black disenfranchisement and to surveil the black community. Ku Klux Klan membership expanded and included policemen and civic leaders.

At the courthouse, the men and women from Ruleville crowded into the circuit clerk's office and announced their intention. Cecil Campbell, the startled and decidedly hostile clerk, stated that only two of them were allowed in the office at the same time. Everyone except Mrs. Hamer and an older man named Leonard Davis went back outside to wait their turn. Sullen white men, some carrying pistols, milled about outside the courthouse; the group waiting to register stood uneasily on the steps and under the portico. Then, without giving a reason, the circuit clerk suddenly closed his office.

Despite the danger Mrs. Hamer and her fellow would-be registrants were facing, my coworkers and I were pleased that they had braved this hostile territory—and that no violence had taken place. I had boarded the bus with the group, and though I had only been in Mississippi for a few weeks, I was already well aware of the dangers of challenging white power in the state. The previous summer, SNCC had begun an intensive voter-registration effort in Southwest Mississippi, and white supremacists had unleashed murderous violence against it.

I was a freshman at Howard University in Washington, D.C., during the campaign in that region of Mississippi and did not plan to become part of the voter-registration effort in the Delta in the summer of 1962. Instead, I intended to participate in a civil rights workshop for young people organized by CORE in Houston, Texas, after finishing my spring semester. CORE had invited me and given me money for a bus ticket because at Howard I had been part of the sit-in movement.

I boarded a Greyhound bus for Houston, but when I reached Jackson, Mississippi—the state's capital—I decided to try to meet students there who were sitting in at segregated public facilities. I could have disembarked in any southern city and met student protesters, but Mississippi was so notoriously racist and violent—wholly associated in my mind, and in the minds of many in my generation, with the brutal 1955 murder of fourteen-year-old Emmett Till—that it was difficult for me to imagine students anywhere in the state being brave enough to sit in. Yet I knew students were doing just that in Jackson. I thought they must have some kind of special courage gene to be protesting in Mississippi. As far as I was concerned, no place in the entire universe was more oppressive and dangerous for a black person. Sit-in protests in the segregated towns and cities of Maryland and Virginia were one thing; sit-in protests in Mississippi were quite another, I thought. So I felt compelled to meet them. I got off the bus and made my way to their headquarters.

But when I told them I was on my way to a civil rights workshop in Texas, Lawrence Guyot, a student at Tougaloo College, rose from his seat and gave me a stern look. He was about to head up into the Delta and become part of SNCC's beginning efforts there. In 1964, he would become chairman of the Mississippi Freedom Democratic Party (MFDP). "Civil rights workshop in Texas!" he scoffed. "What's the point of doing that when you're standing right here in Mississippi?" Guyot (as we most often called him) was a big, intense guy, and his tone was disdainful, almost bullying, conveying without further words what was at once a challenge and a demand: So you're down here just to chatter about civil rights, are you? That's pretty useless. If you're serious, stay and work with us. Jessie Harris, another of the young Mississippi activists, chimed in: "You're in the war zone here."

I got the message. The Greyhound left without me; I never completed my journey to Texas and instead became a part of SNCC's effort in the state. When summer ended, I remained in Mississippi as a SNCC field secretary instead of returning to school. I was nineteen years old.

Although it had happened almost a year before I arrived in Mississippi, I was aware of the September 25, 1961, murder of Herbert Lee, a small farmer and NAACP leader in Amite County. Lee had given strong support to SNCC's efforts in Southwest Mississippi, and his killing—which occurred in broad daylight—was a frightening reminder that death could find you anywhere in the state. It was a lesson I remembered at tense moments, like the one at the Sunflower County courthouse in late August of 1962.

That day, I could feel the tension in the air outside the courthouse. Everywhere in the state, politicians and newspapers were whipping whites into a frenzy over the possibility that in a few weeks James Meredith could become the first black person to enroll in the University of Mississippi. Like school desegregation, voting rights was an explosive issue—the armed white men on the steps of the courthouse were a living testament to that fact.

On the way to Indianola, the fear on the bus had been palpable, but Fannie Lou Hamer had gone a long way toward easing it. She lived a quiet, simple life as a sharecropper and timekeeper on a Sunflower County cotton plantation, and we had neither noticed nor anticipated her strength until she raised her powerful voice in songs of faith and freedom on that bus. Soon her strength and boldness would make her a legendary figure in Mississippi's Freedom Movement.

What happened to Mrs. Hamer after this attempt at voter registration is fairly well known. She returned to the plantation where she and her husband, Perry "Pap" Hamer, had lived and worked for eighteen years. Word of her attempt to register had gotten back to the plantation before she did, and William David "W. D." Marlow, the plantation's angry owner, was waiting for her. He demanded that she withdraw her application and promise never to make such an attempt again; otherwise, she was to get off his land immediately. Mrs. Hamer's reply has entered Freedom Movement lore: "I didn't go down there to register for you," she informed Marlow. "I went down there to register for myself."

Mrs. Hamer's story has become familiar, but the retaliatory violence that soon descended on Ruleville's black community is not so well-known. On September 10 night riders drove through town shooting into the homes of people associated with the voter-registration effort, including the home where Mrs. Hamer had found refuge after her expulsion from Marlow's plantation. In another Ruleville home, that of Herman and Hattie Sisson, located in a black section of town called the Sanctified Quarters, two young girls were wounded: The Sissons' granddaughter Vivian Hillet and her friend Marylene Burks, who were visiting before heading off to college. Hillet's arms and legs were grazed by rifle shots, and Burks was more seriously injured by shots to her head and neck.

Another of the homes attacked by the night riders was that of an elderly couple, Joe and Rebecca McDonald, neighbors of the Sissons. I was staying with the McDonalds along with two other SNCC workers, Charles "Mac" McLaurin and Landy McNair, but as it happened, none of us was in the McDonalds' house when the shooting occurred. I was in town, however, and in a tiny place like Ruleville (population 1,100 then), gunshots fired anywhere could be heard everywhere, especially in the still of a Mississippi Delta night.

I immediately raced back to the Quarters and was told that two girls had been wounded, so I rushed to the North Sunflower County Hospital where they were being treated. I began to ask about their condition and sought to find out, from the Sissons and others, exactly what had happened. Ruleville's mayor, Charles Dorrough, was also at the hospital, and he ordered me arrested for interfering with the investigation by "asking a lot of silly ques-

tions." *Ruleville's town constable, S. D. Milam (the brother of one of the men who had murdered Emmett Till), put me next to a police dog in the backseat of his car and hauled me off to Ruleville's jail.*

Mac, Landy, and I had first encountered Mayor Dorrough a few weeks earlier. We had just come to town and were walking down a dirt road in Ruleville's Jerusalem Quarters—named for a church—when a car suddenly stopped beside us. A white man jumped out and, waving a pistol, announced angrily, "I know you all ain't from here, and you're here to cause trouble! I'm here to tell you to get out of town!" He was Mayor Dorrough, who sometimes engaged in police patrols. In addition to owning the town's hardware store and broadcasting agricultural news on the local radio station, he was president of the local Citizens' Council.

Holding us at gunpoint, Dorrough barked, "You niggers get into this car!" Mac asked why, and the mayor responded, "'Cause this pistol says so!" We got in his car, and he drove us to Ruleville's city hall, where he acted not only as mayor but also as justice of the peace. He accused us of being New York City communists and "troublemakers," shouting that we should get out of Ruleville and go back to New York. In the Mississippi of those days, the Civil War and the Cold War were often conflated, and except for those in Russia, China, and Cuba, New York City communists were considered the worst kind of communists in the world. Mac and Landy were native Mississippians; when Mac explained that "we" were all from the state, I was relieved at being included and kept my Washington, D.C., mouth shut.

Mayor Dorrough seemed to be from another planet, and he certainly ran Ruleville as his own fiefdom. On one occasion SNCC workers were picked up for violating the town's curfew, enforced only on blacks if enforced at all. One of the SNCC workers told the mayor that the Supreme Court had ruled curfews for adults unconstitutional. His response sums up what Mississippi was like at the time: "That law ain't got here yet."

Now, in the wake of the shootings in the Quarters, and on the basis of what could be called Ruleville law, Dorrough came up with another reason for arresting me at the hospital. He claimed that the shooting that had wounded Hillet and Burks was a "prefabricated incident" designed by Bob Moses (SNCC's Mississippi project director), McLaurin, Landy, and myself to generate publicity for a failing political effort in the state. "We think they did it themselves," he told a local reporter, claiming that a "reliable source" had informed him that a civil rights worker had purchased shotgun shells a few days earlier. This accusation and my arrest were so ridiculous that even Dorrough could not hold me for long, and I was released the next morning.

Back at the McDonald home after my release from jail, I found that Dorrough had confiscated Joe McDonald's shotgun, using my arrest as an excuse. Mr. Joe, as we called him, worried aloud about what he would do without it. Like most of the black people in Ruleville and Sunflower County, he was poor, and he depended on a garden in the backyard and his gun to put food on his table, especially now that three young guys were part of his household.

We told Mr. Joe that he had a right to his gun, that the U.S. Constitution gave him that right. He asked us if we were certain. Yes, we told him, and we had a history book with a copy of the Constitution in it. I went and got the book and then read the Second Amendment out loud. "You see," Mac told Mr. Joe for emphasis, "that's where it says so right in the United States Constitution."

Mr. Joe told me to fold over the page I had just read and then took the book from me. A little while later, we noticed that Mr. Joe was not around and we asked his wife, Rebecca, where he was. "He went to get his gun," she told us. "You said it was all right."

We were stunned and fearful. One of our constant concerns in the violent Deep South of those days was that local people would get hurt or even killed for behavior we had encouraged. Herbert Lee's murder leaped into my mind; Mr. Joe going to get his gun raised the terrible possibility that he would be killed too.

We were about to run after Mr. Joe when we heard the familiar rattle of his old truck pulling up. He was back from city hall. We rushed outside. "What happened?" we asked. Mr. Joe said he had leaned into the doorway of city hall and simply told Dorrough, "I come to get my gun." The mayor replied that he didn't have a right to his gun, but Mr. Joe held up the history book he had taken from us, opened it to the page he had asked me to fold over, and told the mayor, "This book says I do!"

It was exactly the sort of action that could get a black man hurt, jailed, or killed in the Delta or anywhere in Mississippi; certainly Emmett Till had been murdered for less. And Dorrough was such an inveterate racist that *none of us could have imagined that he would easily return the shotgun. But we had misjudged the mayor, Joe McDonald, and the entire culture of guns in the Deep South. For now, as Mr. Joe stepped out of his truck, he was triumphantly raising the shotgun above his head.*

1

"Over My Head I See Freedom in the Air"

Slaveholders have no rights more than any other thief or pirate.
They have forfeited even the right to live, and if the slave should
put every one of them to the sword tomorrow, who dare pronounce
the penalty disproportionate to the crime?
—Frederick Douglass, February 9, 1849

Guns and violence are uniquely romanticized in the United States, and they play a leading role in our national creation myth. The American West looms especially large in our historical memory and showcases our obsession and associations with guns: frontiersmen and quick-drawing pistol-toting lawmen like Wyatt Earp and Wild Bill Hickok; the U.S. Cavalry charging to save a wagon train at the last minute; farmers and ranchers fending off angry, dispossessed Native Americans. In their wildly popular family movies, good guys like Roy Rogers and Gene Autry rarely rode without their pistols; the Lone Ranger was never without his six-shooter. Even bad guys—Billy the Kid, Jesse James, Butch Cassidy and the Sundance Kid, Bonnie and Clyde, and Al Capone, all of them killers—have achieved a sort of antihero status and are part of the great American romance with guns and violence. The cowboy movie has been pretty much replaced by digital games today, especially among young people, and this new medium offers players the opportunity to enter into a virtual reality where they can engage in violent fantasies at a level and intensity unimagined a generation ago.

Django, Shaft, and a few other black action figures notwithstanding, most glamorized gunmen are white. For most Americans, the notion of black people carrying guns conjures fear rather than admiration or nostalgia. Rarely is anything romantic associated with the image of a black gun user, despite the heroic black rebellions against slavery in the seventeenth, eighteenth, and nineteenth centuries. The historical connection between black gun use and the freedom struggle has nearly been lost entirely—a fact that undermines our understanding of both subjects.

Time and again, guns have proven pivotal to the African American quest for freedom. It took not just slave rebellions but the Civil War—uniformed and sustained armed conflict—to force open the door to freedom, and it took guns in black hands to begin securing even the limited freedoms gained by that war. Over the following century guns were still being used to help win a promised freedom that was betrayed and had never completely materialized.

Any discussion of guns and black self-defense therefore must begin with the country's origins. Race—a concept far more complex than skin color—is integral to this discussion, and slavery is at the root of any discussion of race in the United States.

Slavery was fundamental to America's beginnings and to life in the United States for most of the nation's history. The lens through which slavery is viewed is typically bifurcated racially, and thus the memory of slavery tends to lead to different observations and conclusions about its effects. To bring into proper focus America's "peculiar institution"—to use a nineteenth-century euphemism for slavery—we have to understand its place in the country's beginnings. And in many ways the country began in the Virginia Colony. Although France and Spain established colonies and slavery in the Americas, the deepest roots of the United States are found in England's North American colonies, and of them, Virginia had the greatest political impact on the founding of the country. Its leaders, especially George Washington, Thomas Jefferson, James Madison, and James Monroe, arguably had the most influence on shaping the design of the emerging United States. Although in 1641 Massachusetts became the first of England's colonies to legalize slavery, Virginia, with a far greater number of enslaved Africans, led the way in regulating slavery throughout the southern colonies. Thus, colonial life in Virginia is the most useful starting point for understanding the beginnings of black rebellion and the accompanying fear of weapons in black hands—a fear that led to America's first gun control laws, which were designed to prevent the possession of weapons by black people.

In the decades immediately following Virginia's founding in 1607 indentured servitude was far more prevalent in the fledgling colony than slavery, although slavery certainly existed. Slave law emerged gradually. But in a racially significant decision on July 9, 1640, in their sentencing of three indentured servants who had run away and been recaptured in Maryland, the Virginia Council and General Court ended the fiction that black indentured servitude was anything less than slavery. One of the servants, James Gregory, was "a Scotchman"; another, Victor, with no last name given, was identified in court minutes as "a dutchman"; and the third, John Punch, was "a negro." Gregory and Victor were sentenced to thirty lashes with a whip and their servitude was extended by four years. Punch, however, was sentenced to indentured servitude for the rest of his life.

Punch's race almost certainly determined the court's decision. Although this early application of the racial double standard took away Punch's prospects of ever living as a free person, there is no mention of slavery in the court's decision—only the fact that John Punch was "a negro." And court minutes give no reason for the disparity in the three escapees' sentences. In other cases before and after Punch's, Virginia courts frequently used the words "negro" and "non-Christian" when specifically prescribing punishment for blacks, but the term "slave" is not used. The discriminatory language of these decisions assumes black inferiority, but the general status of blacks in colonial Virginia appears to be largely undefined by law during the first half of the seventeenth century. Nonetheless, it is only logical to infer that it was an emerging racist *culture* in the "New World" more than explicit legal code that initially described black–white relations.

The discrimination expressed in the judgment against Punch began hardening into actual slave law in 1659 with the passage of a statute reducing import duties on slaves brought into the colony. This was the first overt reference to slavery in Virginia law. The following year a statute was enacted lengthening the servitude of English indentured servants who ran away with enslaved blacks.

By the end of the century indentured servitude had almost disappeared, supplanted by African slavery. There were economic reasons for this, particularly a shortage of available servants from England. But an important political factor accelerating the use of slave labor in the United States—and establishment of the idea of "race"—was the near success of the 1676 rebellion of Nathaniel Bacon and his followers. Bacon's Rebellion was first stirred by his disagreement with the colony's policy toward Native Americans and by onerous new tobacco taxes. Land hungry freemen and smallholders joined him, even though Bacon's argument reflected a quarrel within the colony's wealthy elite, and it quickly became an effort to overthrow the royalist government and replace it with one that would cater to a new class of farmers and entrepreneurs who felt little allegiance to the imperialist obligations of the colony's royalist leadership governing for England's King Charles. Bacon's expanding army of the discontented also included indentured servants—black and white seeking freedom from indenture—who had bonded together regardless of race. They succeeded in burning Jamestown to the ground and driving the colonial governor from the colony. The rebellion collapsed when Bacon suddenly died of dysentery, but Virginia's tiny ruling class of wealthy merchants and large landowners feared the sort of rebellious nonracial unity that had powered the revolt.

Thus, in the aftermath of Bacon's Rebellion, the notion of race as we now know it began to take shape. Formalizing the idea that blacks were inferior just because they were black was easy to do; they looked different. But to have blacks it was necessary to have whites. So not only did laws establish slavery based on the premise of Africans being an inferior race, but "white people" were invented as a collective description of disparate European colonists who had traditionally been defined by their national identities— for instance, Punch's codefendants Victor ("a dutchman") and Gregory ("a Scotchman"). For the purpose of social control, the Virginia Colony's rulers—"Englishmen"—began emphasizing a new, "white" racial identity that encompassed more than those of Anglo-Saxon Protestant heritage. Even "wild" Irish Catholics were included. Colonial leaders enforced the social and cultural separation of blacks and whites with increasing rigor.

Although some blacks were landowners and even held slaves themselves, color prejudice was nothing new to the colony. Differences of skin color and language were obvious and remarked on. Traders brought stories back from Africa that suggested there were even more profound differences between Africans and Europeans, leading to fantastical distortions: Thomas Jefferson, for example, thought that orangutans were sexually attracted to black women. But despite color prejudice, there were sexual liaisons, marriages, and other associations across the color line. Notes historian Edmund S. Morgan, it was "common, for example, for servants and slaves to run away together, steal hogs together, get drunk together. It was not uncommon for them to make love together. In Bacon's Rebellion one of the last groups to surrender was a mixed band of eighty Negroes and twenty English servants."

The colony's rulers worried about the prospect of rebellious unity across racial lines. After Bacon's Rebellion, they were determined to protect their power, wealth, and privilege from similar challenges, and African slavery stabilized their ability to extract tobacco wealth from the colony while giving even the poorest, most exploited "white" an illusory sense of having a piece of the new American pie.

Well before Bacon's Rebellion, though, blacks in Virginia were subjected to degradations and cruelties not inflicted on whites. Disparity in court-ordered punishments for blacks and whites, for example, had begun before and continued after the Punch decision, with blacks sometimes being branded for offenses. More and more blacks were sentenced to a lifetime of bondage. Mixed marriages were outlawed. Court cases increasingly assumed the inferiority of blacks. But as the number of enslaved Africans swelled, fear that they might rebel also grew. In 1680, the Virginia General Assembly was worried enough about the potential danger of black social gatherings to enact a law sharply restricting them. That legislation also made it illegal for any black person to carry any type of weapon or potential weapon; a black person caught carrying a weapon was to be lashed twenty times with a whip. Virginia lawmakers also expressed concern at the possibility of "Christians" being ambushed by runaways and sanctioned whipping and even executing black fugitives from slavery. The 1680 legislation empowered any white person or posse to kill any black escapee resisting recapture:

> And it is hereby further enacted by the authority aforesaid that if
> any negroe or other slave shall absent himself from his masters
> service and lye hid and lurking in obscure places . . . and shall
> resist any person or persons that shalby any lawfull authority by
> imployed to apprehend and take the said negroe, that then in case
> of such resistance, it shalbe lawfull for such person or persons to
> kill the said negroe or slave soe lying out and resisting.

Yet this stricter legislation did not ease fear of black rebellion. In 1719, Virginia governor Alexander Spotswood warned the colony's rulers against deceiving themselves into believing that language differences among enslaved Africans would prevent rebellion. "Freedom," the governor said, "wears a cap which can, without a tongue, call together all those who long to shake of[f] the fetters of slavery." By 1723 racial oppression had been completely codified in Virginia. The law permitted the punishment of slaves by amputation or death for almost any reason. Blacks' voting rights were taken away. Enslaved or free, no black person could hold any public office or bear witness against any white person. Gun law was reinforced, and it became illegal for any black person to possess "any gun, powder, shot, or any club, or any other weapon whatsoever, offensive or defensive." And any black person who raised a hand against a white person, for any reason, was subject to a public whipping of thirty lashes.

Despite these harsh laws, however, whites' fear was not eased. The number of blacks in the colony was growing. Rebellions in Brazil, Jamaica, and other Caribbean and South American colonies of England, France, and Spain were erupting regularly. In 1736 William Byrd II, who was a member of the Virginia Governor's Council and former deputy governor of Virginia, eyed rebellions in Jamaica and warned,

> We have already at least 10,000 men of these descendants of Ham,
> *fit to bear arms* [emphasis added], and these numbers increase
> every day, as well by birth as by importation. And in case there
> should arise a man exasperated by a desperate fortune, he might
> with more advantage than Cataline [*sic*] kindle a servile war . . .
> and tinge our rivers wide as they are with blood.

Byrd's analogy was telling; Lucius Sergius Catilina, also known as "Catiline," was a Roman politician of the first century BC best known for his failed conspiracy to overthrow the Roman Republic. And the governor's worry and warning was clear: given the opportunity, oppressed blacks might bring down the entire white power structure in Virginia.

———

As the colonial era gave way to the early Republic, the position of black people in America only worsened. Like most of the Founding Fathers of the United States, Thomas Jefferson believed that protecting the right of free men to bear arms would help secure the nation's liberty by safeguarding its people from tyrannical government. Ironically, slavery—and the laws protecting it—arguably made Africans the people most tyrannized by government, notwithstanding the subjugation of Native Americans (some of whom were enslaved too).

Jefferson did not consider black people human beings with the rights of free men. He drafted the Declaration of Independence but did not intend to include blacks among those people "endowed by their Creator with certain unalienable Rights." He was a slave owner, after all; Jefferson held almost two hundred men, women, and children in chattel bondage, and though occasionally worrying aloud about the morality and consequences of slavery, he never gave up his supposed right to own and work these human beings as though they were farm animals or to sell them like livestock whenever he felt it necessary. That Jefferson's earliest childhood memory was of being carried on a pillow by an enslaved black person underscores both his privilege and his hypocrisy.

Well aware that slavery was his new nation's great founding contradiction, Jefferson awkwardly separated the oppression and injustice of slavery from his idealistic American project of freedom and liberty. Africans had been enslaved because they were inferior, he rationalized, but for his entire life he was dogged by fear that they might revolt against their slavery or, if freed, might seek revenge against those who had enslaved them. "Are our slaves to be presented with freedom and a dagger?" he asked in an 1821 exchange of letters with John Adams, like Jefferson a founder and former president.

If slavery were outlawed, he and others worried, freed slaves would have the right to bear arms; given their numbers they might also seek and gain political influence and power, especially in Jefferson's beloved South. This concern is essential for understanding the roots of white southern resistance to civil rights. For example, in 1857 the Supreme Court issued a ruling in the case of Dred Scott, a slave who, after he was taken by his owner to a free state, sued in court for his freedom. Chief Justice Roger Brooke Taney ruled that constitutional rights could not be given to black people because "It would give to persons of the negro race . . . the full liberty of speech in public and in private upon all subjects; [the right] to hold public meetings upon political affairs, *and to keep and carry arms wherever they went* [emphasis added] . . . endangering the peace and safety of the state."

Jefferson's racism prevented him from believing that black people could meaningfully participate in the society he envisioned or that they could be equals to white citizens. And given slavery's remorseless exploitation and cruelty, it is easy to understand his fear that free Africans might seek revenge. During a 1961 symposium—135 years after Jefferson's death in 1826—author James Baldwin could still pronounce, "To be a Negro in this country and to be relatively conscious is to be in a rage almost all the time."

Adams's response to Jefferson's letter revealed his sense of personal and political practicality and contrasted his own fear and caution with the anti-slavery zeal of Swedish philosopher and Christian mystic Emanuel Swedenborg and Methodist Church cofounder John Wesley: *I can't deal with this problem* was the attitude he manifested in his reply to Jefferson:

> If I was as drunk with enthusiasm as Swedenborg and Wesley, I might probably say I had seen Armies of Negroes marching and countermarching in the air, shining in Armour. I have been so terrified with this Phenomenon that I constantly said in former times to the Southern Gentlemen, I cannot comprehend this object: I must leave it to you.

Adams, who lived far away from the plantation South in Massachusetts, could opt out of worrying about the prospect and danger of black rebellion, but Jefferson in Virginia could not. He and other planters across the South were dependent on a growing enslaved population for the wealth they gained from tobacco, rice, sugar, indigo, and cotton. They lived with the ever-present threat of rebellions that might destroy their wealthy and— particularly in Jefferson's case—extravagant lifestyle, a lifestyle enabled by the very slave labor that might someday undo it.

The fears of Jefferson and others in the slavocracy had intensified at the beginning of the fight for liberty from England. Deleted paragraphs in Jefferson's first draft of the Declaration of Independence blame George III for slavery in England's colonies—"this assemblage of horrors," as Jefferson denounced it. He wrote the draft without irony or self-examination, acknowledging that enslaved Africans were "people" whose freedom had been taken away through the criminal use of force and violence. At the same time, he excoriated King George for offering slaves their freedom in exchange for joining England's side in its war against American patriots. "He is now exciting those very people to rise in arms among us," Jefferson fumed, "and to purchase that liberty of which he has deprived them, by murdering the people upon whom he also obtruded them; thus paying off former *crimes committed against the liberties of one people* [emphasis added], with crimes which he urges them to commit against the lives of another." South Carolina and Georgia delegates to the Continental Congress did not want to hear anything about Africans being "people" and forced Jefferson to remove these words.

The final draft of the Declaration contains just a single reference to slavery. Brief and indirect, it nevertheless clearly reflects fear of slave rebellion, charging that King George "has excited domestic insurrections amongst us." This complaint is the last of twenty-seven leveled against the English king, but the fear of slave rebellion played an outsized part in the decision of many American colonists in the South to turn against the British Crown. The frightening possibility of slaves joining the British helped convince the southern plantocracy that supporting American independence was necessary, despite the disturbing implications the Revolution's driving political ideals of universal liberty held for the institution of slavery.

The independence movement's egalitarian rhetoric was not lost on those who were enslaved. They agreed with the Revolution's basic premise and promise: freedom is a God-given human right. In 1800 slaves led by Gabriel

Prosser would attempt an insurrection in Richmond, Virginia. The rebellion failed, but before being sentenced to death, one of the rebels proclaimed, while standing in chains before a judge, "I have nothing more to offer than what General [George] Washington would have had to offer, had he been taken by the British and put to trial by them. I have adventured my life in endeavoring to obtain the liberty of my countrymen, and am a willing sacrifice in their cause." This important commingling of Afro-American desire for freedom, willingness to sacrifice to gain it, and Euro-American idealism as defined by the eighteenth-century U.S. independence movement continues to be underappreciated, even though it reverberated across the centuries and into the twentieth century's southern freedom rights struggle. In 1962, for example, Diane Nash—a twenty-three-year-old civil rights activist then six months pregnant with her first child—was on trial in Jackson, Mississippi, for training high school students to engage in nonviolent protests. The judge offered her two choices: pay a fine or be jailed for two years. She chose jail. "[My] child will be a black child born in Mississippi, and thus whether I am in jail or not, he will be born in prison. . . . If I go to jail now it may help hasten that day when my child and all children will be free," she told the judge. Nash eventually served ten days in jail because she refused to move from the white side of the courtroom.

Blacks had served in northern militia units in the decades before the Revolutionary War, especially during the French and Indian War, and some blacks had been active in the agitation leading up to the Revolutionary War itself. Black Minutemen fought in the Battle of Lexington and in the Battle of Bunker Hill. A black man, Crispus Attucks, was the first person killed in the Boston Massacre. Many blacks enslaved in the South, on the other hand, were willing to take a chance with the British. Hundreds joined the British Army's Ethiopian Regiment after the Earl of Dunmore, Virginia's last royal governor, proclaimed freedom for all rebel-owned slaves who joined the British war effort. Jefferson put the number of Virginia slaves who ran away to British lines at 30,000 (although this may have been an exaggeration on his part); some of them fled from his own plantation. Thousands more enslaved men and women in South Carolina and Georgia also fled to the British.

Blacks in America, like whites, were divided by the Revolutionary War.

By the end of the war about 5,000 blacks had fought or served in some capacity on the side of the colonial revolutionists. In Boston, an all-black military company called the Bucks of America was celebrated at the end of the conflict. The company was formed in Boston, but little more is known about them. Their commander, Colonel Samuel Middleton, was the only black commissioned officer in the Continental Army, and he did not hesitate to use weapons when necessary to defend his principles. By one account, when a group of young white Bostonians tried to disrupt an annual, all-black abolitionist rally on Boston Common, Middleton charged out onto the street, leveled his musket at the unruly whites, and commanded them to leave. They did.

On the other side of the battle lines, about 1,000 black men and women had served with the British. A little more than half were soldiers; the rest were cooks and laborers. More would have signed up if the British had permitted them to do so, but Dunmore's order never became general policy. Some black runaways made out better with the British than they would have with the American revolutionists, even though the British lost. At the end of the war, about 3,000 black loyalists were on the British ships that left New York for the Caribbean, Canada, and England.

The new American government, although it was "conceived in liberty," did not abolish slavery. For Jefferson and other slavers, keeping firearms out of the hands of slaves continued to be an urgent matter of personal and public safety. Their fear was justified, as southern history is replete with slave rebellions. Historian Herbert Aptheker has estimated that between 1619 and 1865 more than 250 rebellions by slaves and indentured servants occurred in the United States. Among the most widely known are those of Denmark Vesey, a South Carolina freedman, who planned a slave rebellion in 1822, and Nat Turner, who led a slave rebellion in Virginia in 1831. Although these revolts failed to gain freedom for blacks, they helped germinate a tradition of organized resistance that was the taproot of the modern freedom struggle. Enslaved or free, most black people admired the leaders of slave revolts, people such as Prosser, Turner, and Vesey, and considered them heroes and liberators. And slave revolts were not limited to U.S. soil; nearby Haiti's emergence as an independent black republic after the November 18, 1803, Battle of Vertières, in which rebels defeated some of Napoleon's best expeditionary troops, became both a cause for white nightmares in the new United States and a source of black hope, pride, and inspiration for resistance and rebellion throughout the New World.

————

Slavery persisted for nearly a century after the American Revolution, and enslaved blacks continued to find ways to fight for freedom. Although most did not pick up weapons and engage in armed rebellion, many resisted slavery in subtler and less dangerous ways, such as engaging in work slow-downs, pretending to be sick, or deliberately breaking tools and committing other small acts of sabotage. The last was tolerated by owners and overseers with minimal if any punishment because some slaves purposefully cultivated the notion of black ineptitude and lack of intelligence. Deception—the grin, the shuffle, and the head scratch—was a weapon sometimes as effective as the gun.

Dangerous, angry Negroes hid in plain sight, yet flight, rather than confrontation, was perhaps the most frequently used form of resistance. Escape cost planters money, for slaves were valuable property. And unlike the small Caribbean islands, where slaves worked on the sugar plantations, the North American mainland was vast. It was possible for a slave, even for groups of runaway slaves, to follow river routes and secret trails through swamp and forest to states or territories where slavery was not permitted. Slave intelligence networks ran from the plantation owner's "big" house to the fields, from plantation to plantation, and even beyond the slave states altogether. One escaped slave attempted to marry in Cincinnati, Ohio (a free state). His church's congregation accused him of trying to commit bigamy because they knew he had left behind—"deserted," they said—a wife who was still enslaved in New Orleans. They demanded that he get a release from her in writing. He was able to contact his wife through a waterman who regularly traveled to New Orleans and was part of a black underground communications network. The waterman brought back to Cincinnati a release marked with his wife's X, and the church then approved the new marriage.

Historian Corey D. B. Walker notes that, at a more sophisticated level, black fraternal associations nurtured would-be liberators. He specifically points to Gabriel Prosser's rebellion in Richmond, Virginia, and suggests that black Freemasonry, with its highly organized network of lodges, secrecy, and ritual "similar to the Exodus narrative," gave African Americans "a system and a language" in the American context that helped generate "ideas, ideals and actions for freedom." These associations engaged in more than rituals: they were spaces in which cultural and political ideas were exchanged. Haitians, after winning their own fight for freedom, were especially important in establishing Freemason lodges along the U.S. East Coast. The Haitian presence in the Masonic network in the new United States compares to the shadowy Committees of Correspondence formed on the eve of the American Revolution to coordinate planned rebellion. So too the network of Freemason lodges facilitated planning and communication among Gabriel and his freedom-seeking plotters. It is one of the reasons some white Americans felt that blacks in the United States were "infected by Haiti."

Fraternal societies and the organized black church played a major but rarely-explored role in the ongoing rebellion against slavery. A secret society, barely remembered today, formed when twelve black men from Ohio, South Carolina, North Carolina, Virginia, Alabama, Mississippi, Louisiana, Georgia, and Tennessee gathered in St. Louis, Missouri, on August 11, 1846, and began planning a massive armed assault against slavery. They had been brought together by "Father" Moses Dickson, a Prince Hall Mason and later an African Methodist Episcopal (AME) minister. Dickson had been born free in Cincinnati, but during three years of moving about the South as a barber, he saw slavery in all its horrors. While traveling he had begun discussions about organizing an armed attack against slavery with some of the young men he had met and come to trust. At the St. Louis gathering they named themselves the Twelve Knights of Liberty, and they sought other men who would dedicate themselves to the overthrow of slavery. They were sworn to secrecy; part of their oath was "I can die but I cannot reveal the name of any member until the slaves are free."

Building slowly, they began to drill in secret and to stockpile arms and ammunition. By 1856 their numbers may have been in the thousands and they had changed their name to the Order of Twelve to honor their founders. Undoubtedly the name change also helped cover their activities. Publicly, they were now also a Masonic order named the Knights of Tabor. Their history is murky, for because of the secrecy their plans required, little was written down. And one cannot help but wonder how, given their large number, they managed to maintain secrecy. Nonetheless, buried in the convoluted language of Dickson's *Manual of the Knights of Tabor and Daughters of the Tabernacle,* there are hints of the scale of their underground organization: "In the Darkest hours just before the breaking out of the Civil War, our lives were fixed at all the news centers so that in a few hours, in every hamlet, and in every town, city, and plantation, the members of our Order kept the people posted on that which interested us most."

On Dickson's command, an army organized by the Knights was to converge on Atlanta to begin their assault on slavery. This would have been the largest armed attack against slavery in U.S. history. Dickson made the call in July 1857 but then suddenly called off the planned attack. It is not clear why. There had been an upsurge in insurrectionary actions by blacks in many parts of the South that year. Whites were on high alert, and Dickson had planned a direct attack on Atlanta rather than guerrilla warfare. The chance of keeping the attack a surprise was reduced—and perhaps Dickson could also read the writing on the wall signaling the approaching demise of slavery. By 1857 a man like Dickson, carefully observing political currents, was likely to have foreseen that the increasingly bitter and violent political arguments over slavery's place and legitimacy in the United States would soon tear the nation apart and spark a decisive war over the issue. A Union Army that included black soldiers had to seem more likely to end slavery than any homegrown insurrection, no matter how expansive. And when they were finally permitted, blacks joined the Union Army by the tens of thousands. True to their spirit, most of the Knights of Liberty enlisted.

The Civil War was a watershed. In battle after battle, black soldiers demonstrated their courage, refuting by heroic actions the commonplace notion that they were cowards of dubious worth on the battlefield. After the 1863 Battle of Nashville, Union General George Thomas, seeing the many black bodies, some of them pressed right up against Confederate fortifications, declared, "Gentlemen, the question is settled; Negroes will fight." Years later, W. E. B. Du Bois dryly noted, "The slave pleaded; he was humble . . . and the world ignored him. The slave killed white men; and behold he was a man!"

By the end of the Civil War, about one-fifth of adult black males had joined the Union Army and had engaged in thirty-nine major battles and hundreds of smaller engagements. With this service a new political consciousness burgeoned, fertilized by the black blood that was spilled in combat. In the April 12, 1864, battle of Fort Pillow, Tennessee, 292 black and 285 white soldiers defended the fort. Confederate General Nathan Bedford Forrest, who would later become the first Grand Wizard of the Ku Klux Klan, led 2,500 men against them. Although at first Forrest said he would give the garrison an opportunity to surrender, he soon sent his men pouring into the fort, driving the heavily outnumbered Union soldiers down a bluff of the Mississippi River and into a murderous cross fire. Only sixty-two of the black troops survived. A congressional Joint Committee on the Conduct of the War found that Forrest and his Confederates had shot and bayoneted the garrison's soldiers after it had surrendered; the battle cry for black soldiers fighting with the Union Army became "Remember Fort Pillow!"

The war expanded opportunities for blacks in combat in ways other than picking up a gun to shoot white men. Although black women could not formally join the army, they served as nurses, spies, and scouts. Furthermore, education of slaves had been illegal in the antebellum South, so the Union Army became in part an educational institution for unlettered blacks. For instance, Major General Nathaniel P. Banks, a former Massachusetts governor, assigned members of the American Missionary Society as lieutenants to some of the black regiments for the express purpose of teaching the soldiers to read and write. By war's end thousands of black soldiers were literate, and their newfound abilities to read and write helped foster and deepen their political consciousness, with consequences for the Reconstruction that followed the war. "Knowledge unfits a child to be a slave," wrote the black abolitionist Frederick Douglass, quoting his erstwhile owner, who had quarreled with his wife because she was teaching Douglass to read and write.

———

The era known as Reconstruction that followed the war would remain lodged in black memory in the 1960s. It contained a crucial lesson: no matter what federal law said, the power affecting the day-to-day lives of black people was local, and it was hostile to their efforts to secure civil rights. Black people would have to fight for their rights locally, and unless they protected themselves from reprisal, no one would. So throughout the Reconstruction era, guns guarded many lives and many communities. This lesson, too, would be remembered a century after the end of the Civil War. And though guns could not in the end defeat the resurgent white supremacists once the federal government and its troops abandoned the South, the stories of pushing back against white supremacy—the successes *and* the failures—were an important part of the legacy handed to the civil rights movement of the mid-twentieth century.

During Reconstruction, blacks, joined by white sympathizers, made serious efforts to develop a genuine nonracial democracy in the South, yet today, outside of the black community, this important period is barely remembered. Little of Reconstruction history has made its way into schoolbooks; nor is it much studied in colleges and universities. Indeed, until so-called revisionist historians began to emerge in the 1960s, with the exception of such black scholars as W. E. B. Du Bois, Carter G. Woodson, Rayford Logan, and John Hope Franklin, Reconstruction was typically portrayed as a time of corrupt and incompetent black politicians who were being manipulated by arrogant, mostly white, power-hungry northern carpetbaggers and greedy southern scalawags betraying their native land and their people. This image of Reconstruction burrowed deep into the national psyche of the United States, reinforcing the antiblack prejudices already there. In addition, with no basis in fact at all, the southern rebellion became mythicized as a noble Lost Cause, embraced sympathetically not only in the South but nationally as well. The films *The Birth of a Nation* and *Gone with the Wind*, which stigmatized blacks and celebrated white terrorist groups like the Ku Klux Klan, powerfully tapped into this sympathy.

Reconstruction actually began during the war as southern cities and towns fell into Union Army hands and the army established new governments. Then, at war's end, Congress basically reinstated the old governments of strong Confederate sympathizers. This is generally called the "first

Reconstruction." A "second Reconstruction" began when "Radical Republicans" took control of Congress after the 1866 elections and established new governments in the defeated South that were much more sympathetic—though not wholly committed—to civil rights and black empowerment. In the end, however, Reconstruction was unsuccessful.

But to say that Reconstruction failed does not adequately describe what actually happened in the South after the Civil War. Reconstruction did not fail; it was destroyed, crushed by more than a decade of savage campaigns of violence carried out both by the local governments that had largely remained intact and by vigilante terrorists. Lynchings and other forms of mob violence were the instruments of Reconstruction's brutal death. The overwhelming violence against blacks during this period goes a long way toward explaining why, even though guns were common in twentieth-century black southern communities, there were few black paramilitary units and they rarely attacked or fought back with arms against white-supremacist authority, even in areas like the Mississippi Delta, central Alabama, or southwest Georgia, where blacks were an overwhelming majority of the population. The memories of Reconstruction and its violent demise dictated caution. Overt displays of force, organization, and resistance by the black community might once again trigger an instantaneous and overwhelming reaction from white-supremacist power and its foot soldiers—who were everywhere in the South—with little prospect of federal intervention. This history was very much alive in collective memory, and consequently, in the aftermath of Reconstruction and the restoration of white power, black southerners carefully calculated when and how best to use their weapons.

During the first Reconstruction, white resistance took the form of new "black codes"; they were similar to the slave codes of the antebellum era, designed to deny full citizenship to blacks and to force them into continuing to live in slave-like servitude. These codes were not simply a manifestation of racial prejudice, but were also aimed at blunting the thrust toward black power by former slaves. The southern plantocracy was just as terrified of the remarkably energetic and effective black political organizing that followed the Civil War as they were of the slave revolts that preceded it. "You never saw a people more excited on the subject of politics than are the Negroes of the south," said one plantation manager.

Playing a crucial role in this black surge toward political power were the Union Leagues. They were modeled on the northern Loyal Leagues, which were organized during the war and were mostly made up of white middle-class patriots who supported the Union Army. In the postwar South, however, Union Leagues became the voice and instrument of newly freed slaves. They spread rapidly, holding meetings in black churches, homes, schools, and even in the woods and fields. The southern leagues were semi-secret; members took an initiation oath and pledged to support the Republican Party. Armed men guarded many meetings.

In some places, self-defense organizations were an outgrowth of the leagues, and these organizations took on a militaristic structure, with drilling, armaments, and occasionally even military titles for the commanding "officers." As would be true in the 1960s civil rights movement, many of the Union Leagues' leaders were men with a degree of independence: owners of small farms, preachers, and blacksmiths, carpenters, and other craftsmen. Some came from the North. The December 17, 1867, *New York Times* reported the arrest of an "incendiary negro," George Shorter, thought to be from Illinois, who was calling on blacks in Bullock County, Alabama, to organize a separate black government with its own laws, courts, and sheriff. The leagues also engaged in political education. Members explained the Constitution and the Bill of Rights to their fellows or read aloud from Republican newspapers.

Not surprisingly, the South's former white rulers hated the leagues and the push for black political enfranchisement that they represented. Newspapers kept up a drumbeat of hostile criticism of the leagues and the Republican Party, which the leagues overwhelmingly backed. (The Democratic Party at the time was considered the party of secession, segregation, and the old Confederacy.) Violence was very much a part of whites' attacks, as well. Supposedly upstanding white citizens aided terrorists in burning down black schools, instigating riots, and assassinating black leaders.

Black veterans returning home were considered dangerous, and disarming them was a priority for the white supremacists of the defeated Confederacy. They made systematic efforts to prevent blacks from bearing arms. Among other things, white southerners demanded that black federal troops be disbanded or moved out of the south. A Mississippi law passed in 1865 said in part, "No freedman, free negro or mulatto, not in the military service of the United States government, and not licensed so to do by the board of police of his or her county, shall keep or carry fire-arms of any kind, or any ammunition . . . and it shall be the duty of every civil and military officer to arrest any freedman, free negro, or mulatto found with any such arms or ammunition, and cause him or her to be committed to trial." There is an ironic similarity between the claims made by southern whites then and the argument made by gun control proponents today. Sheriffs and white posses raided black homes to seize "illegal" guns and declared that such seizures were not an infringement of blacks' Second Amendment right to possess guns as part of a militia. Blacks faced strong disincentives to own their guns legally, however, because applying for a license effectively informed local authorities— usually sheriffs—that the applicant had weapons. Blacks were prudent enough not to do this, so most black-held arms were, therefore, illegal.

Although they continued to face violence and repression in the South, blacks did at least enjoy some limited protections under federal law. The 1866 Civil Rights Act outlawed black codes and signaled that black suffrage was the price former Confederate states would have to pay for readmission into the Union. Both the Fourteenth Amendment and the impeachment trial of President Andrew Johnson (for removing Secretary of War Edwin M. Stanton from office) reflect the beginning of this more determined and more radical approach to Reconstruction. The Fourteenth Amendment as it was adopted is best known for its equal protection, due process, and citizenship clauses. But those advocating for it also wanted to nullify state laws prohibiting blacks from possessing guns. To the old plantocracy seeking a return to power in the postwar era, the idea of blacks having those rights was every bit as frightening as it was during the days of plantation slavery. Unsurprisingly, the South resisted the amendment, and the only state of the old Confederacy to ratify the Fourteenth Amendment was Tennessee.

Violent white fury quickly coalesced around a determination to restore white supremacy. Vigilante violence found a comfortable place beside political argument in postwar southern legislatures, as groups like the Ku Klux Klan, the Regulators, the Red Shirts, the White League, the Knights of the White Camellia, the Pale Face Brotherhood, and other white-supremacist organizations began campaigns of terror.

A typical example of this early wave of antiblack terrorism and of black peoples' response to it occurred in New Orleans on July 30, 1866, when a white mob attacked a constitutional convention that was gathering at the Mechanics Institute to establish a new state government that would grant voting rights for blacks. About two hundred blacks—many of them war veterans and members of the Republican Party—had marched to the institute in support of the meeting. This was partly a protest march, for the people participating in it were angry at the state's passage of black codes that "virtually re-enacted slavery."

Suddenly, a white man along the route pushed one of the marchers, who punched him back. A shot rang out; it is unclear from where. The marchers quickly took defensive positions outside the institute, armed and ready to protect themselves and the convention delegates from a growing white mob. For more than two hours a battle raged between the mob and the black marchers. Finally the defenders, outnumbered and outgunned, retreated, and the mob began pushing its way inside the institute. Delegates pleaded with police for assistance and were ignored. One delegate, Reverend Jotham W. Horton, stood in the doorway waving a white handkerchief while crying out to police, "I beseech you to stop firing. We are noncombatants. If you want to arrest us, make any arrest you please, but we are not prepared to defend ourselves." A policeman shouted back, "We don't want any prisoners; you have all got to die." Horton was then shot and killed.

Delegates in the convention hall beat back police and members of the mob and blocked the doors with chairs. Some delegates attempted escape by jumping through windows. Whites fired at the escapees, killing some and chasing others through the streets of New Orleans. In the end, 34 black people were killed, and 119 were wounded. Unofficial estimates of the dead and wounded were even higher.

The bloodshed in New Orleans was not the only manifestation of white rage, fear, and hysteria in the face of what seemed to be the collapse of a way of life they had thought would last forever. Black war veterans were not inclined to be submissive. Two months earlier in Memphis, Tennessee, shooting had broken out between white policemen and black soldiers recently mustered out of the Union Army. The veterans had intervened in the arrest of a black man. Rumors of a black rebellion quickly spread through the white community, and for two days white mobs made up of civilians and policemen rampaged through Memphis's black neighborhoods. On the third day federal troops were finally sent to put down the violence, and an uneasy, insecure peace was restored. By then forty-five blacks had been killed. The scale of the fear and anger over what most southern whites accurately recognized as an attack aimed at destroying their way of life is reflected in the words of the former Confederate chief justice of Texas, Oran Roberts, who in 1868 warned of a pending race war: "Nothing short of the disenfranchisement of the negro race can stop it."

Years later, reflecting on this reign of terror from the ruins of Reconstruction, Frederick Douglass wrote that gaining genuine freedom in the South would require "the ballot-box, the jury-box, and the cartridge-box." Similarly, the forceful antilynching crusader Ida B. Wells-Barnett wrote in 1892, "A Winchester rifle should have a place of honor in every black home, and it should be used for that protection which the law refuses to give." Most blacks had come to the same conclusion long before and had begun to fight back. The Reconstruction era is full of examples of black people raising their voices—and brandishing weapons—to express their intention to fight for the rights due them as free citizens. In Lowndes County, Alabama, in 1868, armed black men gathered in front of the county courthouse demanding that Democrats vacate their local offices as required by recently passed Reconstruction Acts. In Macon, Georgia, a group of black men threatened to burn down the city if one more black man was murdered (leading the city council to call a "meeting of conciliation"). In the same city, in response to threats from the Klan, an armed guard of 150 men protected the homes of Jefferson Long, a tailor and political activist who in 1871 would be elected to Congress, and AME bishop Henry McNeal Turner, the first black army chaplain during the Civil War. When the Klan threatened William Harrison, a black assemblyman in Hancock County, Georgia, he replied that there would be "burning" if any harm came to him or other black Republicans in the county. A former slave, Harrison had the reputation of being "troublesome" and was also thought to have been involved in an 1863 slave insurrection.

Most black responses to white terrorism were self-defensive. Warned James Simms, who published a broadside called the *Freemen's Standard*:

"Let no man or set of men think that the loyal citizens, but more particularly the colored, will tamely submit to being attacked and murdered in Savannah as at Memphis and New Orleans." Yet although black people refused to let themselves be killed without resisting, most were not looking to engage in armed combat with whites, and most were not planning raids on white communities. Many black leaders were concerned that violent black reprisals would trigger even more violence from white supremacists, who continued to hold many positions in state and local governments in the first years of Reconstruction. Appeals to the federal government seemed to be falling on deaf ears.

It is impossible to precisely determine the effect of armed pushback by blacks in the days of Reconstruction. Nevertheless, even though its impact cannot be quantified, it anticipated armed responses to white terror in the twentieth-century civil rights movement. Many of the adult leaders of mid-twentieth-century civil rights struggle were just two generations away from these events and had heard firsthand the stories of ancestors, family friends, or community leaders who had stood up to white authority and won.

Without a doubt there was something new in the black response to the wave of white terrorism that followed the Civil War. For one thing, at war's end, the prevailing attitude and posture of black southerners was very different from what it had been before the war. They could move more freely, though not without restriction at the beginning of Reconstruction. But freedmen held mass meetings protected by armed guards; black people acquired dogs, guns, and liquor, all forbidden under slavery; and blacks refused to yield the sidewalks to approaching whites. In legal principle, if not in actual practice, moreover, black people were now citizens. Assisted by the Fourteenth Amendment, they could organize in ways that had been impossible during the era of slavery.

Blacks had some support from the so-called Radical Republicans who took control of the U.S. Congress in 1867, but they were also able to support themselves as never before. Because of the Civil War, there were weapons in black communities, and black men boasted combat experience. Even gun control efforts aimed at taking weapons out of black hands could not damp a new martial spirit that manifested itself in new and sometimes unprecedented ways. In one of three Reconstruction Acts passed in 1867, the more radical Congress created state militias, which were mostly officered by whites but contained a substantial number of black Civil War veterans.

These southern militias had great impact, especially when state governments used them to protect blacks from the resurgent white-supremacist violence following the Civil War. The Ku Klux Klan made its first appearance in Arkansas in April 1868, just one month after blacks voted in state elections for the first time. The Klan initiated a campaign of terror, murdering and beating blacks and attacking black meetings. On October 22, 1868, Republican James M. Hinds, who represented Arkansas in the U.S. House of Representatives, was assassinated by a member of the Ku Klux Klan, the first sitting member of Congress to be assassinated. In the three months before November's general election, the governor's office received reports of more than two hundred murders by the Klan.

Republican Powell Clayton, a Union general from Pennsylvania who had settled in Arkansas after the Civil War, was elected governor in November. He declared martial law in ten counties he viewed as being in a state of insurrection. "The bullets of the assassin, threats, and every species of intimidation were made use of to prevent the execution of the law, and to rob citizens of the rights and privileges of citizenship," he said in a November 24 address to the state's General Assembly. "A reign of terror was being inaugurated in our State which threatened to obliterate all the old landmarks of justice and freedom, and to bear us onward to anarchy and destruction." Clayton raised a militia of Union sympathizers and former slaves and began an active three-month campaign against white-supremacist violence. The militia fought, arrested, disarmed, and killed Klan members, forcing hundreds of other Klansmen to flee the state. On March 13, 1869, the Arkansas General Assembly made the Klan an illegal organization.

But Clayton's unusually decisive response to white terror was not typical. Militias made up of ex–Confederate soldiers who opposed the efforts of the Reconstruction governments organized to attack their efforts. Many were in militias established before the federal takeover of southern state governments, and they were highly skilled in hit-and-run tactics. They were dominated by the Ku Klux Klan. After the federal occupation, most of the governors, though Republican, feared to use black militias against the Klan and other white terrorist groups because they thought it would trigger a kind of general racial conflagration. What is more, the militias themselves became the target of highly organized white-supremacist campaigns.

The infamous 1873 massacre in Colfax, Louisiana, illustrates both the strengths and the weaknesses of armed black resistance to white vigilante groups. Black power was broken there, signaling an oncoming cataclysm that would sink tentative efforts at democracy in not only Louisiana but in the rest of the South as well: the complete destruction of Reconstruction through armed force. Colfax was the seat of Grant Parish. Republican governor Henry Clay Warmouth, who had been a colonel in the Union Army, created Grant Parish on March 9, 1869, from three other parishes in Louisiana's Red River Valley—Rapides, Natchitoches, and Winn. The Red River Valley was one of the state's strongest bastions of Confederate sympathy. Rumor had it that Simon Legree, the brutal overseer in Harriet Beecher Stowe's antislavery novel, *Uncle Tom's Cabin*, was based on the overseer of the Hidden Hill Plantation near Colfax, which she had once visited. Warmouth's decision to name this new parish for General Ulysses S. Grant was a deliberate slap in the face to Confederate sympathizers, and a reminder that Louisiana's Confederate heartland was administered by a state government dominated by Radical Republicans. But the underlying political purpose of Grant Parish was even more horrifying to the state's white supremacists. It was one of eight new parishes created by the Republican-dominated state government to achieve black majorities in the state, gerrymandering intended to help the state's black communities achieve a political voice, as well as to make Republicans' power more secure.

Since the end of the war extreme violence aimed at intimidating blacks had blighted the region from which Grant Parish was created. In 1867, in a tiny settlement called Holloway's Prairie near the future site of Colfax, armed whites stormed a black church service, shooting and killing any members of the congregation who attempted to escape. Then they randomly selected two men and one woman from the congregation and hanged them. Violence escalated during and after the 1868 presidential election that gained Ulysses S. Grant the presidency. But while white supremacy was growing in strength in Grant Parish, so too was the power of Louisiana's Republican-dominated state government. For a little while at least, as in Arkansas, the state government was able to shield its black constituents from white terror by investing in the armed power of black veterans.

Black militiamen were secreted in various black households in Grant Parish. Warmouth had approved this; they were part of a 5,000-man state militia composed of black and white units. William Ward, the leader of this secret militia unit in the parish and also a captain in the Louisiana State Militia's Sixth Infantry Regiment, had fought during the Civil War in the Louisiana Corps d'Afrique and had achieved the rank of sergeant, the highest rank a black soldier could achieve at the time.

Grant Parish's secret black militia was not shy about flexing its muscles. On March 14, 1871, carrying weapons provided by the state, the militia stormed the Grant Parish courthouse, disrupting the murder trial of a group of white supremacists. At gunpoint and over the objections of the judge, who was thought by Parish blacks to be sympathetic to the men being tried, the militiamen seized the prisoners. "Damn the court," Ward said, claiming jurisdiction in the name of the U.S. attorney in New Orleans. Ironically, his claim was modeled on the power given to federal officials to create special federal tribunals for investigating the legitimacy of owners seeking the return of slaves, as mandated by the Fugitive Slave Act of 1850. That act required the return of proven runaways and also made assisting runaways a federal crime.

Ward's action hardly eased white–black tensions in Grant Parish or in the violently white-supremacist parishes around it. To the contrary, his example confirmed the worst fears of whites everywhere in the state about the new forms of black power accompanying Reconstruction. Yet Ward continued to make similar arrests; empowered by the U.S. attorney in New Orleans, he brought mobsters and murderers before federal tribunals there. He remained unbowed—and he derived support from President Ulysses S. Grant, no friend of Confederate nationalism.

Although notoriously corrupt, the Grant administration nonetheless seemed hopeful to radical black Republicans like Ward, and Louisiana's emerging black power seemed useful to Grant. Traditionally, for instance, crimes like murder by the Ku Klux Klan were considered local cases. Now, under new federal law promulgated by Grant, they could be considered federal crimes. The same law made it illegal for two or more men "to go in disguise upon the public highway" to prevent other people from exercising their constitutional rights, as the Ku Klux Klan did in attacking meetings or the homes of black political leaders. This effectively made the Klan illegal without naming the organization. The law also empowered Ward, a lawman in Louisiana, to make arrests. His Grant Parish militia paraded in old army uniforms.

Meanwhile, white terrorism in Louisiana's Red River Valley was making Colfax a locus of black power—a center for black refugees—and, commented a New Orleans newspaper, "the Mecca of bad and desperate negroes from everywhere." Grant Parish had 2,400 blacks and 2,200 whites according to the 1870 census. This roughly 50–50 racial split mirrored the population of the state as a whole. But what gave Colfax and Grant Parish special significance in the violently rough-and-tumble politics of Louisiana was that it was the headquarters of William Ward and his militia. And Ward had the support of William Smith Calhoun, one of the parish's largest planters.

In the spring of 1873, simmering white–black political antagonism boiled over in the parish. On March 25 Ward and some members of Ward's militia seized the courthouse in Colfax. Whites in Grant and surrounding parishes began organizing to take it back; the chief organizers were the Knights of the White Camellia and another group calling itself the Old Time Ku Klux Klan.

Ward mobilized his militia to take over and defend the courthouse. His men guarded all the roads leading into town and began drilling with arms in front of the courthouse and stockpiling ammunition, while also preventing unknown whites from entering the town. On April 5, black militiamen drove off a group of whites attempting to reconnoiter the town. Ward expected assistance from the newly elected governor, William Pitt Kellogg, an ally of President Grant, but the governor had his own problems, starting with getting recognized as governor. The 1872 election had been bitterly fought, not only pitting Republicans against Democrats but also including a new "Fusionist" Party, led by John McEnery, a former Confederate battalion commander, and widely supported by white-supremacist Democrats and Republicans distressed with the corruption of the Grant administration. The election may have been stolen. Even Grant acknowledged that Kellogg's victory "was not altogether certain." Kellogg and McEnery both claimed the governorship and asked for congressional recognition and federal intervention; both held inaugurations on January 13, 1873. Both appointed a set of local officials for Grant Parish.

Kellogg, still waiting for recognition from Washington, D.C., and insecure without it, decided that he could not come to the aid of Ward. (Grant
finally issued an executive order recognizing Kellogg as governor on September 20, 1873.) Trying to win over former opponents, Kellogg declared
events in Colfax a local matter and said he would not intervene unless the
federal government ordered him to.

On April 13, shortly before noon, hundreds of armed white supremacists approached the courthouse in Colfax. Their leader was Christopher
Columbus Nash, a Confederate veteran and former prisoner of war. Nash
halted his paramilitary group in battle formation within view of the courthouse. Under a white flag, he went into the black community and found a
black man, whom he sent to the courthouse with an offer to negotiate. Out
came the commander of the courthouse defense, a man named Benjamin
Levin "Lev" Allen. "We want that courthouse," Nash told him. Allen pointed
out that Nash's group had already killed several black men at random, men
who were not involved in the takeover, and that the defenders did not feel
safe putting down their arms. Nash and his men could have Allen's own
weapons when he was killed, he added. Both men walked away.

Thirty minutes later, Nash's forces attacked. They were met with heavy
fire from the black militiamen dug in around the building, and for an hour
or so Nash's advance bogged down. Finally, his men brought up a cannon
and opened fire. The heavy weapon surprised the defenders. Some
retreated inside the courthouse building; others fled, only to be chased
down and killed. The attacking white forces torched the courthouse's
cypress-shingled roof, but some of the defenders refused to flee. Those who
did were shot down, as were those who attempted to surrender.

The fighting finally stopped around 3 PM. Nash's forces took prisoners
but summarily executed many with a pistol shot to the back of the head.
The estimates of the number of blacks killed that day vary widely. A military report identifies 105 victims by name. An unspecified number of bodies were found in the Red River; thirteen prisoners were hanged from an
old pecan tree near the courthouse. The aftermath of the Colfax massacre
was as shameful as the event itself: although federal troops arrived on April
21 and some of the attackers were tried, none were convicted or punished
in any way. Nash went on to serve as parish sheriff for several terms.

The Colfax violence set the pattern that would be used to end Reconstruction: white supremacists employing overwhelming violence to cow local blacks, and a federal government reluctant to contain it. Just five months after the Colfax atrocity, on September 14, 1873, some 2,000 White League members defeated 500 black militiamen and 500 metropolitan police officers in New Orleans. They took possession of the statehouse and the New Orleans Arsenal and installed a white-supremacist government. Although soon ousted by federal troops, the White League became the dominant political force in the state, even refusing to pay state taxes. They ruled in defiance of state and federal authority, not in conjunction with it. "Practically, so-called Reconstruction in Louisiana was a continuation of the Civil War," Du Bois would later observe.

The tragedies in Colfax and New Orleans were repeated in other parts of the South. In Vicksburg, Mississippi, at least fifty blacks were killed by white rioters on December 7, 1874. Some accounts put the number of black dead at three hundred or more. Such violence was not random; rather, it was deliberate and political, "an *essential* component in the counterrevolution that rolled back the tide of Radical Reconstruction and restored command of Southern political institutions to white supremacy."

W. E. B. Du Bois wrote with pain in 1935, "The slave went free; stood a brief moment in the sun; then moved back again toward slavery." He was right, but that is only part of the story. Certainly white supremacy and white power achieved and secured "Redemption," as this period has come to be called in many quarters of the white South. For their part, blacks learned that, absent federal support, armed resistance to white-supremacist violence was insufficient, even if it sometimes saved the moment. Moreover, they discerned that any support they received from outside their own communities was unlikely to be timely, permanent, or even genuine.

But the tragic and brutal lessons of Reconstruction's dismemberment did not spell the end of black resistance to white supremacy. The hopes that had animated Reconstruction were never abandoned, and black people nursed the will to resist in the decades to come. Sometimes that will was hidden deeply beneath the surface of black life. And sometimes it erupted suddenly, powerfully, and unexpectedly, as it variously did throughout the entire twentieth century.

2

"The Day of Camouflage Is Past"

*Today we return! We return from the slavery of uniform which the
world's madness demanded us to don to the freedom of civil garb.
We stand again to look America squarely in the face and call a spade
a spade. We sing: This country of ours, despite all its better souls
have done and dreamed, is yet a shameful land. It lynches. . . . It
disenfranchises its own citizens. . . . It encourages ignorance. . . .
It steals from us. . . . It insults us. . . . We return. We return from
fighting. . . . We return fighting. . . . Make way for democracy!*
                                              —W. E. B. Du Bois, 1919

On the cold Monday night of February 25, 1946, armed black men assembled on rooftops in Columbia, Tennessee, intently watching the streets
below. Their eyes were focused on the first block of East Eighth Street,
which housed small businesses and was the Main Street of the town's black
community. The area was called the Bottom by the black community and
Mink Slide by whites. Lynch-mob fervor had been building in town all day,
and when it finally blazed into fierce and furious fire, East Eighth Street
would briefly be turned into a battleground.

The incident that caused that armed black mobilization had taken place
that morning on Columbia's town square when a young black navy veteran
named James Stephenson and his mother Gladys had argued and fought
with two white employees of the Castor–Knott Department Store. The

disagreement seems simple on the surface: In early January Gladys Stephenson had left her radio with the department store's repair shop. But when her youngest son, John Robert, returned for it over a month later, repair shop manager LaVal LaPointe told him that the radio had been sold to an employee of farmer John Calhoun Fleming. The store did, in fact, have a policy that items left longer than thirty days could be sold, but this was the first time the option had been exercised, and the store agreed to retrieve the radio.

Mrs. Stephenson did get her radio back. But when she got it home again, she discovered it still was not working. On the morning of February 25 she went back to the shop, accompanied now by her nineteen-year-old son James, who had just been discharged from the Navy. LaPointe and Mrs. Stephenson got into heated argument about what parts the radio needed and the higher price he was now quoting for the repair. She and her son stalked out of the shop. They were followed by LaPointe and William "Billy" Fleming, an apprentice at the shop and the son of the farmer whose employee had purchased the radio. Near the store's entrance, they passed an elderly white man bringing in a radio for repair. At the same moment, Mrs. Stephenson was telling her son in a loud, irritated voice that the only thing the shop had done was ruin her radio.

Perhaps worried that the Stephensons were impugning the shop in front of its white clientele, or perhaps simply angry at getting an argument from black people, Fleming ordered mother and son out of the store. Apparently something in his tone or body language alarmed James, who placed himself protectively between his mother and Fleming. According to Fleming, James Stephenson looked back at him in a "threatening" manner as he and his mother left the store. That glance, or whatever Fleming read into it, seems to have been the final straw for the irritated radio shop apprentice. He charged through the door and lunged at James Stephenson, striking him in the back of the head with his fist. But Stephenson had been a welterweight boxer in the navy, and he spun around and knocked Fleming through a window next to the closed door.

LaPointe rushed to assist his apprentice, but Mrs. Stephenson grabbed him from behind. He twisted away, slapped her in the face, and tried to restrain her. She pulled herself free and attempted to stab Fleming in the back with a piece of broken window glass, but she missed and only scraped his shoulder. The melee, meanwhile, was attracting a great deal of attention. Another white man ran across the street and jumped into the fray, throwing Mrs. Stephenson to the ground, tearing her coat and giving her a black eye. James Stephenson tried to defend his mother, but the three white men subdued him and called the police.

Columbia's police chief, Walter Griffin, arrived on the scene; mother and son were hustled off to the city jail, charged with breach of the peace, and fined fifty dollars each. They either paid or made arrangements to pay the fine (it is not clear which), but instead of being released as they expected, they were taken back to their cells, where they remained until early afternoon. Police then took them to the county jail; Billy Fleming's father had obtained a warrant alleging they had attempted to murder his son. At the county jail, Sheriff James J. Underwood warned the two that white townspeople were furious and in a violent mood. Indeed, an increasingly inebriated crowd of white people had already begun gathering near the Maury County courthouse calling in loud voices for the Stephensons to be lynched. Fleming's father was among them, but he became so drunk he passed out and had to be carried away.

When Gladys Stephenson's mother, Hannah Peppers, heard that her daughter and grandson were in jail, she had appealed to two black businessmen for help paying the fine: black Columbia's seventy-six-year-old patriarch, Julius Blair, who owned a soda fountain on East Eighth Street, and James Morton, the owner of a funeral parlor on the same street. Both men accompanied Peppers to the town magistrate, who told them that the Stephensons should remain in jail for their own safety. Nevertheless, Mrs. Peppers, Blair, and Morton proceeded to the county jail, and Sheriff Underwood reluctantly released the Stephensons. Mrs. Stephenson was taken home, and James was brought to the Bottom.

As it had in the white community, word of the arrests had spread rapidly through the black community, who felt that James's life and possibly his mother's life were in peril. Black people, many of them armed, streamed into the Bottom: "Probably one hundred-fifty negroes . . . forty to fifty or maybe more [with] guns in their hands, shotguns, rifles of different types and calibers," noted one observer. Julius Blair, never known for bellicosity, declared, "We are *not* going to have any more social lynchings in Maury County."

Blair was referring to an event that lived vividly in the collective memory of the town's black residents: in 1933, after a Columbia grand jury had failed to indict a black teenage boy on charges of molesting a white girl, a mob took him from jail, hanged him, and burned his body. Over the years, such atrocities were tinder for an easily combustible mix of fear and fury in Columbia's black community. The town is only about thirty miles away from Pulaski, Tennessee, where in 1865 six young veterans of the Confederate army first organized the Ku Klux Klan. None of Columbia's blacks doubted that the local white population was overwhelmingly hostile to them and to Afro-Americans generally. Although many blacks were afraid of the harm whites could inflict on them, they were angry, too. And on this winter night in early 1946, that anger flared with unexpected intensity.

When a police car entered the Bottom that evening, a crowd surrounded it and began to rock it, trying to overturn it. Someone near the bumper yelled out that he had "fought for freedom overseas and going to fight for it here." The crowd even threatened Sherriff Underwood himself—a severe transgression of the white-supremacist culture of the time.

Blair, Morton, and other black business leaders tried to lower the temperature of a situation becoming increasingly heated. Morton told Underwood that they did not want any white people in the area. "Get rid of the white people on the square [and] the Negroes [here] would be all right," he suggested. In their effort to quiet things down, Blair and Morton also escorted James Stephenson, who was in the crowd carrying a shotgun he had obtained from a nearby barbershop, out of the Bottom. The two men drove James and his mother to Nashville, about forty-five miles north of town.

As night fell, World War II veterans, a few in uniform, took command of the Bottom's defenses. Around 10 PM, they ordered the lights of the district's businesses turned off, and they shot out the street lights to provide complete cover of darkness. Hearing the gunfire, Chief Griffin and four of his policemen entered the Bottom in two cars. They rode with their lights out, and the Bottom's defenders may not have recognized them as policemen—which may help explain the unrestrained intensity of the defenders' response.

"Here they come!" someone shouted as the two cars approached the

Bottom. Shots rang out. The volley of gunfire wounded Griffin and all four of the policemen and may have caused other casualties as well; a white mob had followed the police into the Bottom, and years later a black carpenter, Raymond Lockridge, told writer Juan Williams that four or five of its members were killed in the exchange. Lockridge described "blood running in the gutters," but he also told Williams that because the victims were white and the killers black, the deaths were covered up. Reporting on events in Columbia later, the *Afro-American* newspaper suggested something similar: "Whites whose obituaries stated [they] died suddenly of heart failures may also have suffered slight cases of Mink Slide bullet poisoning. . . . [Members of the mob] can't admit even to this day that [they] took a beating when colored [people] decided to protect themselves."

This unprecedented show of armed black resistance frightened Columbia's white authorities, and Sheriff Underwood asked the state to intervene. Before the night was over, hundreds of heavily armed state police and National Guard members had arrived in Columbia. Like the white townspeople, they were enraged. They were also cautious, setting up a cordon around the Bottom but waiting until dawn before moving in.

What followed was an orgy of violence and looting. The troopers indiscriminately shot out windows, ripped up the floors of businesses and homes, and broke apart furniture—all under the pretense of searching for weapons, ammunition, and gunmen. They also stole cash and goods from the Bottom's businesses and ransacked Morton's funeral home, scrawling the letters "KKK" on one of the coffins. The NAACP's *Crisis* magazine deplored the invaders' "Gestapo-like vandalism" and reported that when the police and National Guard were finished in the Bottom, "not a single black-owned business in the first block of East Eighth Street was left unscathed. All were damaged through overzealous searching and 'wanton destruction.'" The troopers removed arms found in any home they searched, and they arrested more than a hundred people, two of whom were killed while in custody.

The rampage in the Bottom was much more than a police action innocent of political purpose. After World War II, southern whites feared that black servicemen returning home from overseas would threaten the traditional white-supremacist order. The Mississippi-born editor of Kentucky's *Louisville*

Courier-Journal warned that "militant" blacks "were moving on every front." With growing uneasiness, the southern establishment—planters, businessmen, politicians, and good ol' boys in cities, rural towns, and counties—discerned winds of change rustling the political and social landscape. The widely publicized resistance in Columbia was yet more proof to many whites that if they were to remain supreme in the South, they would have to determine how best to quash any "dangerous Negroes"—especially armed black soldiers—who were trying to assert their opinions and rights in the postwar era.

———

Although the war was responsible for some of the changes that threatened southern whites, change had begun before the war. In the 1936 presidential election, black voters had deserted the Republican Party in large numbers, casting a majority of their votes for the Democrat Franklin Delano Roosevelt. Three months before that vote, Senator Ellison Durant "Cotton Ed" Smith of South Carolina had walked out of the Democratic Party National Convention, enraged over the participation of blacks. "The doors of the white man's party have been thrown open to snare the Negro vote in the North," he protested.

Expanded black participation in the Democratic Party meant that the party could not avoid at least speaking to some of the issues of concern to black people. As limited as the party's interest in black concerns was, however, white southern Democrats were outraged that there was any interest at all. When Hubert Humphrey, then mayor of Minneapolis, made a speech at the 1948 Democratic Party National Convention calling for greater commitment to civil rights, all of Mississippi's delegation and half of Alabama's walked out and formed a States' Rights Party, which nominated South Carolina's Senator Strom Thurmond as its presidential candidate. Southern political leaders who did not join Thurmond's party backed a rump presidential campaign by Georgia's Senator Richard B. Russell to protest the nomination of Harry S. Truman, who had supported the civil rights plank in the party's platform at the 1948 convention. However, these dissidents never really left the Democratic Party and were lumped together as "Dixiecrats."

For obvious political reasons—in particular the growing number of black people in large cities—not everyone in the Democratic Party establishment was angered or fearful of black involvement. Differences over racial policies and practices would continue to alienate Dixiecrats from the national Democratic Party until finally, in 1964, southern whites fled to the Republican Party in overwhelming numbers.

A host of other factors also signaled white supremacy's erosion: President Roosevelt's New Deal programs; Don't Buy Where You Can't Work campaigns in the 1930s and 1940s; the rise of new activist organizations like the Southern Negro Youth Congress (SNYC); the creation in 1941 of the Fair Employment Practices Commission, forced by A. Philip Randolph's threatened March on Washington; the Supreme Court's 1944 ruling against the Democratic Party's white-voters-only primaries in Texas; the Operation Dixie union organizing drive launched by the Congress of Industrial Organizations (CIO) after the war; the steady expansion of the NAACP, with its refocus on giving priority to attacking the legal underpinnings of segregation; and even the status of black athletes like Olympic track star Jesse Owens, boxer Joe Louis, and baseball great Jackie Robinson.

And the world itself was changing. World War II had brought a surge of antitotalitarian rhetoric trumpeting the merits of freedom and democracy. The Four Freedoms articulated by President Roosevelt in his State of the Union address just a few weeks after the bombing of Pearl Harbor—freedom of speech and of worship, freedom from want and from fear—were intended to illustrate what he felt best described American principles, yet they contravened the very essence of southern white power. Many a white supremacist saw fear as a necessary tool for keeping blacks in line; eliminating it was the first step to losing power. And though southern whites could perhaps accept speech and worship as constitutionally protected (though with regard to blacks, Jews, and Catholics, unclear), the U.S. Constitution made no promise of economic well-being, which reinforced argument from some— and not just southern whites—that Roosevelt's New Deal programs crossed the boundary separating capitalism from socialism.

Southern white power recognized that the vision Roosevelt articulated for the country was inherently destabilizing to their way of life. Whatever the merits of establishing or reestablishing freedom and democracy in

Germany, Italy, and Japan, they were still considered white-only prerogatives in Dixie, and in much of the rest of the United States, as well. "Are we fighting this war to destroy everything we inherited from our forefathers?" asked an alarmed Mississippi Delta planter. "This is a conservative war. . . . It is not a war for Fascism, Nazism, Communism, Socialism, New Dealism *or Democracy* [emphasis added]."

The white reaction to these changes was not just political; it was also deeply emotional. In a July 1943 speech, North Carolina governor Joseph Melville Broughton denounced "radical" black leaders who, he said, were "seeking to use the war emergency to advance theories and philosophies which if carried to their ultimate conclusion would result only in a mongrel race." Miscegenation ranked alongside black men willing to kill white men as one of the southern white man's two greatest fears. Cloaked in the language of resistance to "social equality" or presented as defense of southern white womanhood, the need to prevent "race mixing" became an emotional battle cry in charge after charge against the black Freedom Movement. Illustrating the power of this fear is the fact that not until 1967 were statutes outlawing interracial marriages declared unconstitutional—thirteen years after the Supreme Court declared, in *Brown v. Board of Education,* that school segregation was unconstitutional. During and immediately after the war, the idea of racial intermingling, whether casually social or romantic, rallied southern whites. It also focused hostility on returning black servicemen, who while overseas had been treated with appreciation and equality by male and female Europeans. Denouncing black troops from the Senate floor in 1945, Mississippi senator James O. Eastland declared, "There will be no social equality; there will be no such un-American measures when the [black] soldier returns."

Deeper historical currents shaped the white reaction, as well. Spokesmen for white supremacy like Eastland and Broughton considered themselves Jeffersonian Democrats faithful to the country's founding principles. They persuaded themselves that in calling for his Four Freedoms "everywhere in the world," Roosevelt was deliberately undermining states' rights, imposing federal authority on the South, as well as obligating the United States to international authority and values far removed from the Jeffersonian ideal of an agrarian republic in which most authority would be local authority.

The many white World War II veterans raging against the Stephensons almost certainly saw themselves as standing up not only for their southern way of life but also, more broadly, for the American way of life. Translated into the values and mores of their time and place, that meant that if a white man hit a black man, as Fleming did to James Stephenson, the black man was not to hit back. Nor was any black person to argue with any white person, as Gladys Stephenson had. Like the ideals of freedom and democracy, the right to stand one's ground was held to be an exclusively white prerogative. Even when threatened by a mob, black people were to back down or submit—never to stand up for themselves.

All these complex factors shaped the decision of exasperated blacks to pick up the gun in Columbia in February 1946. An editorial in the *Columbia Daily Herald* made it unmistakably plain that the local and state response was aimed at protecting white supremacy: "The white people of the South . . . will not tolerate any racial disturbances without resenting it, which means bloodshed. The Negro has not a chance of gaining supremacy over a sovereign people and the sooner the better element of the Negro race realizes this, the better off the race will be."

Black Americans, however, interpreted what had happened in Columbia very differently. "Negroes even in small communities like Columbia where they were outnumbered almost three to one, do not intend to sit quietly and let a mob form, threaten, and raid their neighborhood," editorialized *Crisis* magazine. Columbia's black community agreed. Their resistance had changed the everyday experience of being black in Columbia and Maury County. Five years later, Sol Blair, a barber and the eldest son of Julius Blair, told journalist Carl Rowan, "Before, Columbia was a hellhole, but we've got a good city now. Used to be that when a Negro went into a store uptown, the clerks didn't see him until he started to walk out. You go in [a store uptown] now and ask for a pair of galluses [suspenders] and those [white] clerks will button 'em up for you."

Blair was not alone in thinking that 1946 had been a turning point. A few days after speaking with him, Rowan traveled into the countryside of Maury County to meet and interview Henry Clay Harlan. In 1927, with the help of the sheriff, Harlan's grandson, eighteen-year-old Henry Choate, had been seized from the county jail by a white mob and hanged from the courthouse's second-floor balcony. When Harlan's wife warned her husband against talking to Rowan about the murder, Harlan assured her,

> There won't be no more trouble. . . . That's the one thing I learned from 1946. They now know Negroes have guts. The Blairs and Mortons was the first Columbia Negroes ever to stand up like men. Blood was shed, but it paid off. I dare say times has changed. A colored man used to not have the chance of a sheep-killing dog. But 1946 changed that.

———

It was no coincidence that Columbia's sea change occurred so soon after World War II. Unprecedented numbers of black people had served in the U.S. military in the preceding decades: 380,000 in World War I and more than 1 million in World War II. They had encountered vicious racial discrimination at every level. Even blood was segregated by race during World War II, despite the fact that Charles R. Drew, the doctor whose research had made blood transfusions possible, was an Afro-American. But even though black soldiers faced enemies within the U.S. military, it was the experience of travel and combat that truly changed them. Warfare exposed black servicemen to a wider world, gave them the discipline and know-how to organize and fight, and gave many of them the experience of killing white men. Black soldiers returned home changed and with a new willingness to fight for and defend their rights, with guns if necessary.

To be sure, Afro-American soldiers have participated in warfare since the American War of Independence, and their experiences have always intensified the black fight for freedom. But the twentieth century was nevertheless exceptional. With World Wars I and II, a strong and sustained translation of war experience into black civil rights activism began to permanently change the political landscape of race. World War I began closing the doorway through which so much of the nineteenth century's racial presumptions and practices passed into the twentieth century. Just four decades after the white-supremacist Redemption from Reconstruction, World War I began to make it plain that black silence and submission could not be guaranteed by violence alone. Yet this slowly closing doorway was still partially open as World War II approached, and even at that war's end the door was not yet locked nor firmly shut.

Both wars, however, helped a diverse range of organizations to put pressure on the South and on the federal government to recognize the civil rights of black people. Gaining civil rights did not mean simply ending discrimination and violence against black people in the South; rather, it meant establishing black people's long-denied citizenship and granting their claim to all the accompanying rights and privileges—a claim that the southern Redemption of the past century had sought to deny. SNCC's Bob Moses would later characterize the question of access to citizens' rights as one of "constitutional personhood": who gets to be a full citizen of the United States? As the twentieth century progressed, it became clear that this question not only remained unresolved but also applied to more than black people. It is also contingent on another question: does the federal government have the disposition and will to fulfill its duty of protecting the life and liberty of all its citizenry?

For much of the twentieth century, local, state, and federal governments demonstrated little interest in guaranteeing either blacks' safety or their political rights. They often, in fact, stubbornly resisted calls to do so and responded ruthlessly and brutally against those pressing them to meet their responsibilities. With World War I and World War II, however, it became increasingly apparent that the black community could no longer be ignored or silenced and whites' claim to racial superiority and grip on power would face a powerful challenge and greater pressure to change.

Prior to World War I, many southern whites also thought that the violence of Redemption and the continuing violence of terrorist groups like the Ku Klux Klan had successfully tamped down threats to white supremacy. They had persuaded themselves that black people had come to accept their inferior standing in southern society. The fact that a new wave of antiblack mob violence surged after World War I can be attributed to white surprise, fear, and anger at discovering they were wrong, that blacks were not content with the southern white-supremacist system or, indeed, with discrimination in the North, for that matter. And this discovery led to more sophisticated and systematic attempts to restructure and reinforce white domination.

Influential personages in the federal government shared the South's alarm and joined southern authorities in blaming civil rights efforts—and even the kind of back talk engaged in by the Stephensons—on subversive ideology, individuals, and organizations. They believed that anarchism, communism, and unions explained black discontent.

———

Worries about new black threats grew during World War I and World War II and frequently revolved around fears that whites would be outnumbered and that blacks would engage in armed rebellion. A federal official in Texas reported with alarm in 1917 that "Negroes are organizing all over the state under the name of the 'National Association for the Advancement of Colored People' and are buying up all the high-powered rifles and ammunition they can possibly buy." In Georgia during World War II a rumor spread that black soldiers were using the absence of white bosses to stockpile weapons in preparation for a general uprising. But perhaps most bizarre was the rumor that spread at the start of World War II, a rumor that had nothing to do with guns directly, except for what it reveals about the irrational fear held by many white southerners. It was said that black maids influenced by Eleanor Roosevelt—"Eleanorites"—were organizing Eleanor Clubs whose members planned to disrupt the existing social order by refusing to wear servants' uniforms, work unlimited hours, or respond when addressed by their first names. Surly maids were supposedly going to try to enter white-owned homes by the front door instead of the back door. The alleged Eleanorite motto: "No colored maid in the kitchen by Christmas." The FBI actually began a formal investigation into the supposed existence of these clubs in 1942.

Though the American public had never had a problem with employing black women as domestic servants, the U.S. military had always been reluctant to use black men as soldiers. In World War I especially, the military would rather have used blacks behind the front lines than place them in combat. The old myth of black cowardice undoubtedly still prevailed as well, alongside the old fear of guns in black soldiers' hands. Accordingly, even as Afro-American troops set about risking and often sacrificing their lives for the United States, they were constantly reminded of their second-class status in it.

A vivid illustration of the discrimination black soldiers faced during World War I is provided by the August 7, 1918, memorandum *Secret Information Concerning Black American Troops*, which was issued to France's military by the French mission that was liaising with American forces. The French mission had been pressured into issuing the memo by the headquarters of General John Joseph "Black Jack" Pershing, commander of U.S. expeditionary forces in Europe. He, along with other members of the U.S. military brass, objected to the fact that black U.S. soldiers under French command were being treated as the equals of French soldiers—especially because they were also comfortably associating with French civilians in their homes and in public places. The document stressed that French officers needed to understand the sensitivities of race in America and recognize that black people would pose a dire threat once they returned home unless they were consistently separated from whites while overseas. "The increasing number of negroes in the United States (about 15,000,000) would create for the white race in the Republic a menace of degeneracy were it not that an impassable gulf has been made between them," the document asserted. "The vices of the Negro are a constant menace to the American who has to repress them sternly." To the credit of the French government, it ordered all copies of the document collected and burned.

The experiences of black soldiers in World War I are intimately connected to several developments unfolding in the United States at around the same time, events that would recast the racial dynamic in the United States for the rest of the twentieth century. A Great Migration of black people from the South to the North began in 1910. It continued for more than half a century and gradually transformed the U.S. black population from primarily southern and rural to primarily northern and urban. Industrial cities like Detroit and Chicago began to swell with incoming black southerners. Although the migrants found greater opportunity outside the South, they did not escape discrimination and racial friction, especially with regard to housing and the workplace. "The South," observes one historian, "was never another country even though for much of its history it may have felt and acted like one."

Blacks moving north may have found more freedom in terms of job opportunities and even political participation, but in many ways their plight remained the same. In a letter written just a few days after Woodrow Wilson's inauguration in 1913, W. E. B. Du Bois reminded the new president that he had gained the office with the help of black voters. They had sided with him despite the fact that he was a Democrat, a leading member of a party notorious for its white-supremacist outlook. Wilson owed black people something in return, said Du Bois. "The forces of hell in this country are fighting a terrific and momentarily successful battle," he wrote in his open letter to Wilson. "But the fight is on, and you, sir, are this month stepping into its arena." Almost immediately, however, Wilson, a Virginian, began the racial segregation of Washington, D.C., starting with government buildings, dismissing many black government employees. In so doing, he sent a powerful signal that the highest level of U.S. authority was committed to white supremacy. It was yet another reminder that black people could expect little or no help from the federal government.

World War I and the presidency of Woodrow Wilson are part of a period in post–Civil War black life in America that has come to be called "the nadir." Stretching roughly from the end of Reconstruction in 1877 until the end of World War I in 1918 (and, some would say, several decades beyond that), these were the years in which race relations in the United States were at their lowest ebb. Stripped of the rights and political opportunities they had begun to enjoy during Reconstruction and rarely finding any white allies in the federal government, blacks either fled to the relative safety of the North or struggled to survive in the South in an almost unimaginable climate of antiblack terror. Between the end of Reconstruction and the U.S. entry into World War I, thousands of lynchings took place, mostly in the South, and often under the pretense of protecting southern white womanhood. Speaking from the Senate floor in 1919, Mississippi senator John Sharp Williams endorsed lynching, and particularly if a black man was accused of raping a white woman. "Race is greater than law now and then," he asserted, "and protection of women transcends all law, human and divine."

Violence continued to be the main tool of white-supremacist authority during the first half of the twentieth century, because the white power structure had not yet completed construction of the more sophisticated legal edifice it would use to protect white supremacy from the 1950s on. Across the rural South, moreover, a system of debt peonage not far removed from slavery was firmly in place. Still, whites were perpetually wary of any black display of self-reliance or assertion of human rights, and their fears frequently erupted in hysterical rampages. In late July 1900, for instance, white rioting swept New Orleans for days during the manhunt for a black laborer and back-to-Africa advocate named Robert Charles. A white policeman had beaten and shot at Charles for sitting on the porch of a white friend; Charles had shot the officer in response but had not killed him. Charles battled infuriated whites alone, allegedly killing several policemen as well as a few vigilantes before being shot and killed himself.

However, not everywhere was black resistance so successfully hunted down and crushed. In 1906 whites rioted in Atlanta, whose black population, more than most in the South, embodied black resilience. Walter White, who would eventually lead the NAACP, was a boy then and remembered black resistance to it. His family had learned that a mob intended to invade their Atlanta neighborhood, which was close to the city's downtown, and "clean out the niggers." There had never been guns in their house, but White's father acquired some at the insistence of his wife. Recalls White:

We turned out the lights early, as did all our neighbors. Toward midnight the unnatural quiet was broken by a roar that grew steadily in volume. Even today I grow tense in remembering it. Father told Mother to take my sisters, the youngest of them only six, to the rear of the house, which offered more protection from stones and bullets. . . . There was a crash as Negroes smashed the street lamp at the corner of Houston and Piedmont Avenue down the street. In a very few minutes the vanguard of the mob, some of them bearing torches, appeared. . . . In a voice as quiet as though he were asking me to pass him the sugar at the breakfast table, [my father] said, "Son, don't shoot until the first man puts his foot on the lawn and then—don't you miss!"

The mob moved toward the lawn. I tried to aim my gun, wondering what it would feel like to kill a man. Suddenly there was a volley of shots. The mob hesitated, stopped. Some friends of my father's had barricaded themselves in a two-story brick building just below our house. It was they who had fired. Some of the mobsmen, still bloodthirsty, shouted, "Let's go get the nigger." Others, afraid now for their safety, held back. Our friends, noting the hesitation, fired another volley. The mob broke and retreated up Houston Street.

White's memory of the Atlanta riots reveals the same strategy—and many of the same tactics—that blacks used to protect their neighborhood in Columbia, Tennessee, some four decades later and throughout the Black-Belt South in the 1950s and '60s. Yet even in 1906 this was not an isolated incident of blacks arming themselves for self-defense, nor was it unique to White's neighborhood. During the same riots, W. E. B. Du Bois, then a sociology professor at Atlanta University, bought a double-barreled shotgun and sat on his front porch, determined to protect his wife and daughter. "If a white mob had stepped on the campus where I lived," he wrote later, "I would without hesitation have spread their guts over the grass."

Across the country, with and without guns, black people like Du Bois were willing to resist white-supremacist power—especially violence—by any means necessary. If we exclude here the more complex Native American resistance to settlers seizing their land, it can easily be argued that today's controversial Stand Your Ground right of self-defense first took root in black communities.

Most self-defense was personal rather than consciously political, and most was manifested as a local response to white terror rather than as any sort of national movement. Certainly, political modes of resistance cannot be disregarded, and even when white-supremacist terror raged at its worst during the nadir, blacks organized to repel it. In 1887, for instance, T. Thomas Fortune and AME bishop Alexander Walters formed the first national black civil rights organization, the Afro-American League (which changed its name to the National Afro-American League in 1890). Neither the Afro-American League nor later national organizations were organizing armed resistance. But they were organizing political struggle, which reinforced communities engaged in local struggles, where armed resistance was sometimes necessary.

In these communities, where the law was generally weighted against them, armed self-defense was a natural response to white terror. This was illustrated most dramatically on the Georgia coast in August 1899, in an episode that has come to be known as the Darien Insurrection. A young white married woman in Darien, Georgia, gave birth to a nonwhite child and accused her black neighbor, Henry Denegale, of raping her. Denegale turned himself in, logically—if perhaps naively—thinking that jail would be the safest place for him. Fearful that their father might be seized from jail and lynched, Denegale's sons mobilized blacks in the community, who then surrounded the jail to protect him. Every time the sheriff tried to move Denegale "for safekeeping," his allies rang the bell of a nearby church, signaling that more armed men were needed to prevent his removal. Finally, claiming he was faced with "insurrection," the sheriff appealed to Georgia's governor, who sent in a state militia unit that placed Denegale on a Savannah-bound train—to the cheers of his black protectors. Denegale was later found not guilty of the rape charge and released, although twenty-three of the so-called insurrectionists were tried, convicted of rioting, fined, and given jail sentences of up to a year of hard labor. Interestingly, instead of the enraged antiblack violence that typically followed such acts of black resistance, a biracial committee was formed in Darien and began working to ease tensions in the town.

Although this incident of collective armed action seems to have been more the exception than the rule during the nadir, it may be that similar black responses have been ignored or have gone entirely unrecorded. This may have been especially true in the coastal region of Georgia, where the Darien Insurrection occurred; although at this time Georgia's lynch-mob terrorism was perhaps worse than in any other part of the South, the Georgia coast had the fewest lynchings of anyplace in the state.

———

Black struggle was slowed but not stopped by the southern white Redemption. Although a willingness to use armed self-defense was certainly alive in many black communities, much of the resistance during the nadir also took the form of political action. Between 1900 and 1906, blacks mounted a boycott movement against Jim Crow streetcars in many southern cities. A surge of intellectual activity around this time also challenged what some considered Booker T. Washington's overly accommodating approach to white power. Most notable in this regard was the Niagara Movement, an organization that grew from a 1905 meeting at Niagara Falls (on the Canadian side) of twenty-nine black intellectuals led by W. E. B. Du Bois and his former Harvard University classmate Monroe Trotter. This movement led to the formation of the NAACP, undoubtedly the most significant development in civil rights struggle during these early years of the century.

Yet although groups like the NAACP would prove crucial in aiding and inciting black resistance, its impact during the nadir itself was limited, as was the impact of most other groups, with the possible exception of Marcus Garvey's Universal Negro Improvement Association (UNIA) for a time. The NAACP grew slowly, never quite taking root in the South until a new black leadership supplanted the sometimes condescending white do-gooders who dominated the organization in its early days. Three men were significant to this transformation: poet, educator, and diplomat James Weldon Johnson, who in 1920 became the NAACP's first black executive director; a grown-up Walter White, who in 1930 succeeded Johnson as executive director and who, as an African American with very fair skin, blonde hair, and blue eyes, went undercover at scenes of southern lynchings to covertly investigate them for the NAACP; and W. E. B. Du Bois, the prolific intellectual who would launch and edit *Crisis* magazine. The thinking of these three reshaped the organization around a black consciousness and self-reliance. In a 1914 letter to his good friend and prominent NAACP supporter Joel Spingarn, Du Bois expressed the thinking of "new Negroes"—men such as himself, White, and Johnson—who were now taking center stage in the NAACP: "No organization like ours ever succeeded in America; either it became a group of white philanthropists 'helping' the Negro like the Anti-Slavery societies; or it became a group of colored folks freezing out their white co-workers by insolence and distrust." The color line was ever-present, Du Bois noted. "Everything tends to break along [it]. How can this be changed? By changing it. By trusting black men with power."

The idea that black people should take control of their own destinies was not limited to the NAACP or confined to the thinking of black intellectuals like Du Bois; rather, it reflected the attitude of many in black America at the dawn of the twentieth century. A new generation of men and women was consciously distancing itself from the thoughts and habits of their parents and grandparents who had suffered under slavery and the terror of the Redemption. These "new Negroes" asserted themselves, exchanged ideas, and planned action. In addition to *Crisis* magazine, a host of other black publications—newspapers with national reach such as the *Chicago Defender*, the *Baltimore Afro American*, the *Pittsburg Courier*, and Marcus Garvey's *Negro World*, as well as the *Messenger*, the *Emancipator*, and the *Crusader* magazines—were read by black people around the country, expanding black aspirations and promoting a more public black militancy. Black soldiers going off to fight in World War I carried with them the thoughts and attitudes promulgated in these publications and discussed at their kitchen tables. They, too, were new Negroes.

Black leadership was divided over the question of whether or not black men should join the war effort. But even in their disagreement, the political effect of the war can be seen in the intensifying debate—which would continue for the rest of the century—about the relationship of black people to the American government and about their obligation to sacrifice themselves for its priorities. Although Du Bois favored enlistment, Monroe Trotter argued that fighting for democracy within the United States—"making the South safe for Negroes"—was the greater need. Similarly, A. Philip Randolph (who in 1919 would become president of the Brotherhood of Sleeping Car Porters, the country's largest black labor union) argued that black leaders so eager to make the world safe for democracy should go to France themselves and fight. He himself, he said, "would rather fight to make Georgia safe for democracy."

While these disagreements over whether to support the war effort were straining the unity of black leaders, within the ranks of blacks in the armed forces something new appeared: open defiance of, and sometimes even physical resistance to, the racial discrimination and oppression that was the norm in military life.

A 1917 confrontation in Houston, Texas, provides a particularly graphic example of black troops standing up to white power—and of the risks they ran in doing so. At about noon on August 23, a little over four months after the United States entered World War I, Mrs. Sara Travers, a housewife and mother of five, was ironing clothes when she heard gunfire. She stepped out of the house to investigate and encountered two white policemen, Lee Sparks and his partner Rufe Daniels. The officers were searching for two men who had been shooting dice, and Sparks demanded to know if Mrs. Travers had seen "a nigger jumping over the yard."

Mrs. Travers lived in the predominately black San Felipe district of Houston's Fourth Ward. Sparks was well-known for his racist brutality, and his reputation may have played a part in her decision to respond with a simple "No, Sir." Nevertheless, without asking permission, Sparks barged into Travers's house and began searching it—routine behavior by Houston police in black neighborhoods.

As Sparks was coming out of the house, he heard Mrs. Travers telling one of her neighbors that she thought Sparks had been firing at some gamblers. Sparks called her a liar, claiming he had fired into the ground. Then, suddenly, he flew into a rage. "You all God damn nigger bitches!" he shouted, "since these God damn sons of bitches nigger soldiers come here, you are trying to take the town." His outburst over, Sparks went back inside the house to continue searching it.

This time Mrs. Travers followed Sparks and asked him what he was looking for. He replied, "Don't you ask an officer what he want in your house." Where he was from, Sparks told her, white men "don't allow niggers to talk back to us; we generally whip them." Then he slapped Travers. Her scream brought Daniels into the house, and he and Sparks decided to place the housewife under arrest because she was acting like "one of these biggity nigger women." Pinning Mrs. Travers's arms tightly behind her back, Daniels marched her outside to wait at a nearby call box for a police patrol wagon to carry her to jail.

By now, Mrs. Travers's neighbors were gathering, and a soldier, Private Alonzo Edwards, who was also a military policeman, approached the two white policemen and asked that Mrs. Travers be allowed to dress; she was barefoot, wearing an "ol' raggedy" slip and her underwear. He also asked that she be placed in his custody. Sparks responded by striking Edwards across the head several times with his sidearm and arresting him.

A short while later, another black soldier, Corporal Charles W. Baltimore, stepped off a streetcar in the neighborhood and learned of the arrests of Travers and Edwards. Baltimore approached Sparks and Daniels, who were still patrolling the area, and asked what had happened. In particular, he wanted to know why the policemen had beaten and arrested Edwards. Baltimore was with the military police (MPs), and there was a standing agreement that the city police and military police would share the duty of policing soldiers, although black MPs would patrol unarmed. Houston's police chief had also said he would order his policemen to call black MPs "colored" instead of "nigger"—an order that either had not reached Sparks or made no difference to him.

Sparks told Baltimore, "I don't report to no niggers." He and his partner then began pistol-whipping Baltimore, who fled. The two policemen gave chase, firing several shots at the soldier. Baltimore ran into a house and hid under a bed but was caught and arrested. He was bleeding badly from the beating, but Sparks claimed Baltimore had sustained his injuries from running through a door. Sparks later told a city board of inquiry that he did not mind black military police "as long as they would stay in their place."

That evening, almost two hundred black soldiers met at Camp Logan, a military base still under construction, which they had been sent to Houston to guard. Their anger over the virulent racial hostility of Houston's white residents had been simmering since their arrival, and they had little trouble believing two rumors spreading through their ranks: that Baltimore had been shot and killed and that a white mob was on its way to attack them.

The soldiers stole guns from the camp and, ignoring the orders of officers, marched into the city and toward the police station. As they passed through Houston's all-white Brunner neighborhood, whites attacked the column, and the troops defended themselves. As they marched, they shouted out protests; one soldier yelled, "We ain't gonna be mistreated!" Another was heard to exclaim, "God damn white people!" Baltimore, now released from jail, joined them—but although the troops could see for themselves that he had not been killed, they could not turn back now. A white mob formed and joined the police in the street. A shootout ensued.

Of the twenty people who died in the exchange of fire, only two were black troopers; the others were five white policemen (one of them Rufe

Daniels), and thirteen white civilians. A police car was riddled with fifty bullets. This was not, however, a mindless black rampage, nor did it display the savagery of white rioting. Writing in the November 1917 *Crisis* magazine after her investigation into the incident, Martha Gruening, an attorney associated with the NAACP, offered a nuanced and commonsensical conclusion about the event: "It was not a cold-blooded slaughter of innocents but the work of angry men whose endurance had been strained to the breaking point, and who in turn committed injustices."

Martial law was declared, and the Illinois National Guard, which was also in Houston, arrested and confined 163 of the rebellious soldiers to a prison stockade. After a three-week court-martial in November, 54 were found guilty of murder and mutiny, and 13—Corporal Baltimore among them—were sentenced to be hanged; 41 received life sentences. Neither President Wilson nor the secretary of war reviewed the death sentences, as was required when a court-martial handed down a death penalty sentence. Just before dawn on December 11, 1917, accompanied by army trucks carrying lumber for scaffolding and trap doors, the thirteen men were taken to an isolated mesquite thicket near Salado Creek outside San Antonio and hanged. A *New York Times* reporter wrote, "The negroes, dressed in their regular uniforms, displayed neither bravado nor fear. They rode to the execution singing a hymn, but the singing was as that of soldiers on the march." The men refused blindfolds. It was only after the hangings had occurred secretly that the convictions, sentencing, and executions were announced publicly. "Thirteen young strong men . . . have gone to their death," wrote a dismayed Du Bois with a restrained mixture of grief and anger; "soldiers who have fought for a country that was never wholly theirs; men born to suffer ridicule, injustice and at last death itself."

Houston was a tragedy, but it was also a lesson. The clash and its aftermath demonstrated to blacks again a lesson learned during Reconstruction and Redemption in the previous century: that the use of firepower was not likely to defeat the coordinated power of wrathful federal and local authorities reacting to black anger and aspiration. It is a lesson that has endured, in some form, in black consciousness to this day. Individually and collectively, black people have always been fairly hardheaded and cautious in appraising what is doable and desirable in the pursuit of equal rights. Experience taught then and teaches now that blacks should never underestimate the level of violence that could be brought to bear against them by white authority, and that they should never overestimate the prospects for receiving understanding and support from white people.

Houston was rare, in that black troops took action in a white neighborhood. Despite the deep anger that existed among black troops, incidents of such retaliatory or offensive violence were not typical. Even during the so-called Red Summer of 1919, when black communities in city after city across the country were besieged by white mobs, ex-soldiers sometimes provided defense but generally refrained from assaults on white people and white communities. This restraint was in part due to some very practical as well as political considerations. Retaliation would surely have been viewed as an assault on government, and though local governments—and many parts of the federal government as well—were undeniably racist, such action would have been akin to launching a civil war.

It would be a mistake, however, to think that blacks' anger and ambitions were abandoned at the war's end. Strong underground currents of thought and activism flowed with greater force in and from black communities in the aftermath of the war, eroding the white-supremacist order. Propelling these currents was blacks' shared desire to promote and safeguard genuine democracy in the United States and also, on occasion, overseas. Black soldiers in the war, declared veteran William N. Colson in the July 1919 issue of the *Messenger*, "were fighting for France and for their race rather than for a flag which had no meaning." The war had exposed more of the terrain of struggle, wrote Du Bois. "There is not a black soldier but who is glad he went—glad to fight for France, the only real white Democracy, glad to have a new, clear vision of the real inner spirit of American prejudice. The day of camouflage is past."

———

There was clearly a new Negro in the new century, in a milieu typically portrayed in terms of art, literature, and music or encapsulated in the Harlem Renaissance. But this new Negro had a corresponding political existence much larger than New York City's Harlem and the arts, and with the threat to free expression and civil liberties somewhat eased after the war—at least above the Mason–Dixon Line—the demands of this new generation became less muted.

One of the most prominent and influential voices of what is sometimes called "the new Negro movement" belonged to the writer and political activist Hubert Harrison. Harrison felt that an organization more radical than the NAACP was needed, and he founded the Liberty League. Self-defense was high on his list of necessary action. "If white men are to kill unoffending Negroes, Negroes must kill white men in defense of their lives and property," Harrison wrote in 1917. "This is the lesson of the East St. Louis massacre." He was referring to a riot that had taken place just a few weeks before the Houston confrontation in East St. Louis, Illinois. Black laborers had replaced striking white workers, and false reports warned that blacks were planning to attack white communities. In response, whites went on a rampage; huge white mobs indiscriminately stabbed, clubbed, and lynched blacks, driving 6,000 people from their homes. They also demanded that guns be taken away from black people. Before the carnage was over, forty-two blacks and eight whites were killed.

Harrison died in 1927 at the young age of forty-four. But many blacks thought as Harrison did, that guns were needed to stop mob atrocities. Lynching continued to be a powerful tool of white supremacy and was ignored at every level of government. Rioting whites were an ever-present threat. An editorial in the *Messenger* magazine noted these dangers and spoke for many when it declared, "Negroes can stop lynching in the South with shot and shell and fire. . . . A mob of a thousand men knows it can beat down fifty Negroes, but when those fifty Negroes rain fire and shot and shell over the thousand, the whole group of cowards will be put to flight."

Another outspoken member of the new Negroes was William N. Colson, who had served as a second lieutenant during the war and was afterward closely associated with the *Messenger* magazine. In one of a series of articles written decades before the sit-ins of the 1960s, he urged direct action against train and bus segregation. "Each black soldier, as he travels on jim crow cars, if he has the desire, can act his disapproval," Colson wrote. "When he is insulted, he can perform a counter-action." Colson did not elaborate on what he meant by "counter-action," although nonviolence is not likely to have been in his mind. But he did envision a vanguard role for black veterans that in some respects came true, especially after World War II: "The function of the Negro soldier, who is mentally free, is to act as an imperishable leaven on the mass of those who are still in mental bondage." Sentiments like these are the seeds from which subsequent civil rights organizations like SNCC, CORE, and even SCLC sprouted. They were fertilized not by nonviolence but by the idea of resistance, and they were planted well before those organizations rose to prominence in the 1950s and '60s.

South Carolina native Osceola McKaine was another of the "new crowd Negroes"—a term coined by the *Messenger,* perhaps to distinguish them from the more favored and slightly older "new Negroes" like Du Bois, Johnson, and White. McKaine too had been radicalized by the war and would become a major figure in the League for Democracy, a short-lived organization of black veterans that described itself as "an organization of soldiers, for soldiers, by soldiers." Its intent was to "keep alive the military spirit of the race." Although the group fell far short of its goal of becoming the "predominant race organization in the Republic" and of having a presence in every town containing more than a thousand black people, it did get the attention of military intelligence. For a time, military intelligence considered the League for Democracy to be a greater threat than Marcus Garvey's nascent UNIA. In 1944 McKaine helped organize the Progressive Democratic Party (PDP) in South Carolina, an alternative to the state's all-white Democratic Party that foreshadowed by two decades the Mississippi Freedom Democratic Party (MFDP), which challenged the legitimacy of the all-white state party to represent the Democratic Party.

Not all veterans, of course, took as radical a posture as Colson or McKaine. Dartmouth College graduate Lester B. Granger began working with the Urban League after his military service and eventually became its president. The Urban League, originally founded in New York as the Committee on Urban Conditions Among Negroes, concentrated on breaking down barriers to employment and over the years developed close relationships with potential employers. Charles Hamilton Houston, another World War I veteran, decided to become an attorney; as dean of the Howard University law school and NAACP special counsel, he would become the godfather of the 1954 Supreme Court *Brown* decision by initiating the NAACP plan to attack the validity of "separate but equal." Houston later remembered, "I made up my mind . . . that if luck was with me and I got through this war, I would study law and use my time fighting for men who could not strike back." Yet wherever these veterans fell on the political spectrum, whites considered them all tainted by their overseas military service.

Black veterans were thought to be largely responsible for the black agitation that white Americans saw in evidence all around them, from the black nationalism of Marcus Garvey to the expanding NAACP. Mississippi senator Theodore Bilbo surely echoed the attitude of many white supremacists toward the black soldiers of World War I and World War II when he declared that they had been "poisoned with political and social equality stuff."

Although most black veterans of the world wars would not become civil rights leaders, they generally returned home unwilling to surrender their humanity and dignity by submitting to the old codes of behavior demanded by white supremacy. Many found ways to personally resist its strictures, even with force when necessary. Their military experience was a crucial factor in their willingness to use force: for men who had been shooting at Nazis or at Japanese and Italian fascists, to shoot back at attacking Klansmen simply was not a very difficult choice to make, especially because, despite having fought for democracy overseas, they did not encounter much of it when they returned home.

The nation's blacks were becoming increasingly impatient for the rights that had long been denied them. In the years between the two world wars, black people were demanding desegregation and equal rights much more insistently than before the wars. They became even more intent on gaining full citizenship, with all of the rights that accompanied it. This was an affirmative demand, distinct from the protests about the racist practices and barbaric horrors (like lynching) that had dominated black concerns earlier in the century. Blacks no longer felt they had to prove their worthiness. Rather, they were convinced that democracy was a human right and that participation in making the decisions that affected their lives was not a privilege to be earned but a right guaranteed to them—along with all U.S. citizens—under the Constitution.

The experience of facing off against Germany in World War II helped solidify many black Americans' commitment to accelerating their struggle for democracy at home. Germany's claim to be the fatherland of an Aryan "master race" made it white supremacist in a way that it had not seemed to be in World War I. To fight Adolf Hitler's Nazism, therefore, was to strike a blow against the ideology of white supremacy in the United States as well, if only because it intensified discussion about democracy and citizenship. As Walter White expressed this change in tone, "The Nazi philosophy crystallizes all and every anti-colored, anti-Jewish, anti-liberal and anti-freedom principle." A January 1942 editorial in *Crisis* magazine even more explicitly connected the war abroad and the war at home: "The fight against Hitlerism begins in Washington, D.C., the capital of our nation, where black Americans have a status only slightly above Jews in Berlin."

Even so, some influential black intellectuals' experiences in World War I, as well as their stance against colonialism, led them to lean toward isolationism when war once again broke out in Europe. "So far as the colored peoples of the earth are concerned," wrote columnist George Schuyler "it is a tossup between the 'democracies' and the dictatorships. . . . What is there to choose between the rule of the British in Africa and the rule of the Germans in Austria?" This attitude, which reflected both emotional and political ties to anticolonial struggle, continued well into the 1960s and encouraged the young people of SNCC and CORE to take a great interest in Africa's independence movements and the continent's armed liberation struggles.

Dissident voices notwithstanding, the civil rights establishment saw that World War II—as a war against fascism—presented a significant political opportunity. Linking the fight against fascism overseas with the fight for full citizenship and democracy at home could both continue and accelerate the reframing of the civil rights struggle that had begun with World War I. Anticipating the entrance of the United States into the war, *Crisis* magazine editorialized in its December 1940 issue, "This is no fight merely to wear a uniform. This is a struggle for status, a struggle to take democracy off of parchment and give it life." There was broad agreement within the civil rights community that the war should be fought on two fronts, and on February 7, 1942, the *Pittsburg Courier* launched a "Double V" campaign, which called for victory over fascism abroad and victory over racism at home. As pioneering black journalist Edna Chappell McKenzie recalled years later: "We were in war and in war you don't have friendly relationship[s]. You're out to kill each other. And so that's the way it was with *The Courier*. . . . We were trying to kill Jim Crow and racism. . . . Now what [the government] didn't seem to understand, that we had every valid reason to fight for full citizenship at home if we expected to give our lives overseas."

Not all black Americans signed onto the Double V campaign, however. After America's entry into the war, the black leadership establishment outside the South slowly—and somewhat contradictorily—began to deemphasize protest and direct-action challenges to the federal government. Indeed, a year after it was launched, the Double V campaign had almost entirely disappeared from the pages of the *Pittsburg Courier* and many other black newspapers. Instead, these newspapers—and most civil rights organizations—signed on to the war effort, explaining that America's fight was their fight and easing the pressure on Washington for the duration of the war. Despite his initial success in pressuring President Roosevelt to issue Executive Order 8802 banning discrimination in defense industries, Randolph's March on Washington Movement and plans for protest and civil disobedience in cities across the country fizzled out, receiving no encouragement from nationally prominent black leaders. Randolph himself backed the war effort, taking a different stance than he had during World War I. "We, all of us, black and white, Jew and Gentile, Protestant and Catholic, are at war. . . . What shall the Negro do?" he asked. "There is only one answer. He must fight."

Racial discrimination persisted in the ranks of the military and at all levels of U.S. society during World War II, despite what appeared to be the more liberal presidency of Franklin D. Roosevelt. But in the final analysis, whether or not World War II marks a precise watershed moment in the evolution of black struggle in the United States, it certainly gave it an enormous boost. Even a casual observer of the southern Freedom Movement cannot fail to notice the prominence of the war's black veterans in that effort. Clearly something had changed in the perspective and behavior of many of the returning veterans. And it is clear, too, that this change took place independently of mainstream black organizations. Rather, it occurred at the grass roots, where—not coincidentally—the staunchest resistance against white power could soon be found, as well.

3

"Fighting for What We Didn't Have"

*It is impossible to create a dual personality which will be on the one
hand a fighting man toward a foreign enemy, and on the other hand
a craven who will accept treatment as less than a man at home.*
—Judge William H. Hastie to U.S. War Department, 1941

Armed white men surrounded Medgar and Charles Evers when they
appeared at the Newton County courthouse in the logging town of Decatur,
Mississippi. It was 1946, not long after the two brothers had been discharged from the U.S. Army, and they were planning to register to vote.

The Everses knew many of the gun-toting white men around them; as
boys they had even played with some of them. The frightened circuit clerk
knew the Evers brothers, too. As Charles Evers years later recalled of him
and other white Mississippians like him, "Like almost half the whites in
Mississippi . . . [they] didn't want murder and bloodshed, but they didn't
dare embrace us and get branded 'nigger lovers.'"

Despite the risk of ostracism, the clerk brought the two returned veterans inside and sat them down in a back room, where he tried to persuade
them to abandon their attempt. When they refused, he finally permitted
them to register. "Medgar and I had always wanted to vote," wrote Charles
Evers in his autobiography. "As soldiers we'd worked like dogs, risked our
lives fighting for freedom, democracy, and all the principles this country
was founded on. But we couldn't vote. The law said we could, but the whites
of Mississippi made sure we couldn't."

That the Evers brothers had succeeded in registering to vote in a rural Mississippi community like Decatur was unusual, but registering was only half the battle. They wanted to actually cast ballots on Election Day. The stridently racist Theodore Bilbo was seeking a third term in the U.S. Senate, and Charles and Medgar intended to help defeat him.

Some fourteen years earlier—in 1932, when Medgar was nine and Charles was eleven—the brothers were sitting on the steps of the same courthouse amid a white crowd gathered for a Bilbo campaign speech. For the two boys, it was entertainment in a small town that had very little. "We ignored all the nigger baiting," Charles remembered later. "Northerners can't appreciate a southern rascal. I always could." Because Medgar and Charles were so young, they were not likely to encounter the kind of violent reaction that would almost certainly have met any black man daring to sit on the courthouse steps to listen to Bilbo's rants. But Bilbo noticed them, and, pointing at them, he emphasized the necessity of maintaining white supremacy. "You see these two little niggers setting down here?—these two nigger boys right there will be asking for everything that is ours by right. . . . If you don't keep them in their place, then someday they'll be in Washington trying to represent you."

The day before the 1946 primary, the unintentionally prescient Bilbo was back in Decatur, and in a familiar racist harangue in the town square he appealed to his white listeners to target black registered voters, even though they were very few in number: "The best way to keep a nigger from the polls on election day is to visit him the night before," Bilbo said to a receptive crowd that understood exactly what he meant.

No one in Newton County was likely to be foolish enough to show up at the Evers's home attempting to frighten and intimidate anyone. The boys' father, James, was sometimes called "Crazy Jim" Evers. Undaunted by white-supremacist authority, he would not hesitate to shoot any attacker regardless of race. But elsewhere in town—particularly around the locus of white power that was the courthouse—the Evers family had to be much more careful, although on more than one occasion James Evers had refused to step aside to let whites walking toward him pass.

The effects of Bilbo's encouragement were plain to see when Medgar, Charles, and four of their friends—all of them World War II veterans—

went to the courthouse to vote on July 2. They found awaiting them a crowd of "rednecks . . . holding shotguns, rifles, and pistols," recalled Charles Evers. But the white men standing guard at the courthouse may not have realized that at least one of the six men before them had come prepared for a fight.

Charles Evers would later claim that he was carrying a pistol and a switchblade knife. The county sheriff was on the scene watching as the two groups eyed each other, but he said nothing and did nothing, so Charles told Medgar he intended to try to enter the Courthouse and vote. "I meant to die fighting for Negro rights," he later wrote. "The 'Klukkers' [Ku Klux Klansmen] were cowards. They liked defending white rights but they didn't want to die doing it."

Medgar, who was always less hot-tempered than his older brother, decided that it was not worth the risk and that they should leave. "We'll get them next time," he told his brother. Charles let Medgar lead him away. "I'd stopped guarding my life," he recalled, "but Medgar guarded it for me." Still, Charles's weapon would come in handy. Some of the whites who had been at the courthouse followed the group home and continued to threaten them. "We pulled our guns. . . . They turned heel and ran," Charles wrote.

Medgar told a slightly different story and the two stories help show the differences between the two brothers. According to Medgar, the six had walked to the courthouse and did actually enter it, but armed white men surged around them, so they split up and returned home. They regrouped and drove back to the courthouse with guns hidden in the car. They left the weapons in the car and attempted to walk into the polling place but were once again blocked by a white mob. "We decided not to pursue it," said Medgar later without elaborating. The group of veterans left the court-house. They were followed by some of the whites, who waved guns from their cars. But when the Evers group showed their own weapons, the whites stopped following them.

Like many black men returning home after World War II, the Evers brothers and their friends had resolved not to be intimidated or pushed around and not to submit to the old, familiar restrictions and oppressions ordained by white supremacy. And though Charles and Medgar did not use their guns or their military training on primary day in 1946, many veterans were willing to do so when they felt it necessary and practical. "Fighting World War II woke up a lot of us," says Charles Evers. "We had to ask ourselves . . . Why were we second class citizens?"

Men like the Evers brothers would prove vitally important to the Freedom Movement in the 1960s. And while black–white shootouts were by no means common in the postwar South, the threat that they might occur increased markedly with the return of black veterans. Indeed, it became apparent almost immediately at the end of the war that the region was on the cusp of change largely because, more than any other group within the black community, veterans were the least accepting of white supremacy. They were dangerous. White power recognized that they were dangerous. And this is where the modern civil rights movement truly begins.

Mississippi native Amzie Moore exemplifies the link between World War II veterans and the modern movement. More than any single person, Moore would be responsible for SNCC's presence in Mississippi and its movement into grassroots organizing for voting rights. He was drafted in 1942, and despite the discrimination and segregation he encountered at every posting, his army service changed him. As he entered a new world far removed from the Mississippi he had grown up in, his experiences began opening his mind, and he found himself thinking in ways he never had before. "For a long time I had the idea that a man with white skin was superior because it appeared to me that he had everything," he recalled. "And I figured if God would justify the white man having everything, that God had put him in a position to be the best." His military service and the travel it entailed radically changed this outlook. "You can leave Calcutta, you can leave Egypt; you can go down the Red Sea through the Suez Canal; you can hit the Indian Ocean, you can go up the Gulf of Said [Port Said, Egypt]. . . . You going to find black people all the way over," Moore observed. "You go for miles and miles and that's what you're going to see." Amzie Moore's wartime travels led him to conclude that European civilization had been lifted from barbarism largely by the achievements of much earlier and superior civilizations, such as that of Egypt. He was stunned: "All *civilization* was black. . . . And I was so surprised. And since then, I have not had [an inferiority] complex." Before being discharged, Moore joined the NAACP.

Back home in Cleveland, Mississippi, after the war, Moore saw that conditions for black people had not improved. The city's white residents had even organized a home guard to protect white women from the black veterans supposedly lusting for them, and there was an upsurge in murderous antiblack terrorism. Despite his newly expanded black consciousness, however, Moore did not organize protest or resistance. Instead, he planned to get rich. He got a job at the post office where he had worked before the war, built a brick house, and—with a loan from Standard Life Insurance Company—opened a service station with a small café attached. His wife operated a beauty salon on the premises.

Then one day Moore visited a black family living on a cotton plantation not far from his home. He found fourteen "half-naked children" without beds, and the family was burning cotton stalks in an old metal barrel to keep warm. They had, Moore recalled, "no food." Moore too had grown up on a Mississippi plantation. "I'd been hungry in my life. . . . And I could tell how a hungry child felt, because I knew how *I* felt. Just looking at that I think really changed my whole outlook on life. I kinda figured it was a sin to think in terms of trying to get rich in view of what I'd seen."

After that visit, Moore redoubled his commitment to the NAACP. In 1955 he was elected president of the organization's Cleveland branch. His selection surprised him; he had not even been present at the meeting when the vote was held. Later, he became vice president of the State Conference of NAACP branches. He was, in 1960, the first black Mississippian adult civil rights leader to embrace SNCC, a student-led organization founded that year with the assistance of Reverend Martin Luther King Jr.'s SCLC.

The convergence of older activists—many of them veterans, like Moore—with the generation of Afro-Americans who came of age following World War II would spark a critical new phase in the Freedom Movement struggle. In Moore's case, a significant connection occurred during the late summer of 1960, when a Harlem-born, Harvard-educated teacher named Bob Moses was traveling the South recruiting students to participate in a SNCC conference being planned for October. Ella Baker—SCLC's acting executive director and a highly respected adult adviser to SNCC—sent Moses to Moore. Although Moore admired the sit-ins that had become SNCC's main mode of action, he was not interested in having them in Cleveland; instead, he encouraged Moses to consider a voter-registration campaign. "Amzie was the only one I met on that trip giving the student sit-in movement careful attention, aware of all that student energy and trying to figure out how to use it," remembers Bob Moses. "He opened up his home to me, had conversations with me and that was really an education for me." Mississippi and the Black-Belt South in general had been largely invisible to Moses, and although news like that of Emmett Till's lynching and of school desegregation issues reached him in New York City, he had no idea that southern blacks were still being denied the right to vote. During the previous decade, says Moses, "I was taught about the denial of the right to vote behind the Iron Curtain in Europe; I never knew that there was denial of the right to vote behind a *Cotton Curtain* here in the United States."

Amzie Moore attended the October SNCC conference that Moses had been promoting, although it cannot be said that Moore's voter-registration proposal was met with great enthusiasm. A larger, more intense discussion about filling up the jails with nonviolent protesters dominated participants' thinking—"jail without bail." The invitation to the October conference had stated, "Only mass action is strong enough to force all of America to assume responsibility and . . . nonviolent direct action *alone* [emphasis added] is strong enough to enable all of America to understand the responsibility she must assume."

By the summer of 1961, the Kennedy administration was watching sit-ins, and especially Freedom Rides, nervously—and with no small degree of hostility. President John F. Kennedy and his brother Attorney General Robert Kennedy felt that they threatened their administration's domestic and foreign policy agenda by embarrassing the United States and angering powerful Dixiecrats, and so—in what must be one of the great political miscalculations of the 1960s—they pressed student activists to abandon direct-action protests and work instead on voter registration. They thought that such work would be much more acceptable to southern white power than sit-ins seeking desegregation. Therefore, the Kennedys and other high-ranking administration officials concluded, a voter-registration campaign would be met with less white violence than desegregation efforts. In turn, because voter-registration efforts would be far less dramatic—not likely to be seen on television or on the front pages of newspapers—civil rights struggle would be less embarrassing to the United States as it competed with the Soviet Union for influence with newly independent nations in the Third World—nations that, crucially, were mostly Asian, African, and Latin American. Robert Kennedy offered assurance that money from tax-exempt foundations his family controlled or influenced could be made available for voter-registration campaigns.

Many Freedom Movement activists viewed the Kennedy administration's gesture with suspicion. Some of SNCC's key leaders felt strongly that they would be selling out by devoting time and energy to voter registration when more immediate and everyday forms of discrimination persisted all across the South. They also felt that the moral dimension of the movement would be lost to political opportunism. The Kennedys' willingness to help pay for voter-registration campaigns only added to their suspicion, for it seemed like a cynical political ploy, an attempt to use money to divert the movement from the sort of militant, direct-action protest they knew the Kennedy brothers hated. The Kennedys' indifference to enforcing existing civil rights law and their hostility to protests challenging segregationist violations of those laws had already led many in the movement to come to disturbing conclusions: that the administration's own political needs took priority over the enforcement of civil rights law, and that the Kennedys were more than willing to compromise with southern bigots in order to achieve their political goals. Furthermore, some of these student leaders believed that electoral politics was inherently immoral because, more often than not, it required that principle be sacrificed for political advantage, a belief that only added to their resistance to turning to voter-registration drives.

There was, however, interest in voter registration by some within the newly formed SNCC, not because of the persuasiveness of the Kennedys but because of Moore, Baker, and other older movement stalwarts who had been fighting for civil rights much longer than the youthful activists of SNCC. They were moving toward organizing for voter registration along a different political track than the one laid out by the Kennedys: real power for real change. So, lukewarm interest by SNCC activists notwithstanding, the following summer Bob Moses returned to Mississippi, as he had promised Amzie Moore, to begin SNCC's first voter-registration project in the state. In so doing, he foreshadowed an important shift in SNCC's strategy, a shift that brought it into line with the broad black consensus in the South, which held that voter registration was the primary need and should be the primary struggle. Indeed, despite the ambivalence of many young activists toward voter registration, SNCC's October 1960 conference—converging as it did with Moses's "discovery" of Moore and Mississippi—marks the beginning of SNCC's slow movement away from the kind of religiously rooted ideals of love and redemptive suffering expressed in its founding statement, and toward an appreciation of the more secular practicalities of grassroots political organizing in the violent, rural Black Belt.

Nonviolent direct actions would bring other young people—southerners for the most part—into the older tradition of community organizing, and they would become deeply involved with both SNCC and CORE, rapidly moving those organizations into grassroots efforts to expand black voter registration. The SNCC-driven voter-registration effort in Mississippi initiated by Moses first got off the ground in the southwestern corner of the state and then a year later moved into the Delta. There, in the northwestern corner of Mississippi, SNCC dug in. Amzie Moore's Cleveland home served as an early command center, a stopping-off point for a breakfast of scrambled eggs or a dinner of spaghetti and meatballs (often with canned peaches in thick syrup for dessert). Moore's house had a telephone and an extra bed or floor space if needed, and it was always churning with ideas, conversation, and planning.

The local people in Moore's network guided these young organizers as they worked to get potential black voters registered in the rural communities of the Delta. Moore's network included members not only of the NAACP but also of the small churches on the plantations. Moore sometimes sang in them with a traveling gospel group before making a political pitch for voter registration. He was also a well-known Prince Hall Mason, and the connections the fraternal network gave him helped spread the word about voter registration. These were networks organic to the community. Some, like the Freemasons or the black churches, had roots going back to slavery. Others, such as the almost underground NAACP branches, were newer. There were even a few remnants of Marcus Garvey's UNIA. In any case, they kept communities and the people within them connected.

As was true during the days of slavery, word of mouth was a key component of communication.

One of the subjects of wide comment within these Mississippi Delta networks was that Moore did not segregate his gas station and café. There were no "white only" or "colored only" signs on his restroom doors, and anyone could sit at any table. Given that his service station was located on State Highway 61, then a highly trafficked route south to New Orleans, Moore's refusal to toe the segregationist line also attracted angry attention from local white supremacists. They tried to mount a boycott against him, and he was certain that night riders would eventually attack his home. They never did, but Moore did not take any chances. Floodlights washed across his backyard every night, and movement organizers who stayed with him can recall falling asleep secure in the knowledge that Moore was sitting in the bay window of his home, keeping careful watch, his rifle and pistol within easy reach.

———

Although Amzie Moore, Medgar Evers, and other World War II veterans did become civil rights leaders in the decades after the war, most veterans did not. It was however, not uncommon for them to personally (as distinct from politically) defy the rules of white supremacy, as James Stephenson did in Columbia, Tennessee, in 1946. On July 6, 1944, Army Second Lieutenant Jackie Robinson—who would become a baseball legend when he played with the Brooklyn Dodgers following the war—refused to move to the back of an army bus at a training camp at Fort Hood, Texas, when the white driver ordered him to. Although buses on military bases had officially been ordered to desegregate, Robinson was arrested by the military police and court-martialed for insubordination. He was acquitted, transferred to another military base, and honorably discharged four months later.

Such acts of defiance, though obviously having political implications, were usually not planned in advance and did not benefit from organized public political support. When the Evers brothers and a handful of fellow veterans attempted to vote, for instance, there was no corresponding effort to register or vote by any of Decatur or Newton County's nonveteran blacks. Nor did black veterans themselves tend to band together in any sustained effort to claim the rights promised under the law. They did not attempt to vote en masse; most often, like James Stephenson and Jackie Robinson, they demonstrated their defiance—and sometimes their willingness to defend themselves—in personal ways rather than in organized political actions.

Moreover, it is unclear what the subgroup of black veterans who did become politically visible activists had in common (aside from the obvious, their experience of military training and, for many, of using guns in combat). Within the Evers family, for instance, there was a strong tradition of defying the rules of white supremacy. Yet before Medgar became involved in 1951 with a newly formed organization in the Delta, the Regional Council of Negro Leadership (RCNL), and then in 1954 became the NAACP's first Mississippi field secretary, there seems to have been no tradition of membership in civil rights organizations or of civil rights leadership. Age, geography, education, work, income, family, social status, and class all contributed to these leaders' decisions to join the movement, but the relative importance of these factors is hard to measure. Generally black veterans took greater political risks than nonveterans; their military experience gave them a confidence most nonveterans lacked, but pinning down exactly what caused them to emerge as Freedom Movement leaders is difficult. "The only thing you can say is that probabilistically, *on average,* these guys [veterans] are more likely than guys who never served to be [leaders]," thinks Christopher Parker, who has studied their attitudes and experiences. "After all, they had survived serving in a racist military in which they were often forced to wage two wars: one in the battlefield, the other on base."

To be sure, many of these veterans-turned-leaders had personalities that suited them to leadership. Shortly after Medgar Evers married his wife Myrlie, they visited his parents. During the visit, Medgar would sometimes wander off—to where, Myrlie did not know. Once, after Myrlie exclaimed, "He's disappeared again!" Medgar's mother took her aside and told her, "Don't worry about him daughter, he's my strange child." As a boy, "Mama Jessie" told Myrlie, "Medgar would play with his friends, tell them what to do, and then sometimes he would disappear. But I always knew I could find him under the house. I would ask him, 'What are you doing?' And he would always say, 'I'm just thinking mama, just thinking.'"

Witnessing antiblack violence at an early age, while growing up on a small farm just outside of Decatur, had greatly affected Medgar Evers, his brother Charles, and others in the core group of Mississippians who would be critical to the survival of young civil rights organizers in the 1960s. The murder by white men of Willie Tingle, a close family friend, for allegedly looking at a white woman in the "wrong" way—what whites sometimes called "reckless eyeballing"—greatly affected the two brothers. Tingle was dragged through the streets of Decatur by a wagon and then hanged from a tree, where whites used him for target practice. For days the two Evers brothers passed the bullet-riddled body on their way to school.

Despite such horrific violence, or maybe because of it, even as boys Medgar and Charles organized "little rebellions." For example, they let the air out of the tires of the white salesmen who would burst into Decatur's black homes without invitation; or they hid behind bushes and threw rocks at the buses that carried white students to their school, which was far better equipped than the one-room school that black children walked to.

Medgar Evers was also shaped by his father, James Evers. Many in Decatur saw James's refusal to step off the sidewalk in deference to approaching whites as a sure sign that he was crazy. But his sons understood that his behavior was much more principled than most of Decatur's townsfolk could acknowledge. He taught his children that blacks should not be unnecessarily apologetic, and that whites should treat blacks with dignity. He even predicted that black people would regain the voting rights that they had won after the Civil War but that had been taken away by the violence of Reconstruction and the resulting Redemption of the Southern white-supremacist order.

"Crazy" blacks like James Evers were sometimes killed, sometimes driven off, and sometimes left alone—but whatever became of them, their spirit and example most certainly influenced many of the key adult figures in the southern civil rights movement who took young organizers under their wings in the early 1960s. Faith S. Holsaert, a New Yorker who in the summer of 1962 joined SNCC's work in Southwest Georgia, remembers project director Charles Sherrod explaining to her that "southern white folks didn't mess with a few intransigent black people who would rather die than lose their dignity. It would be more trouble to control such souls than to leave them alone."

Some of these "crazy" black people were women. It was common knowledge in Sunflower County, Mississippi, that Lou Ella Townsend, the mother of famed civil rights leader Fannie Lou Hamer, could be dangerous if pushed too hard. Walking out into the cotton fields to work, Mrs. Townsend would put a pan on her head and carry a bucket in each hand. One of them was always covered by a cloth and in that bucket there was always a 9 mm Luger pistol. Once, when a plantation overseer hit her youngest son in the face, she warned him not to do it again. Laughing, perhaps as much in disbelief that she could or would do anything to stop him, the overseer grabbed Townsend, spun her around, and raised his arm to strike her. She caught his arm and forced him to the ground. When she let him up, he fled; he never bothered her children again.

On another occasion, a white man on horseback rode into the fields where Townsend was working. The man spied her young niece Pauline and told Mrs. Townsend that he intended to take the girl back home with him, and also that he was going to beat her niece so she would know her place. Mrs. Townsend responded, "You don't have no black children and you're not going to beat no black children. If you step down off that horse, I'll go to Hell and back with you before Hell can scorch a feather." He too left, unwilling to tangle with this "crazy" black woman. This plantation predator could not have known that his attempt to lay claim to Mrs. Townsend's niece would trigger a particular anger in her. Of twenty-two brothers and sisters in her family, she and two others were the only children who were not the product of rape by white men.

Stories of black resistance like those passed on orally within the families of Medgar Evers, Fannie Lou Hamer, and others helped form a black consciousness that was very much alive throughout the first half of the twentieth century, and they also underlay a deep and powerful collective memory that was invisible to whites but greatly affected the shape and course of the modern Freedom Movement. Mrs. Hamer, for instance, could talk vividly about the oppressiveness of the Mississippi she grew up in, and through her mother and grandmother she knew much about the oppression black people had endured before her birth. But she could also recall with pride not simply that her family and others had survived their enslavement, but also that they had retained some measure of their human dignity and, on occasion at least, were able to draw some lines that whites dared not cross.

The powerful influence of men and women like James Evers and Lou

Ella Townsend on the generations of younger southern blacks who joined or observed the civil rights movement of the 1960s cannot be underestimated. Without a doubt Mrs. Hamer was deeply inspired not only by her mother's sad past but by the efforts her mother made to ensure that the Townsend family could survive physically and spiritually. She was "the quintessential 'outraged mother,' moved by anger and determined to 'make a way out of no way,' if only for her children's sake." James Evers had the same determination and outrage.

Charles Evers remembers that he and his brother Medgar once accompanied their father to the commissary of Decatur's sawmill to settle a bill. Although he could hardly read and write, James Evers could work out sums in his head. He saw that he had been overcharged and said so.

"You callin' me a liar, Nigger!" yelled the commissary manager.

"I don't owe you that much and I won't pay it," replied Evers softly—and, to those who knew him well, dangerously.

"I'll kill you, you black sonofabitch!" shouted the manager, and he began moving toward the counter to get the pistol he kept behind it. Jim Evers blocked his path, grabbed a large coke bottle from a crate nearby, smashed it on the counter, and thrust the bottle's jagged edge at the clerk. "You better not go around that counter," Evers told him. "Move another step and I'll bust your damn brains in."

According to Charles, there were other "mean whites" in the commissary at the time, but they remained frozen in place. The clerk, terrified now, was "shaking like a leaf." Jim Evers ordered his sons to leave the commissary. "Don't run," he told them; "they're nothing but a bunch of cowards." The elder Evers followed the boys, backing out of the commissary, his eyes never leaving the clerk or the other shocked patrons. It is amazing that Evers got out of the commissary—let alone made it home—alive, but, as Charles Evers explains it, "Daddy stopped them [because he] wasn't scared and he'd have killed a few of them before he died. They knew that." At home that night, Jim Evers sat up with his rifle. "Don't ever let anybody beat you," he advised his two sons. "Anyone ever kicks you, you kick the hell out of him." Describing the character of men like James Evers and explaining how some of them survived in racist communities like Decatur, Charles Evers wrote of his father, "He didn't smell like fear, he smelled like danger. White folks can be pretty dumb, but most of them leave danger alone. They couldn't make daddy crawl, so they called him a 'crazy nigger' and let it go."

Medgar Evers's wife, Myrlie Evers-Williams, says it is important to understand the impact of the commissary confrontation if one is to grasp a key aspect of her husband's character: his pride, even in a state that sought to destroy it in black men. "That was one of the stories Medgar shared with me in terms of the respect, love and admiration for his father. He told it with great pride. Charles also has a very vivid memory of this and still tells this story. He told it to me again just the other day."

Yet acts of direct defiance like the ones that helped shape the characters of Mrs. Hamer and the Evers brothers were certainly the exception and not without risk—risk of death especially. Mississippi's tradition of responding with violence to black demands for civil rights and human dignity endured throughout the 1950s and '60s. Medgar Evers was ambushed and killed in the driveway of his Jackson home in 1963. In 1955, voting-rights activist Lamar Smith, like Evers a World War II veteran, was shot to death on the lawn of the county courthouse in Brookhaven, and Reverend George W. Lee, an NAACP leader, suffered a similar fate in Belzoni: gunfire from a carload of whites blew away the left side of his face. In 1961, NAACP leader Herbert Lee was gunned down by a state legislator, Eugene Hurst, in broad daylight at the cotton gin in Liberty, the county seat of Amite County; Louis Allen, a black witness willing to testify about the shooting, was shot and killed in front of his house after more than a year of harassment that included beatings and jailing. Five years later, on January 11, 1966, the NAACP leader and successful farmer Vernon Dahmer was killed when his farmhouse outside Hattiesburg was firebombed. Thirteen months after that, on February 27, 1967, Natchez NAACP leader Wharlest Jackson, a Korean War veteran, was killed when a bomb planted in his truck exploded. This hardly finishes the roll call of the many murdered across the South in the 1950s and '60s because of their civil rights activities.

Such violence frightened most blacks away from directly challenging the entrenched white-supremacist order. By the 1960s, however, the way white-supremacist terrorists were able to exercise violence was more limited than it had been in previous decades. Part of the reason for this was the 1957 Civil Rights Act, which established a Civil Rights Division in the

U.S. Department of Justice that, for all its shortcomings, helped create what Bob Moses has called "a little piece of legal crawlspace" in which blacks' legal defenders could operate. The act gave the Department of Justice the right to intervene in areas like Sunflower County, where racist violence had previously fallen under the jurisdiction of local white authorities, who often had no interest in investigating it—and who in many cases even abetted or participated in it. Yet although the Department of Justice was permitted to intervene, it did not always exercise that prerogative.

The Civil Rights Division of the Justice Department, and the limited expansion of federal authority it represented, did not represent a newfound federal commitment to extending civil rights to black people. The federal government remained reluctant to rein in white supremacists and often allied with them. Mississippi politicians such as Senator James O. Eastland—indeed southern Democrats in general—were reelected over and over again precisely because blacks were denied voting rights. Their seniority made these Dixiecrats so politically powerful in Congress that even presidents—Democrats like Kennedy especially, but Republicans also—did not want to alienate them, for presidents often need such powerful personages to achieve their administrations' legislative and policy goals.

By the 1950s and '60s, it had become amply evident that state and federal governments had little interest in supporting the black struggle for civil rights. The Kennedy administration constantly admonished nonviolent activists to "go slow," be patient, and give southern racists a chance to change. Even some prominent figures in the national civil rights establishment, who were largely ensconced in northern offices, felt that parts of the Deep South were too difficult and dangerous to take on directly. Between this attitude and growing white violence, many southern blacks, especially in rural communities, increasingly felt alone and isolated. Into this vacuum—sometimes sooner and sometimes later, and for reasons as varied as they were—there stepped new political leaders, drawn disproportionately from the ranks of black veterans.

Sometimes it was tragedy that galvanized brave black men and women to take up the Freedom Movement's standard. In 1954, in a postwar climate that, at least to some degree, encouraged civil rights efforts, Medgar Evers attempted to gain admittance to the University of Mississippi law school and also became Mississippi field secretary for the NAACP—the organization's first in the state. Charles Evers's postwar ambition, by contrast, took him in an entrepreneurial direction, and he left Mississippi in the mid-1950s. Only after Medgar's assassination in 1963 did Charles commit to full-time civil rights work in Mississippi, picking up his slain brother's mantle as NAACP field secretary. Later he became a political leader in Jefferson County, Mississippi, where in 1969 he was elected mayor of the city of Fayette. Except for the all-black Delta town of Mound Bayou, Charles was the first black mayor of a Mississippi town since Reconstruction.

World War I veteran and South Carolina native Osceola McKaine traveled an even more circuitous route to southern political activism and leadership. For a time he tried to organize veterans in Harlem, but he became angry, disillusioned, and alienated because of intransigent antiblack discrimination everywhere he looked in the country. He left the United States and became a cabaret owner in Belgium. In 1939, when Hitler invaded that country, McKaine returned home with what he described as "at least a splinter on my shoulder." In 1944, he, South Carolina NAACP chairman James M. Hinton, and the editor of the *Lighthouse and Informer* newspaper, John Henry McCray, helped found a new political party in South Carolina, the Progressive Democratic Party (PDP). But although the party intended to galvanize black voters, the white-supremacist system blocked it from any meaningful participation in state politics. South Carolina's General Assembly had repealed laws regulating primaries, and the state's Democratic Party immediately excluded blacks from voting in them, thus effectively strangling the PDP in its cradle.

Many veterans seem to have had prewar dispositions that, perhaps activated by military service, were manifested politically after the war. A good example is Aaron Henry, who would become president of the Mississippi NAACP in 1960 and president of the Council of Federated Organizations (COFO) in 1962. Henry thought it was "a fortunate thing" that he was drafted into the army in 1943, shortly after he turned twenty-one. He was already considered "uppity" by some whites because he wanted higher education and because, unusually, he worked as the night manager of a white motel in Clarksdale. Even in a paternalistic planter town like Clarksdale, where such ambitiousness might not normally have been considered a threat or an attempt to step above one's place, Henry's aspirations generated some hostile who-does-this-Negro-think-he-is grumbling. But Henry was also, as he put it, "good at avoiding trouble." After the war he went to college on the GI Bill and became a pharmacist. He opened a drugstore in Clarksdale.

Henry's story was, up until this point, a familiar tale of determined upward mobility within the limitations of Jim Crow Mississippi. But he felt that, as a black man, he needed to do something more than own a drugstore. This sharpened racial consciousness—and its attendant ambition—began before his military service. Encouraged by a favorite high school teacher, Henry read Richard Wright's *Native Son,* learned of historic black leaders like Frederick Douglass, and became a youth member of the NAACP. But military service deepened his understanding of both his own potential and the challenges he faced. "Three years in the army taught me that racial segregation and discrimination were not unique to Mississippi," Henry recalled, "but confirmed my feeling that the situation was worse in my state." As Henry encountered "separate but equal" in the army, he saw that although the U.S. military's idea of "equal" was closer to equality than Mississippi's, "it was still a sham. No matter how equal the facilities, the idea of white superiority and Negro inferiority remained, and we knew it was incongruous with the American idea of democracy that we were fighting for."

When he returned home after the war, Henry found that little had changed, but he "sensed undercurrents rising to the surface." At Coahoma County's annual black agricultural fair, for example, the crowd booed local newspaper editor J. D. Sneider when he declared in a speech that blacks would never vote in Mississippi. Sneider was followed onto the stage by the editor of a black newspaper in Little Rock, Arkansas, who stated that black people would be voting soon and that gaining this right would be accomplished by bloodshed if necessary.

As if to prove just how wrong Sneider was, Henry registered to vote. No mob had greeted him when he went to the Coahoma County courthouse in Clarksdale, but there had been resistance. The circuit clerk denied knowing that GIs were exempt from paying a poll tax. Henry borrowed a poll-tax-exemption certificate from a white veteran to prove the exemption existed and was finally permitted to register. He began working with the Progressive Voters League trying to get others to register, as well.

Henry was the first black person in Coahoma County to vote in a Democratic Party primary election, and his experience at the poll may have been the tipping point that cleared the path for his emergence into active leadership in the civil rights movement. When he arrived at the courthouse on Election Day, several blacks he knew were standing around. Like Henry, they had recently registered to vote, but when he asked why they had not yet voted, they told him it was because they were trying to decide who would have "the honor" of being the first to go inside and cast his ballot. "Actually I believe they were waiting to see what would happen to the first Negro who tried to vote," Henry wrote later. Some of the men were veterans like Henry, but at this moment his particular blend of experiences inside and outside the military seems to have set him apart from even his former comrades in arms. He walked inside the courthouse and voted. "There was no reaction from the whites," he remembered, "and the other Negroes began to file in and vote."

———

The political assertiveness of men like the Evers brothers and Aaron Henry marked an important shift in America and in the white-supremacist South after World War II, but it was not the only change wrought by the war. The Soviet Union and the United States were locked in an escalating struggle for advantage. And the United States, which during the war had proclaimed it was fighting for the preservation of freedom and democracy, now found those claims being thrown back in its face from both inside and outside its borders. The plight of black people was being held up as concrete proof that America was not an all-inclusive democracy.

America's demonstrable racism, segregation laws, and antiblack violence were seriously undermining the image of democratic virtuousness that Washington wanted and needed to project around the world. In the wake of World War II, liberation movements were stirring in the colonies of European nations, many of them critically weakened by the war. America had the opportunity to take the lead in supporting and influencing these freedom struggles abroad by demonstrating a commitment to freedom at home. But if it did not, the Soviet Union could point to conditions in the

United States and would have the advantage in the contest for influence in the emerging new nations. Much of the colonized world was populated by nonwhite peoples who took a decidedly dim view of America's state-sanctioned racism. Meanwhile, many of these emerging Third World nations were discovering that playing the two powers against one another assisted their efforts to secure footholds in their bids for independence.

Black leaders were quick to use geopolitics to advance the cause of civil rights. In 1945 NAACP leader Walter White, who had fallen out politically with W. E. B. Du Bois, brought him back into the organization's fold as director of special research. Du Bois's specific task was to ensure that the newly formed United Nations understood the connection between freedom for the colonized world and racial equality in the United States. All of this made Jim Crow an inconvenience and embarrassment to Washington in a way it had never been before.

Below the Mason–Dixon line, these signs of global change triggered a fierce political argument among white politicians: on the one hand were those still spewing the coarse racist demagogy of the likes of Theodore Bilbo, and on the other were those trying to use more carefully modulated tones, such as Mississippi's Senator John Stennis, Georgia's Senator Richard Russell, and South Carolina's Governor James F. Byrnes, who was also a former Supreme Court justice and secretary of state. These men had reached the conclusion that the South needed a more refined political rhetoric when it came to race. To do this, argued Senator Stennis, it was necessary to win national sympathy for the white South, and that would require white southerners, especially politicians, to downplay regional appeals and racist rhetoric. "I shall make no appeals based on prejudice or passion, even if the prejudice happens to be one that I share from my natural experience of growing into maturity in the South," the Mississippi senator said in a 1948 press statement. "We must divorce our thinking from (a) the so-called racial question, (b) the war between the states, (c) the South as a geographic region."

Additionally, southern leaders like Stennis also felt it necessary to cultivate certain blacks and accord them the status of "responsible Negroes" whom white people would accept as nonthreatening political leaders—for black people, of course, not for whites. It is white power's tolerance of these black "leaders" as *political* voices that makes this chosen few somewhat different from the traditional "house negro" of slavery or the obsequious "Uncle Tom" afflicted with what SNCC's Courtland Cox, borrowing from Malcolm X, sometimes mockingly used to call the "Is we sick, Massa?" syndrome.

The white establishment believed that the black leaders they selected actually reflected what the black community thought and wanted, which partly explains their angry surprise on discovering that black people still felt they were being treated unfairly and wanted independent leaders. Many whites found new ways to support their delusions about black satisfaction, placing the blame for blacks' increasingly public discontent and escalating protest on "outside agitators," who they imagined were stirring up and generally manipulating contented but ignorant blacks—"good niggers" or "*our* niggers*," to use the white southern idiom of the time.

Following World War II a political rhetoric emerged that muted explicitly white-supremacist calls and began instead to incorporate phrases like "states' rights" and "protecting our American way of life" into the white-supremacist lexicon. After the Supreme Court's 1954 *Brown v. Board of Education* decision, which ordered desegregation of the nation's schools, the federal government's intrusion into states' jurisdictions was regularly denounced in the South, and many whites supported the "nullification" of federal authority by state and local government—an old idea first forcefully argued by South Carolina senator John C. Calhoun as an intellectual argument for slavery's legitimacy in the years leading up to the Civil War; the argument is that, as members of a confederation of sovereign states, individual states could constitutionally nullify federal actions that subverted their rights. A singing group, the Confederates, became the Barbershop Harmony Society's 1956 International Quartet Champion with the song "Save Your Confederate Money, Boys; the South Shall Rise Again."

Although the southern white elite was growing less and less comfortable with crude redneck racism, it was also disquieted by a changing economic terrain. The war had created a great demand for labor, allowing tenant farmers, sharecroppers, and others on the bottom rungs of rural employment to abandon their jobs and pursue new, more promising opportunities. Many left for jobs in cities, and not just in northern and western cities but in southern cities as well. Labor unions, meanwhile, were growing in power. Union organizing had been quickening just before the war and continued afterward.

Tens of thousands of textile workers had struck throughout the Southeast in 1934. The integrated Southern Tenant Farmers Union (STFU) had made some headway organizing in rural communities in the 1930s, and despite its internal difficulties in the 1940s, STFU influence lingered. Between 1946 and 1953 the CIO engaged in Operation Dixie, a union organizing campaign in twelve southern states. "White employers throughout the South complained that only the poorest quality of workers remained on the farms, and they noted that particularly Negroes (and in the Southwest, Mexicans) were becoming 'too independent' and having to be humored."

Although antiblack violence and terrorism shot up dramatically after World War II, as it had after World War I, it was not working as a means of staunching black challenges to white supremacy. Those challenges were increasing and intensifying. In the political arena, especially, blacks were taking advantage of newfound strength. Afro-American migration to the North and West had made black voters increasingly important to the Democratic Party. And even in the South—in Georgia especially, but elsewhere in the region as well—following the war, it briefly seemed possible that white reformers, union members, veterans, and blacks, all seeking good government, greater fairness, and modernization, might form an effective political coalition. Ellis Arnall, who served as governor of Georgia from 1943 to 1947, had ended the state poll tax and did not resist when the Supreme Court ordered that the state's historically all-white primary elections be opened to voters of all races. (The Democratic Party primaries had excluded blacks, which, in the one-party South, meant that they were effectively excluded from the electoral process.) In an effort at electoral reform, some white veterans even began working with the black veterans who had organized the Georgia Voters League, which aimed to increase voter-registration numbers and voter turnout in elections. In 1946, when Representative Robert Ramspeck resigned from Congress, a special election was held to fill his vacant seat in Georgia's Fifth Congressional District, and it was thanks in large part to Atlanta's black voters that attorney Helen Douglas Mankin won; she had been the only one of seventeen candidates to actively seek black votes.

Still, this political progress had its limits. In Georgia, for instance, the state's county unit system (similar to the presidential Electoral College) gave rural Georgia disproportionate power in primary elections. Even as blacks seemed to be gaining ground politically—at least in Atlanta—the county unit system remained the key determinant of Georgia elections until it was ended in 1962. It had not been used in the special election that Mrs. Mankin won in 1946, but it would cost her victory in the next election—even though, with significant help from black voters, she would win the popular vote.

For many whites in Georgia and other states in the South, any "representative democracy" that included black people did not, should not, and could not represent white people. Racist political campaigning continually raised the specter of communism and "mongrelization" or—as that deep southern white fear was sometimes more softly expressed—"social equality." During the fiercely fought 1950 North Carolina senate race between the virulent racist Willis Smith and the prominent liberal Frank Porter Graham, Smith issued a flyer titled "White People Wake Up" that read in part, "DO YOU WANT Negroes beside you, your wife, and daughters in your mills and factories? Negroes eating beside you in all public eating places? . . . Negroes teaching and disciplining your children in schools?" By successfully fusing racial fear and anticommunism, Smith won the election by nearly 20,000 votes.

There really was no substantive white support for blacks' freedom struggle in the South. Many white southerners who thought of themselves as liberal because of their opposition to old-school racial demagoguery and corruption were in truth liberals or progressives only in the most limited sense. Even many of those members of Georgia's white community who—like Mrs. Mankin—were beginning to take meaningful steps away from the old racist order did so mainly because they needed black people in new and very specific ways. The "essence of the liberal position in Georgia in 1946," wrote journalist Laura Wexler in her investigation of the lynching at Moore's Ford Bridge of two black couples in Walton County, was that "black people didn't deserve equal rights, but they did deserve a safe environment in which to work for white people." The new, more moderate language of racism, meanwhile, made the ugly ideology and policies it was employed to defend more politically palatable to northern whites, winning wider and more open sympathy and support for segregation and white supremacy, especially from the radical right-wing fringe outside the South that described itself as "conservative."

As the war decade drew to a close, the loud, angry race baiting of southern white demagogues quieted somewhat in the upper levels of the political
establishment—on the floor of Congress, for instance—although Senator
Eastland and others still delivered periodic inflammatory rants against
blacks. Lower down on the political ladder, however, on the levels that
affected everyday black life, not much had changed. Although the white-
supremacist system of the old South was weakening in spite of Klan terrorism and other violent attempts to prop it up, it was still very much in
place. But increasingly blacks were unwilling to abide it socially or politically. Furthermore, blacks had also been affected economically by significant changes that had been unfolding since before the war.

Following the war, black veterans were prepared to contribute to the
labor force in new ways. The military had trained them, had provided
many of them with the basic education they had not received at home, and
had given them new skills. Mostly deployed in the army's Quartermaster,
Transportation, and Engineering Corps, a great many black soldiers had
been employed in areas from which they had been excluded in civilian life.
And although many of their jobs were officially designated as "unskilled,"
the soldiers nevertheless got useful training and experience—as truck drivers, road builders, construction workers, and so on—that were transferable
to civilian life. The Red Ball Express—trucks driven by black soldiers, often
under heavy enemy fire, to supply combat units moving across Europe after
D-day—is a good example of the way wartime experiences provided blacks
not only with military training but also with technical and logistical know-
how that would give them an advantage in the civilian labor market after
the war. According to Ulysses Lee, a member of the Office of the Chief of
Military History from 1946 to 1952, the variety of ways black troops were
employed in World War II "far outstripped" anything seen in World War
I. The rank-and-file black soldier of World War II was also much better
educated than his counterpart in World War I. "Not surprisingly," Lee continued, "black soldiers anticipated parlaying [their] wartime training into
better jobs when they returned home." According to the Army Research
Laboratory, 61 percent of black soldiers believed their military training
would help them find a better job than they had before the war. Only 39
percent of white GIs shared this optimism.

The effects of this economic transformation were potentially just as earthshaking as blacks' strengthened political presence in the United States. Many black soldiers, especially southerners, had been unskilled laborers before the war, but on returning home only a third planned to return to their previous occupations and employers; two-thirds planned to find other work. Such intentions and abilities—to say nothing of the desire for and anticipation of upward mobility that underlay them—threatened the southern agricultural system, for southern agriculture, although rapidly mechanizing, still depended on black labor. But these changes in the black workforce also threatened to disrupt the region's dominant sociopolitical system, which assumed black servility. Many black veterans' newfound ability to support themselves and their families with work that earned more than a minimal wage undermined the submissiveness on which the system depended. At the same time, it bolstered black veterans' self-esteem and increased their demands for respect and a better life.

Even the guarded public posture of many veterans after the war could not hide their desire for something better than they had known before it. One Clarksdale, Mississippi, veteran described both his ambition and his caution on returning home: "We didn't push anything in that time because [whites] was running everything. . . . I didn't entertain the idea that I was going to change it. No, but I had the idea, look I'm trying to better myself." However careful they were politically, he and many other veterans agreed of their military service that—as one veteran put it—"we were fighting for what we didn't have." Their military experiences gave black veterans a depth of determination whose importance to the oncoming southern freedom struggle cannot be overstated. And it sometimes manifested itself in an aggressive assertiveness that stoked tensions with white supremacists back home. Doyle Combs, who was seriously wounded in the war and went on to become the leader of the Toccoa, Georgia, NAACP, recalled his feelings after returning home with a distinctly militant anger that would resonate mightily in the decade to come: "Since I lost a portion of my body to protect my own rights, I would die for my rights and I would kill for my rights. And I was going to vote if I had to kill somebody to vote."

———

Monroe, North Carolina, does not usually feature prominently on the map of black political struggle, but in the two decades following World War II the town embodied these crucial trends in the black freedom struggle—and it was perhaps their most dramatic illustration. Whites there, as elsewhere in the postwar South, were worried both by small-scale black political insurgencies and by perceptible and growing changes in blacks' attitudes toward the white-supremacist system. Defiance of the established order was becoming more and more common, and resistance to white rule seemed to be breaking out all across the region.

Monroe would come to represent not only black veterans' refusal to submit to the old white-supremacist order once they returned from the war, but also their willingness and capacity to engage in well-armed and well-organized self-defense in the pursuit of their long-denied liberties. This vital aspect of the freedom struggle in Monroe lasted well into the era of nonviolent protest, and, perhaps more than in any other part of the South, it illustrates the complex relationship between nonviolence and armed self-defense. Sit-ins, or more precisely stand-ins, began in Monroe in 1957, almost three years before what is now generally considered the first instance of this form of student-led nonviolent direct action in the South, but that has been forgotten. Guns always accompanied nonviolent struggle in Monroe, and that is well-remembered and has always been a much more awkward subject.

Black political struggle in Monroe is often associated with the leadership of Robert Williams, whose dramatic expulsion from the NAACP and subsequent exile from the United States have overshadowed what should be the main focus of his and Monroe's story: a strong black community that would not be pushed around by white supremacists. Leadership, after all, does not negate community, and although military veterans featured prominently in the black leadership that emerged in Monroe after the war, they were not the only important actors there. Williams would become the most visible personality among those veterans, but the story of the black campaign of armed self-defense in Monroe did not begin with him. Rather, it began in 1946 with what should have been a relatively inconsequential event: an argument between a white man and his black employee. As events in Columbia, Tennessee, and elsewhere in the postwar American South attest, however, nothing in the interactions between blacks and whites was inconsequential if it involved Afro-American defiance. And indeed, the argument in Monroe led to the most explosive of events: the murder of a white man by a black man.

Bennie Montgomery had served in the army during World War II and had been severely wounded. He came back to Monroe with a steel plate in his head, and according to Williams, his high school classmate, he was never the same after his injury. After the war he returned to work on the W. W. Mangum farm just outside Monroe. One Friday night at the end of May 1946, Montgomery, drunk, wrecked his father's car. The next day, after half a day's work, he asked for his wages so that he could go into Monroe and have his father's car repaired. It has not been reported *how* Montgomery asked for his pay and half a day off, but Mangum seems not to have liked his tone or manner, and the farmer began kicking and slapping him. Montgomery fought back. At some point during the ensuing struggle, Montgomery pulled out a pocketknife and slit Mangum's throat, killing him. Not long afterward he was arrested while sitting in a Monroe restaurant drinking beer, his clothes still covered in blood.

The local Klan wanted to lynch Montgomery, but he was rushed out of town, tried, found guilty of murder, and put on death row at the Central Prison in Raleigh, North Carolina. On March 28, 1947, he was executed in the prison's gas chamber.

That should have been the end of the story. However, when the state of North Carolina sent Montgomery's body back to Monroe for burial, Ku Klux Klansmen—still angry that he had been whisked out of town before they could snatch him from jail—demanded that his body be turned over to them, not to his family. The Klansmen wanted to mutilate his body, probably by dragging it through Monroe's streets as a public display of the fate that awaited black men who assaulted whites. They also threatened to kill the funeral parlor director if he dressed the dead soldier in his uniform for burial or allowed an American flag to be draped across the casket, as was customary in burial services for veterans.

As these threats mounted, a group of local black veterans met in the barbershop of Booker T. Perry, himself a World War I veteran, and decided that none of this was going to happen. They began planning for the defense of the funeral parlor, its director, and Montgomery's body. Williams was among them. Like most of the other men who gathered at Perry's barbershop, he was not long out of the army.

When the Klansmen approached the funeral parlor, three dozen rifles, including Williams's carbine, were trained on their motorcade. No one fired a shot, but it was unmistakably clear to the Klansmen that the black men lined up in plain sight outside the funeral parlor were prepared to use the weapons they carried. Whatever plans the Klansmen had disintegrated. They fled. "That was one of the first incidents," said Williams years later, "that really started us to understanding that we had to resist, and that resistance could be effective if we resisted in groups, and if we resisted with guns."

This may have been one of the first instances of concerted, armed self-defense by black people in Monroe, but it would not be the last. Monroe resident Dr. Albert E. Perry is not nearly as well remembered as Williams, but the next major confrontation with the Ku Klux Klan would center on him. In the summer of 1957, after a child drowned in one of the dangerous, unsupervised swimming holes the area's blacks were relegated to using, Perry and Williams took a group of black children to Monroe's municipal swimming pool. It was located on the grounds of the Monroe Country Club, which had been built with $200,000 of federal funds plus another $31,000 in local tax money. They were denied entrance but "stood in" wearing their swimming suits and holding towels. They repeated this over several days.

Dr. Perry was well-off and well-educated, and he had come to represent a renewed spirit of activism—and a revived NAACP—in Monroe. As president of the Union County Council on Human Relations, he had already written a mild letter to the city's Recreation Board requesting that the board "provide supervised swimming for all citizens." The World War II veteran was relatively new in town: a native of Austin, Texas, he had trained in Monroe at Camp Sutton during the war, fallen in love with a local girl, married her, and settled in the city as a doctor after finishing at Meharry Medical College in Nashville, Tennessee, following the war. He was also a member of the NAACP.

Perhaps because the Union County branch of the NAACP was rather like a social club for Monroe's small black bourgeoisie, the town's white population had tolerated it. But the Supreme Court's 1954 *Brown* decision ended that tolerance; suspicion of and hostility to NAACP branches, regardless of their local character, intensified across the South. Under pressure from Monroe's white powers and a resurgent North Carolina Ku Klux Klan, which reacted angrily to the Court's decision, most of the middle-class members of the Monroe NAACP branch deserted. Only six members remained in 1955 when they voted the rough-hewn Robert Williams into the presidency of the dying branch; most of those remaining members then canceled their own memberships. Dr. Perry stayed with the organization as its vice president.

Perry and Williams slowly rebuilt the branch. They reached out to working-class blacks in Monroe and to other members of Union County's grass roots—laborers, farmers, domestic workers, the unemployed—getting many of these people involved with the NAACP for the first time. They also reached out to ex-servicemen, several of whom had helped safeguard Bennie Montgomery's body almost a decade earlier. "We ended up with a chapter that was unique in the whole NAACP," Williams wrote later, "because of [its] working class composition and a leadership that was not middle class. Most important, we had a strong representation of returned veterans who were very militant and didn't scare easily." The Monroe chapter of the NAACP would prove itself unique in another way, as well. After becoming NAACP branch president, Williams took the unusual step of establishing a National Rifle Association chapter—the Monroe Rifle Club, also called "the Black Guard"—whose ranks soon filled with black members. Williams also secured "better rifles" via mail order and secondhand purchases.

Dr. Perry's prominence in the black community, his education and relative affluence, and even his Catholic faith had all made him a target of white fear and resentment. But the swimming pool controversy raised the antipathy to a new level. From a Ku Klux Klan perspective, bare black skin in the water with bare white skin was akin to sexual assault. As the swimming-pool protests continued and white-supremacist anger mounted, the Klan stepped up its efforts at intimidation and began regularly driving through the black community, shouting insults and threats, and shooting randomly into the air—and sometimes at homes. Such piecemeal assaults on the black community were only the beginning.

On the night of October 5, 1957, after holding a rally complete with a cross burning, a heavily armed motorcade of Klansmen headed toward Perry's home on the outskirts of Monroe. However, an attack had been anticipated. Helmeted men from the NAACP, with automatic weapons, were dug in behind sandbag fortifications and hidden in other strategic places around the house. When the Klan convoy arrived at Perry's home and opened fire, they were immediately met with disciplined, withering volleys from the defenders. The men shooting back at the Klansmen were apparently not shooting to kill, for the gunfire was aimed low, but they were definitely determined to drive the Klansmen away with the threat of death. "We shot it out with the Klan and repelled their attack," Williams recalled later. "And the Klan didn't have any more stomach for this type of fight. They stopped raiding our community." The next day Monroe's City Council banned Ku Klux Klan motorcades.

Neither Williams nor Perry could possibly have imagined then how controversial—or how influential—their branch of the NAACP would become. Because of their leadership, the tactics and strategies of armed self-defense—as practiced by persons and communities under assault for their civil rights efforts—became nationally visible. It was in Monroe, moreover, that the principled practice of armed self-defense first converged with the modern civil rights movement's emergent tactics and strategies of nonviolence. Yet this confluence has often been oversimplified as a clash between violent and nonviolent ideas and approaches to civil rights struggle. This oversimplification ignores the more complex tensions between the priorities of local black communities and the priorities of national civil rights organizations—tensions that are embedded in and that much more accurately describe events in Monroe between the swimming-pool protests of 1957 and Williams's eventual exile from the United States in 1961.

Williams's militant self-defensive tactics quickly attracted the attention of the national civil rights establishment. Arguing for the necessity of organized self-defense in a September 1959 article in *Liberation* magazine, Williams praised Martin Luther King Jr. as "a great and successful leader of our race," but he also insisted that black southerners often had to face "the necessity of confronting savage violence" with violence of their own. "I wish to make it clear that I do not advocate violence for its own sake, or for the sake of reprisals against whites," he wrote. "Nor am I against the passive resistance advocated by Reverend Martin Luther King and others. My only difference with Dr. King is that I believe in flexibility in the freedom struggle."

Responding in the same magazine a month later, King acknowledged that nonviolence as a philosophy could be difficult for the average person to grasp, but he also worried that even the sort of restrained violence that Williams was advocating put the black struggle at risk because it could "mislead Negroes into the belief that [violence] is the only path and place them as a minority in a position where they confront a far larger adversary than it is possible to defeat in this form of combat." In this, King was expressing a reality that southern blacks had long understood: overt or preemptive displays of force by black people—like that organized by black World War I veterans in Houston, Texas, in 1917—ran the risk of eliciting an overwhelming and brutal response by local and national authorities.

But King also acknowledged that there could be value in armed self-defense. "When the Negro uses *force* [emphasis added] in self-defense," the advocate of nonviolence wrote in his response to Williams, "he does not forfeit support—he may even win it, by the courage and self-respect it reflects." In this exchange, King seems to have misunderstood Williams as inviting blacks to kill whites with impunity. For his part, Williams may have equated nonviolence with pacifism, not fully understanding the forcefulness of nonviolent direct action.

This exchange between Robert Williams, a gruff working-class leader, and Martin Luther King Jr., a prince of the black Baptist church who was rapidly rising to national prominence as a civil rights leader, forecast the political and class tensions that would be increasingly significant inside the southern Freedom Movement of the 1960s. Tensions between local grassroots organizers and the national civil rights establishment were growing rapidly as the 1950s drew to a close. One telling episode was the infamous 1958 "kissing case" in Monroe, when a young white girl, six-year-old Sissy Marcus, playfully kissed a seven-year-old black boy, David "Fuzzy" Simpson, as nine-year-old James Hanover Thompson—also black—stood by. The two boys were quickly arrested for "molestation" and sentenced to reform school until they reached the age of twenty-one. After the boys had been detained for three months, North Carolina's governor bowed to public outrage, international media attention, and outside legal assistance and pardoned them. The legal assistance came primarily from New York attorney Conrad Lynn, who became involved because the NAACP said it would not take the case, arguing that it did not take on "sexual" cases. Eventually, however, embarrassed by its lack of involvement, the organization did involve itself with the case.

Whether because of political disagreements with Williams or because of his strategic choices, the national NAACP hierarchy simply had no respect or affection for the Monroe branch leader. NAACP executive director Roy Wilkins dismissively called him "the Lancelot of Monroe," and NAACP counsel and future Supreme Court justice Thurgood Marshall even suggested to the FBI that the agency investigate Williams. Yet ironically, whatever the basis of the NAACP's objection to Williams, it does not seem to have had anything to do with his use of guns. In 1959, at the very convention that suspended Williams from the NAACP, the organization passed a resolution affirming the right of self-defense.

4

"I Wasn't Being Non-Nonviolent"

Every what the Mississippi white man pose with, he got to be met with. I said, "Meet him with ever what he pose with. If he pose with a smile, meet him with a smile, and if he pose with a gun, meet him with a gun."

—Hartman Turnbow, Mississippi farmer

Now you can pray with them or pray for 'em, but if they kill you in the meantime you are not going to be an effective organizer.

—Worth Long, SNCC field secretary

As the 1960s opened, white-supremacist terrorists, galvanized by mounting challenges to the South's racist status quo, increased their attacks on civil rights workers and leaders and on the ordinary black men and women who made up their constituency. Local and state governments supported this violence, and it was largely ignored by the federal government. And as the attacks and assassinations went on unabated, the question of how best to deal with such dangers also grew.

Most southern organizations formed to struggle for civil rights did not adopt the tactics of armed self-defense as visibly as did Robert Williams and the NAACP branch in Monroe and Union County, North Carolina. However, many local NAACP leaders routinely traveled armed because they were in constant danger of murderous attack, especially following the

Supreme Court's 1954 *Brown v. Board of Education* decision. At the same time—and quite unexpectedly—the use of nonviolent forms of direct action was also growing, especially among younger participants in the movement. Perhaps the most renowned campaign of nonviolent protest was the Montgomery bus boycott of the mid-1950s, but student sit-in protests—which erupted in Greensboro, North Carolina, on February 1, 1960, and spread rapidly—made nonviolence, as both tactic and philosophy, an even larger part of black political conversation. However, as the Freedom Movement began to emphasize work in rural communities, it became clear that nonviolence—both the practice and the idea—had its limits. Activists and organizers associated with nonviolent organizations such as SNCC, CORE, and SCLC increasingly found themselves working with local supporters who were strongly inclined to shoot back at night riders and other terrorists.

Most of these activists and organizers were young and inexperienced, fresh off college campuses or high schools. For many of them, grassroots community organizing was a new approach to the civil rights struggle, and it posed new, unexpected challenges. Their key supporters in local communities—men and women who were often their parents' age or older—had survived white-supremacist terrorism earlier in the century and were able to openly aid these organizers in part because they were willing to use their guns. This presented the young activists with an unanticipated dilemma. How should they respond? Should they resist the possession and use of guns by the local people they were involved with in rural communities? Or should they accept it, knowing that the very weapons that seemed so out of place as part of a nonviolent protest movement might also save their lives? Few had any training in nonviolence beyond a few workshops to prepare them to sit in or walk picket lines. Even fewer had any grounding in nonviolence as a philosophy or way of life. So, to put it simply, what would these young men and women do when confronted with guns—and, indeed, what *could* they do? The answer to these questions would be found not in the classroom or church but, rather, in the day-to-day work of community organizing.

The story of Joe McDonald reclaiming his shotgun in Ruleville, Mississippi, in the summer of 1962, told in the prologue, offers a window onto the ways young organizers could influence the attitudes and behavior of the men and women at the grassroots level. Yet it also reveals the ways the organizers had to change in order to win their trust and support. For although organizers might have come to these communities with at least a vague notion of nonviolence as a tool for change, the reality was that black men and women in the Deep South had developed their own ways of coping with the threat of white violence, and in engaging with these local community organizers found themselves being transformed at the same time that they were effecting transformation.

Ruleville mayor Charles Dorrough confiscated Joe McDonald's gun following nighttime attacks in the black community by night riders. The mayor accused SNCC organizers—myself among them—of planning and executing the attack. Mr. Joe needed the gun not only for self-defense but also for the simple but primary purpose of putting food on the table, so he took a copy of the U.S. Constitution to Ruleville's city hall, pointed to the Second Amendment, and demanded his gun back. It was an act of profound bravery, but it and Mayor Dorrough's response both speak to the complex range of challenges, risks, and small victories found in civil rights struggle at the grassroots level. Clearly, neither segregation nor white-supremacist power was defeated by the mayor's returning Joe McDonald's shotgun. But victories in the South were almost always small. To be able to organize in rural communities like Ruleville, organizers had to win the support of people like Mr. Joe, people willing to work with them despite the danger. The problem was large and movement efforts only addressed part of it, so organizers had to be realistic about how much change they could effect and had to be careful to temper the expectations of the people they worked with. "One of the things I felt in Mississippi was that you always had to understate everything," explained SNCC's Bob Moses years later. "What you had to show people was that you were actually biting off a small piece of the problem. . . . [You] were always afraid that you were going to get people thinking that something was going to happen that wasn't going to happen." This concern affected priorities and even the language organizers used in these communities. The problems facing black people in the Deep South were hundreds of years old, and intimately familiar to local people. There was not much about the local dimension of the problem that they did not already know, so they would see through any exaggerations about change organizers might make. Approaching them required a hardheaded honesty that was consistent with their lived experience, the facts of their lives, which organizers had to learn as they worked.

In attempting to build meaningful relationships with black people in these rural communities, organizers quickly came to appreciate the fact that, in their lives, danger was always nearby. Understanding and organizing local black communities in the Deep South was not the same as mobilizing for a protest march or a sit-in. "It isn't [done] by getting people who are going to respond to the big speech," says Bob Moses, thinking back to those dangerous days. It was slow, mostly quiet work, because any public challenge to the existing order of white supremacy could get organizers or their local supporters killed. Danger was not abstract; it was immediate and intensely personal, affecting the entire community—family, neighbors, and friends. This was quite different from putting ourselves at risk. And we organizers knew, as surely as we knew the sun would rise, that it was our presence that triggered white violence. One of the most painful movement memories is of the funeral of NAACP leader Herbert Lee, when the murdered man's anguished wife walked up to Bob Moses and SNCC chairman Charles "Chuck" McDew and devastatingly charged, "You killed my husband! You killed my husband!"

Yet risk was already a fact of life for many black people in the South, and although they could not eliminate it, southern black communities had learned how to minimize risk long before the existence of SNCC, CORE, SCLC, and even the NAACP. They knew when they were in danger and when they were not, and they did the best they could to protect themselves. It made perfect sense, therefore, that local blacks responded cautiously to the arrival of our small group of organizers in Ruleville, while measuring the value and consequences of the new risks that accompanied our presence.

The presence of civil rights workers stoked a deep-rooted fear among local Afro-Americans. Often confused with apathy, this fear was complex. One obvious reason for it was the terrorism that local blacks knew could be brought to bear against them at the slightest hint of a challenge to the prevailing white-supremacist order—terrorism that ranged from Ku Klux Klan violence to Citizens' Council reprisals, from individual attacks to collective punishment. Another component of what could look like apathy was the fact that local people generally did not have the option of leaving; they were held by family, work, even loyalty to place, or sometimes simply debt. Movement organizers—almost all of whom came from outside the community where they were working—always had the option of leaving. And finally, through the use of force and violence, fear had been cultivated in black communities for centuries.

There was widespread concern in Ruleville's black community that the very presence of organizers was dangerous. "They were afraid of us because the white folks didn't like us," remembered Mac McLaurin. There was also concern for the young workers themselves. Whether or not local Afro-Americans were willing to work with them, no one in the black community wanted to see the organizers killed. McLaurin recalled that when Mayor Dorrough picked him, Landy McNair, and me up at gunpoint as we walked along the side of the road in Ruleville's Jerusalem Quarters, "People were peeping out of the windows, scared. And after we got back they told me, 'we never expected to see you all again.' Why? I asked. What did you think was going to happen? 'We thought you all was gonna be in the river.'" The fact that we were not murdered was a small victory and became part of the local conversation about the presence of "the nonviolents" in town, advancing our work in Ruleville and Sunflower County.

As organizers we needed to convince the black populace that we would remain present and committed when—as it inevitably did—the going got terrifyingly rough. That sort of trust could not be built overnight. People would judge our commitment much as they judged the weather or crops or the danger they faced from the Klan, the county sheriff, and his deputies. And they would judge at their own pace, using skills that the necessities of survival had forced black communities to develop over centuries in America. "The basic first step was earning the right to involve the people you were working with," remembered Bob Moses of those early organizing days when life-threatening danger hung over every potential action. Organizers needed to fit into the local culture while at the same time challenging oppressive and restrictive parts of it. And since they were, after all, asking people to put their lives at risk, they had to earn the right to organize. That could not be accomplished by pretending to be more capable of defending themselves or the people who cooperated with them than they actually were. As Moses noted,

> It's all dangerous. You are carrying danger with you [and the local people] have to figure out whether or not *you're* for real. You have to *earn* that. You don't earn that [by engaging in] some kind of charade about being violent—they know better—or by being boastful about what you're going to do to whoever messes with you. They've already been through too much to think that that kind of talk means anything. Their very lives have depended on the ability to *read people* as distinct from reading books. And that ability is what allows you to earn their respect.

Organizing this way literally and figuratively required putting one foot in front of the other; going from door to door and field to field, knowing that even those men and women most open to joining them would be cautious.

Although Moses's observations reflect his experiences in rural Mississippi, organizers confronted similar challenges everywhere they went in the South, in cities as well as in the back country. In a 1961 field report describing his first days in Albany, Georgia (a small city, not a rural town), SNCC's southwest Georgia project director Charles Sherrod explained what was involved in taking the first steps toward earning the right to organize:

> The first obstacle to remove . . . was the mental block in the minds of those who wanted to move but were unable for fear that we were not who we said we were. But when people began to hear us in churches, social meetings, on the streets, in the pool halls, lunchrooms, nightclubs, and other places where people gather, they began to open up a bit. We would tell them of how it feels to be in prison, what it means to be behind bars, in jail for the cause. We explained to them that we had stopped school because we felt compelled to do so since so many of us were in chains. We explained further that there were worse chains than jail and prison. . . . We mocked the system that teaches men to be good Negroes instead of good men.

These first steps of contact and conversation were what ushered in serious publicly visible challenge to white power. Most people in these communities were accustomed to keeping their dissatisfaction well hidden. In 1896, a time of great antiblack violence across the South, Paul Lawrence Dunbar wrote poetically,

> We wear the mask that grins and lies
> . . .
> We sing, but oh the clay is vile
> Beneath our feet, and long the mile.

Humor, double entendre, and misdirection in tone and language were all traditionally used to conceal dissatisfaction behind a variety of masks. Historian W. Fitzhugh Brundage provides a useful descriptive label: "Resistance assumed the guise of what may be called discursive insubordination." This "language of dissent," as Brundage calls it, can be seen in the spirituals that were born in the bondage of slavery and are still admired for their beauty but are rarely appreciated as songs of resistance. Although many black people projected a sense of deference and subordination to whites, that did not mean they accepted the injustices done them; rather, it meant they had learned the practicalities of survival in a world where the odds were heavily stacked against them. Movement organizing in the 1960s was an attempt to change those odds—an attempt connected, it must be emphasized, to similar efforts much older than SNCC, CORE, SCLC, or even the NAACP.

That Joe McDonald slipped his mask by asserting his gun rights cannot be disconnected from the links of trust forged by the conversations Charles Sherrod describes or the earned respect that Bob Moses considers so crucial. The relationship with the community was everything. And slowly the community began to reveal its real face. The first impressions organizers made counted for a lot. For instance, McLaurin and his SNCC colleagues— myself among them—were brought to Ruleville by local NAACP leader Amzie Moore. Significantly, he did not introduce us to the black community by placing us at the head of a protest march into the town square; rather, he brought us to a Sunday service at Mount Galilee Missionary Baptist Church, where we were introduced to the congregation. After the service, Amzie handed us over to the McDonalds and left.

We got to know the local people and the community in conversations driven as much by curiosity as by political purpose. We learned from Joe McDonald and others what it was like to live and work in Ruleville and Sunflower County. At the same time, he, his neighbors, and others wanted to know about the family history and personal backgrounds of the three young SNCC workers now living among them. They were asking the "Who are your people?" questions that form—or at least once formed—so important a part of relationships in southern culture. We moved with careful, deliberate steps, because even within the confines of the black community it was impossible to avoid danger, as demonstrated by Mayor Dorrough's sudden pistol-toting appearance as we walked down one of the dirt roads in Jerusalem Quarters.

It was this kind of presence that earned cooperation and support. People made small commitments that were visible in the choices they made, often at great risk, and those choices had a profoundly persuasive wider effect. It helped put eighteen people on the bus that left Ruleville for the Sunflower County courthouse in Indianola; it informed Fannie Lou Hamer's decision to stand up to the owner of the plantation where she worked; and it helped Joe McDonald go down to city hall and demand his shotgun. Individual choices like these were the starting points for a much broader, organized, and collective effort to challenge white supremacy. "To battle institutions we must change ourselves first," SNCC's Lawrence Guyot once observed, and it was not difficult to see those sorts of personal changes everywhere in the Deep South in the early 1960s.

———

Mississippi in 1962 was a totally repressive state, the most repressive in the country. It was a "closed society," choking in the tight grip of white supremacy. And what helped keep white supremacy so powerfully in place was not simply violence but also old habits of thought. Black people had been taught to believe in their own inferiority and to accept that white power determined all their rights and could not be dislodged or challenged.

Organizers going from door to door trying to encourage voter-registration attempts often heard in response to their efforts, "That's white folks business" and "Ain't foolin' around with that mess."

In this context, Joe McDonald's decision to use a book to assert his gun rights was a critical breakthrough. Mr. Joe could neither read nor write, noted Charles McLaurin, and he had also never stood up to white authority in the way he did that day. "Joe McDonald had never looked a white man in his face and demanded anything in all of his life," said McLaurin years later,

> and now here he was, this seventy-six-year-old black guy who can't read or write inspired enough by these young Negroes to go down to city hall and challenge the mayor with this book. Think about it! The mayor was known to carry a pistol; he'd pull a gun on any black person who challenged him. He pulled a gun on *us*! But Joe McDonald went down there. We gave Mr. Joe the ammunition he needed to face the [white] man. And I think the mayor gave Mr. Joe his gun back to try and keep down "trouble"—folks in Ruleville responding to us. He probably said to himself, "Let me give Joe his gun back 'cause I don't want no more trouble from these boys." We empowered Mr. Joe and that helped [our work] in the community.

McLaurin's recollection of McDonald's victory that day speaks not only to the intimate relationship between organizing and grassroots struggle but also to the boldness required of individual men and women who, having been raised in a system that often brutally crushed challenges to white authority, responded to encouragement from young organizers to take control of their own lives.

McDonald's assertion of his gun rights and Mrs. Hamer's attempt to register to vote were bold examples of direct action by people who had never before raised their voices to speak for themselves. Together, men and women like these formed the heart of the fledgling movement in Ruleville and Sunflower County. They were sharecroppers, day laborers, domestic workers, housewives, and grandmothers—people like three older women who, a week before Mrs. Hamer's group tried to register, were brought to the Sunflower County courthouse by McLaurin. They were the first from Ruleville to attempt to register since the early 1950s; McLaurin called them "my little old ladies" and insisted, "They made *me* a man."

Examples like these certainly did not represent mass movement, but they were an indication that some new current was flowing through black Mississippi. They represented, as Bob Moses put it in a 1961 letter smuggled from the jail cell he shared with student protesters in McComb, Mississippi, "a tremor in the middle of the iceberg."

These tiny tremors were felt in both the black and white communities in Ruleville and elsewhere across the South. They helped erode the paralyzing fear that had defined black people's relationship with white people for the entire twentieth century. They were also part of the potential "trouble" that McLaurin thought had alarmed Dorrough. McDonald's demand for the return of his shotgun suggested a loss of the white power controlling the lives of black people, a power that had been secured by fear, force, and violence. Even with voting rights still denied, even without attempts to desegregate public schools and without lunch-counter sit-ins in Ruleville and Sunflower County, a demand by one elderly man was enough to trigger alarm.

In the 1960s whites began to learn that black people were not as docile as they had thought. That bred fear in them, and their range of options for quashing black resistance was shrinking. "Spectacle lynching" was common in the first four decades of the twentieth century. Newspapers sometimes gave advance notice of hangings and burnings as public events for whites, and even children were brought to watch. Now, though such events were not impossible, it was far more difficult to participate in one without facing penalties. After World War II, antiblack violence began to take on a more covert character: assassination, kidnapping, bombings.

Although new federal laws were forcing white violence underground, so too were black-owned rifles and shotguns. "Nighttime marauders had learned to keep a more respectful distance from their targets because the targets were increasingly prone to shoot back," notes Charles Payne. Night riders could not be certain that they would not get killed by the blacks they assaulted. Since the end of World War II, black veterans had been consistently proving themselves willing to repel violent attack with gunfire, which helps explain why night riders turned to drive-by shootings—not lingering on the scene—or to bombs planted beneath churches and homes in the dead of night. Also, many blacks—not just veterans—were gun owners. Mrs. Hamer's mother would go to the cotton fields with a pistol in her possession. And Mrs. Hamer, like her mother, also kept weapons nearby in case she needed them: "I keep a shotgun in every corner of my bedroom and the first cracker even looks like he wants to throw some dynamite on my porch won't write his mama again."

As organizers embedded themselves in local life and culture in the Deep South, they discovered that people had different relationships to guns and self-defense. The specifics varied from community to community. Rural Holmes County, Mississippi, for example, was radically different from Sunflower County; 70 percent of the land in Holmes County was owned by black farmers, the legacy of a New Deal Farm Security Administration program, and that in turn had encouraged a strong tradition of black independence and mutual cooperation, including armed self-defense. There was considerable and sometimes violent white opposition to independent black farming communities like the ones in Holmes County, but black farmers, proud of their landownership, were used to cooperating with each other—there was a cooperatively owned cotton gin in Holmes County, for example—and they were determined to protect themselves and their land from attack.

This tradition of organized armed self-defense was already well entrenched in other parts of the South when movement workers arrived. One noteworthy example of a Holmes County community that employed sophisticated defensive tactics was the community of Mileston, where Hollis Watkins began working as a SNCC field secretary in 1963. A native Mississippian raised in the tiny southwest Mississippi hamlet of Chisholm Mission (named for an AME church), Hollis was brought up in a family with its own share of "crazy Negroes." (As a boy his father had to leave home because he fired a shotgun at a white man who was cursing his mother.) Recalls Watkins of the approach to Mileston:

> You had to turn off the highway, cross the tracks and make a loop
> on a narrow dirt road to get back to the highway. You're gonna
> be passing houses, and a few had telephones. Mr. Dave had one
> at the beginning of the road, Miss Epps at the other end. Mr.

Howard's daddy and his brother lived in between; they had phones. If after a certain hour, you know after dark, a vehicle didn't give the proper signals, then telephone messages would be relayed. Usually Miss Epps would call Mr. Howard's daddy or his brother; they would call Mr. Dave and ultimately that vehicle would be approached from the front and the rear and checked to see who it was. In most cases it would be met head-on with bright headlights ... with two people in a car. And from behind by four people in a pickup truck ... two of the people would generally be in the cab. And two would generally be in the back with the guns raised over the cab.

Terrorists approaching Mileston could not be absolutely sure they would get home alive.

Yet most black people were not organizing paramilitary units or much self-defense beyond that which protected their own homes and immediate community, which helps explain why the mayor of Ruleville returned McDonald's shotgun to him. Dorrough obviously thought it unlikely that Joe McDonald would use his gun in any type of aggressive or retaliatory violence. Like denim overalls, shotguns and pistols were an ordinary part of everyday southern life. Indeed, Mississippi's gun culture proved so powerful that in 1954, when state legislator Edwin White expressed alarm that too many blacks were buying firearms and introduced a bill requiring gun registration "[to protect] us from those likely to cause us trouble," the bill never even made it out of committee.

Like many in the generally impoverished rural South—impoverished for many white as well as black people—Joe McDonald mainly used his gun to put food on the table. Mayor Dorrough surely knew that. Guns were undeniably possessed for self-defense too, but to a lesser extent, and blacks exercised caution when it came to this, and the mayor certainly knew that as well. Moreover, Joe McDonald was seventy-six years of age and known to be a man of great dignity and probity; his having a gun posed no danger of aggressive violence to anyone in the black or white community. He was not going to climb into his pickup truck and drive through town shooting into the homes of his neighbors or lead a posse of black vigilantes into the white community; Dorrough, his racial prejudices notwithstanding, had to have known this too.

This is not to say that whites did not worry about black retaliation. Hodding Carter III, who was editor of Greenville, Mississippi's *Delta Democratic Times* in the 1960s, explained,

> You don't even have to put it in terms of race. If you have run a society in which basic to its sense of itself was the use of violence, its use of murder, its use of weapons to hold control firmly in its hands . . . it's almost inevitable that being who you were you would think that those to whom you had been doing this would consider it worth *their* while to use the same tactics.

Whites, in other words, feared and perhaps expected that the same sort of terrorism they had used against the South's black communities would someday be turned against them. This fear could take bizarre turns. In November 1965, the Ku Klux Klan contacted Deputy Sheriff Earl Fisher in Washington County, Mississippi. The Klan told Fisher that Louisiana's Deacons for Defense and Justice, notorious at the time for providing armed protection to nonviolent CORE organizers in that state, and the Nation of Islam, which had been made prominent by Malcolm X and his Black Nationalist rhetoric, had joined forces to organize a black uprising against whites. Arms and ammunition, the Klan said, were being smuggled into the county seat—Greenville—via the Mississippi River and were being hidden in coffins at a black cemetery on the edge of town. The Klan urged state police to place armed guards at every black cemetery in Mississippi and actually persuaded Fisher to exhume the grave of one elderly black man. No guns were found. Fisher called a press conference to assuage the fears of the white community, which was panicking about the rumors of a pending black uprising. Fisher also announced that the sheriff's office was launching an investigation of the Ku Klux Klan.

Although the likelihood of armed insurrection by blacks was practically nil, trumpeting the threat of such an uprising—as the Klan did in Washington County—was demagogically useful to some whites and played to fears held by others. "Almost all of the planter-farmer types believed that *their* blacks, *their* 'niggers,' their whatever, felt themselves better treated than others' and were not likely to be insurrectionists," says Carter, "but [they] felt they couldn't be sure that their neighbors' [black] 'bad guy' wouldn't show up, and kill them."

Yet remarkably, even in the midst of panics like these, whites did not attempt to disarm blacks. The precedent for disarming blacks went as far back as the antebellum and colonial eras, when laws across the South were written to keep weapons out of black hands. But another aspect of southern culture appears to have trumped these precedents. Even within the framework of white supremacy, if there was no overt or apparent political challenge to the social order, a peculiar intimacy could exist in rural communities like Ruleville, and even in cities. Sometimes—and the word *sometimes* must be stressed here—whites' collective delusion that blacks were satisfied with the way things were loosened long-standing segregationist practices and eased more generalized and abstract fears of black insurgency. After all, blacks across the South performed intimate domestic services for whites, from nursing and caring for white babies to cleaning and caring for white peoples' houses and lawns and cooking their food, often spending as much time in white homes as in their own. Even in the 1960s, as white anger increased over black protest and political assertion, one could still hear some whites declare how close they were to their "mammies" or tell of a black "uncle" or kindly Old Black Joe teaching them to hunt and fish. In some respects, day-to-day life was less segregated in the South than in the North.

But none of these everyday relations challenged white supremacy, which was always understood to be fundamental to black–white interactions. The codes coordinating racial contact and behavior were more finely calibrated than suggested by the raw violence and crude language of the Ku Klux Klan and their ilk. Hodding Carter described this relationship succinctly, noting, "There was a great deal of contact between black and white in Mississippi and in the Deep South. The contact was that of master and slave, of subordinate to superior, of serf to master. It was a contact in which the illusion of familiarity on the white part bred [their] contempt. . . . It was togetherness under very rigid rules. It was a joke."

There was certainly no sympathy among most whites for the notion of freedom rights that drove black struggle. When a black boycott of white businesses began in Port Gibson, Mississippi, a small town where every-body knew everybody, whites were hostile to even such modest black demands as asking that adults be addressed by the courtesy titles of "Mr." and "Mrs." In one telling illustration of this hypocrisy and resistance, a supermarket owner said that she didn't "feel like it was a good idea" to hire a black cashier because blacks could not be trusted—they would lie and steal—but she nevertheless also explained that when she had young chil-dren she was able to work at the store because "you could get [black] help pretty reasonable and they were pretty dependable."

Most white reaction to black political action for change across the South was characterized by hypocrisy and paranoia, frequently taking the form of both a claim and an accusation: "Our niggers" are happy and satisfied with their lives because we whites are good to them, and all this violence and "trouble" is "instigated" by "outside agitators" for their own destructive political, probably communist, purposes. One variation of this claim held that charges of white violence made by civil rights workers and organiza-tions were fabrications designed to embarrass the South as part of the process of destroying "our way of life." Another variation justified arresting nonviolent sit-in students and Freedom Riders for disorderly conduct or breach of the peace instead of members of the violent white mobs swirling angrily around them and sometimes assaulting them. Whites in the South recognized that their way of life was under serious attack and had to be defended—with arms when necessary.

This intransigence could only be challenged effectively by local people. It meant little if McLaurin, McNair, or I said that black people in Ruleville were dissatisfied; we could be ignored or dismissed. But it meant a lot if Mrs. Hamer or Joe McDonald said *they* were dissatisfied, and it forced attention on black life in a white-supremacist culture. Our explanation to Mr. Joe that he had a right to his gun had nothing to do with any interest we might have had in his—or our—self-defense at that moment, and every-thing to do with a basic principle that defined grassroots organizing in Ruleville, Sunflower County, and across the South: if there was going to be meaningful change, ordinary people needed to find their voices and begin speaking for themselves. SNCC and CORE field secretaries took advantage of every opportunity to help people understand that they had rights and to help them see exactly what those rights were. It was an obvious and necessary part of the process of building a local consensus around the idea of challenging a powerful white-supremacist system like that which existed in the state of Mississippi. Telling McDonald that he had a right to his gun was an opportunity to do just that.

Mr. Joe's decision to retrieve his gun, although unexpected and certainly *not* organized by the SNCC workers in Ruleville, was as important an assertion of his rights as going to the county courthouse to try to register to vote. And it is indicative of the budding strength of the Freedom Movement in this hostile territory that Mayor Dorrough returned the gun to Mr. McDonald.

Although black people across the South recognized that without federal protection they would sometimes need to take up arms in defense of their persons and property, they had to be cautious. Black community leaders had long ago concluded that retaliatory violence was off-limits and that, in addition their constituents always needed to weigh their right to self-defense by any means, including the use of guns, against the negative reaction that would result from their use of guns. Armed aggressive assault against state or local government or attacks against police would almost certainly alienate potential allies and might bring an overwhelming armed retaliatory response.

Carrying weapons for self-defense was viewed quite differently. NAACP field secretary Medgar Evers customarily traveled around Mississippi armed, with a rifle in the trunk of his car and a pistol beside him on the front seat. His national headquarters in New York did not challenge him; it was a commonsensical and acceptable approach to increasing his chances of staying alive. But using guns for one's own defense and for punitive retaliation were two different things. In 1959, in Monroe, the county seat of Union County, North Carolina, a white man escaped conviction for assaulting an eight-months-pregnant black woman; Robert Williams, president of the county's NAACP branch, angrily responded, "We must be willing to kill if necessary. We cannot take these people who do us injustice to the court. . . . In the future we are going to have to try and convict these people on the spot." The NAACP removed him from his position. Williams was not the first to speak in this manner, and many in Monroe, the county, and other black communities agreed with his sentiments. The NAACP's national leadership, however, felt he had crossed a line that made the organization vulnerable to political attack from both local and federal governments.

Unlike the NAACP, which was silent on nonviolence in its stated policy, the newer organizations—SNCC, CORE, and SCLC—all had policies of nonviolence. But as their work in rural communities progressed in the 1960s, the necessities of survival blurred the line separating their organizational commitment to nonviolence from armed self-defense. In Mississippi as in Monroe, this blurring of the line—even crossing of the line—did not begin with young political radicals. Rather, it had started well before the 1960s among impatient, determined, and sometimes embittered southern black men of an older generation, who were seeking the traditional rights that were supposedly the birthright of all Americans but that they had long been denied. The surge of white supremacist violence that forced him to leave also reveals its limits.

Theodore Roosevelt Mason "T. R. M." Howard, chief surgeon at the Taborian Hospital of the Knights and Daughters of Tabor in the all-black Mississippi Delta town of Mound Bayou, was one of the most prominent of these older men. His story, in 1950s Mississippi, illustrates the practical use of armed self-defense and demonstrates what would be true in the 1960s as well: that armed self-defense was connected to the broader stream of community organization.

In 1951, the successful and sometimes flamboyant doctor founded the Regional Council of Negro Leadership (RCNL), in some ways a forerunner of the movement that would emerge a decade later as the Council of Federated Organizations (COFO). That organization, founded in 1961, was the umbrella organization under which all civil rights organizations in Mississippi worked. Creation of the RCNL coincided with increased activity by the NAACP in the state, and though the RCNL was sometimes at odds with NAACP leadership in New York, for all practical purposes local NAACP leaders and RCNL leaders were interchangeable.

Although the RCNL had only a small dues-paying membership, it had an outsized influence. Interestingly, most of its leadership came from Mississippi's tiny class of black doctors, entrepreneurs, landowners, and craftsmen. Not only did these men (the RCNL leadership was entirely male) have something to lose, but they had won their property and status against great odds, and they were inclined to protect them. Unlike many laborers, for instance, they had trucks and automobiles, a fact that helped shape their activism: the RCNL mounted a boycott of Delta gas stations that refused to have restrooms for black people, distributing bumper stickers that read "Don't Buy Gas Where You Can't Use the Restroom." The RCNL also persuaded the NAACP to organize a national campaign urging black associations and businesses to deposit money in the black-owned Tri-State bank in Memphis, Tennessee, and to make this money available for loans to black businesses suffering from economic reprisal in Mississippi—not an effort likely to be launched by sharecroppers. This was not a group that placed integration or desegregation high on its agenda; instead, it sought political influence with white power. The RCNL's members saw themselves as leaders of the vast majority of Mississippi's black population, a population that was impoverished and generally had little formal education but that desired an end to white supremacy all the same.

Dr. Howard was a charismatic, affable leader and an eloquent speaker whose pointed wit delighted black audiences. And he had no shortage of audiences; thousands attended the RCNL's annual Freedom Day rallies held in Mound Bayou where they were addressed by prominent black leaders of national stature. Chicago congressman William Dawson spoke at the first of these in 1952; he was the first black congressman to speak in Mississippi since the nineteenth century. Gospel great Mahalia Jackson sang there the same day. Addressing a 1955 Freedom Day rally, Howard joked that the virulently racist Mississippi senator Theodore Bilbo, who had died in 1947, was living in hell and had "recently sent a direct message to the capital at Jackson asking [whites] to stop treating the Negroes so badly in Mississippi and to give them a break, because they have a Negro fireman down there that keeps the fire mighty hot."

Because of his highly visible militancy and his organizing skill, Howard was constantly in danger of being attacked by white-supremacist groups, and so guns were as important to him as his medical instruments. Mississippi law permitted the open display of firearms, and Howard often wore a pistol on his hip; a rifle was also always visible in the back window of his air-conditioned Cadillac. And although a license was required to carry a concealed weapon, reportedly there was also a secret compartment in the Cadillac housing a pistol and a similar compartment in his leather-upholstered Ford Skyliner convertible. The *Pittsburg Courier* reported that Howard would sometimes "take the gun from its secret hiding place and put it in his lap . . . always cocked!" Howard was not unique in this regard; all the RCNL leadership traveled armed, especially after the Supreme Court's *Brown* decision, which triggered a rapid expansion of the Ku Klux Klan in Mississippi and escalating antiblack violence.

The RCNL maintained strict security. Strangers visiting Howard's home were required to pass through a checkpoint, and armed guards were on duty around the clock. Emmett Till's mother, Mamie Elizabeth Till-Mobley, stayed at Howard's home while attending the trial of her son's murderers. A heavily armed RCNL caravan escorted her daily to the Tallahatchie County courthouse thirty-four miles away in the little town of Sumner. *Jet* magazine's Simeon Booker, who stayed in a two-bedroom guest cottage across from what he described as Howard's "mansion," had never been to Mississippi before the Till murder trial. He was a Baltimore native and acknowledged being "scared as hell most of the time; but the object was to get the story." Booker recalled that his photographer, David Jackson, "was even more frightened than I was, and he carried a pistol." At the trial, Tallahatchie County sheriff H. C. Strider wanted to keep Booker—along with the few other black reporters in town to cover the event—out of the courthouse, but he was overruled by the judge. "Demonstrating that he bore no resentment at being overruled by the judge," Booker recalled later, "[Sheriff Strider] greeted us every morning at our press table with a cheery, 'Good morning, niggers.'"

Howard's home was safe haven for the black reporters covering the Till trial. *Ebony* magazine's Cloyte Murdock, having difficulty opening the front door wide enough to bring her luggage inside, found that a stack of weapons was blocking the door. Another visitor saw a magnum pistol and a .45-caliber pistol at the head of Howard's bed; a submachine gun rested at its foot. He also saw "a long gun, a shotgun or a rifle in every corner of every room."

The defensive measures of the RCNL were more informal than those of the well-trained units formed by black military veterans that would later emerge in Monroe, North Carolina; Jonesboro, Louisiana; and Tuscaloosa, Alabama; but the armed RCNL leaders shared with these later groups a sense of political activism. Gun ownership by RCNL members represented a great deal more than simple possession of firearms, long routine in individual black households. The organization could speedily mobilize substantial and deadly firepower. For instance, when a rumor spread that Howard's wife, Helen Nela Boyd, had been assaulted by whites, fifteen carloads of armed men quickly appeared at the Howard home prepared to provide assistance and protection anywhere it was required.

In the early 1960s, robust and organized defensive measures were an absolute necessity for any prominent black civil rights advocate who valued his or her life. These were especially strong men and women. The terror of the preceding decade had selected leaders who were willing to stand up to white terrorism, with force if necessary. A combination of economic pressure, violence, and murder had savaged the ranks of black leadership after the Supreme Court's *Brown* decision. Those leaders who survived and who chose to remain and continue to risk their lives in the pursuit of civil rights tended to be dogged, militant, and willing to engage in armed self-defense.

The decimation of the black leadership in the 1950s had been abetted by new, more sophisticated tactics that emerged from the white-supremacist establishment in Mississippi in response to postwar civil rights activism. Many in Mississippi's white political and business leadership had come to recognize that mob violence undermined the support they sought from the rest of the nation. Similarly, some political and economic leaders considered "Bilboism"—a neologism that referred to the unabashedly racist rhetoric of Mississippi senator Theodore Bilbo—ineffective. So by the 1950s the language of white supremacy was gradually softening in some quarters, becoming less shrill in an attempt to gain respectability for racism. Phrases like "states' rights" and concepts such as the need to protect "constitutional liberties" from communist subversion and federal interference were becoming stand-ins for raw racist rhetoric.

The Citizens' Council—a new tool for white supremacy—was born in

Indianola, Mississippi, on July 11, 1954, called together by former paratrooper and plantation manager Robert "Tut" Patterson just two months after the *Brown* decision. The council began "pursuing the agenda of the Klan with the demeanor of the Rotary," urging "concerned and patriotic citizens to stand together forever firm against communism and mongrelization." The fourteen men who gathered for the first Citizens' Council meeting reflected all the councils that would quickly spread first across the Delta and then across the state and the South. They were middle-class businessmen and managers. By November 1954, Citizens' Councils had been organized in scores of Mississippi towns and cities; by 1956 the council claimed 25,000 dues-paying members in the state. Their agenda was to force anyone, white or black, who dissented from white supremacy and racial segregation back into line or out of the state.

What happened in Yazoo City, Mississippi, following the formation of the Citizens' Council is typical of what began to happen everywhere across the South. Fifty-three people in Yazoo City had signed a petition in favor of school desegregation. The Citizens' Council arranged for the names, addresses, and telephone numbers of all fifty-three to be published in the local newspaper as a full-page advertisement. The last line of the ad read, "Published as a public service by the Citizens' Council of Yazoo City." All the people whose names were listed in the advertisement lost their jobs or had their credit cut off. In Clarksdale, the names of those petitioning for school desegregation in that town were published in the *Clarksdale Press Register* along with the editorial comment, "These people are the agitators and troublemakers."

The Citizens' Council officially eschewed violence but legitimized it with their campaigns on behalf of white supremacy. Reprisals for the Clarksdale petition case "came swiftly," recalled local pharmacist Aaron Henry, who would eventually preside over Mississippi's NAACP. "Whites looked at the petition list and if your name was on it, you just caught hell." In this period, even being accused of civil rights activity could get one killed. Columbus dentist Emmett J. Stringer, who was president of the Mississippi NAACP in 1953 and 1954, dramatically increased the organization's membership during his presidency, but his efforts earned him continual threats against his life. He and his wife began sleeping in the middle bedroom of their home, thinking they might be safe from bombings there. Knowing his life was at risk, Stringer took steps to protect himself as best he could. "I had weapons in my house, and not only in my house, I had weapons on me when I went to my office, because I knew people were out to get me. I would take my revolver with me and put it in the drawer, right where I worked.

All around the state, the pace of deadly violence steadily increased as the councils grew. In Belzoni, the county seat of Humphreys County, Reverend George Lee and Gus Courts, a grocer, organized an NAACP branch in 1954. Its membership grew rapidly. The following year, just a few days before the anniversary of the Supreme Court's *Brown* decision, Lee was driving home from an RCNL meeting. A car pulled up beside him and someone inside shot him to death. Sheriff Ike Shelton suggested that Lee had somehow lost control of his car and that the lead pellets found in what was left of his jaw might be teeth fillings. As the *Jackson Clarion-Ledger,* Mississippi's main daily newspaper, headlined Lee's murder: "Negro Leader Dies in Odd Accident." Six months later, Courts barely escaped death when a car pulled in front of his grocery store and the occupants opened fire. Bullets hit Courts in the left arm and stomach. Shortly thereafter, he left the state for Chicago.

With all the levers of power in white hands, and with stepped-up antiblack terrorism being encouraged by the state governments and largely ignored by the federal government, civil rights advancement had essentially come to a halt in the Deep South. Black voter registration, which had been showing modest increases in the first half of the decade, declined sharply in the second half as white intimidation intensified. In 1955, before Courts was driven out of Belzoni, a Citizens' Council member showed him a list of ninety-five black registered voters and told him that everyone on the list who failed to remove his or her name from the voter lists would be fired. Within a year, the only black registered voter in Belzoni was a T. V. Johnson, an undertaker, wrote Aaron Henry in his autobiography. And Johnson, according to Henry, "was afraid to go to the polls."

Courts was by no means the only black leader to flee Mississippi. Testifying before the Senate Subcommittee on Constitutional Rights on February 16, 1957, Courts pled for help and protection:

My wife and I and thousands of Mississippians have had to run away. . . . We had to flee in the night. We are the American refugees from the terror in the South, all because we want to vote. Not only are they killing colored people who want to vote and be citizens, but they are squeezing them out of business, foreclosing their mortgages, refusing them credit from the banks to operate their farms.

Rumor had it that there was a $1,000 price on T. R. M. Howard's head, so three months after the September 25, 1955, acquittal of the murderers of Emmett Till, and shortly after his wife had had a stroke, he moved to Chicago. "I feel I can do more alive in the battle for Negro rights in the North than dead in a weed-grown grave in Dixie," he was quoted as saying.

Not everyone fled, however. Among those who stayed was Amzie Moore, a leader in the RCNL and the Bolivar County NAACP president. Another who refused to leave the state was Aaron Henry, the Clarksdale pharmacist. Like Moore, he had been active with the RCNL, and he was also a leader of young Turks who in the mid-1950s began challenging Mississippi's older, more cautious and conservative NAACP leadership. Though not recorded, Amzie Moore was almost certainly aligned with Henry. In 1960 Henry became NAACP state president, and two years later he was named president of COFO. Medgar Evers stayed in Mississippi, too. He was regional representative for T. R. M. Howard's Magnolia Insurance Company and had become deeply involved with the RCNL as its program director. Despite mounting antiblack violence, Evers also devoted himself to full-time work for the NAACP.

These men—all three World War II veterans—reflected changing times not only in Mississippi and the United States but also in Africa, Asia, and Latin America, where armed anticolonial resistance and political protest were receiving a great deal of coverage in the postwar black American press. Evers, Henry, and Moore were sharply aware of the changing world around them. Evers, for example, was watching with great interest the Mau Mau insurgency against British colonial rule in Kenya that was also known as the "Land and Freedom Movement." For a time in the early 1950s, the Kenyan leader Jomo Kenyatta, who some thought was covertly leading the insurgency, "dominated" Evers's thinking, says his wife Myrlie. "Kenyatta, Medgar felt instinctively," she recalled, "was a man driven to violence by the brutal oppression of his people." Evers even considered trying something similar in Mississippi. Even if guerrilla activity could not win in Mississippi, he thought, it might attract much-needed attention to the plight of black people in the state. Charles Evers reflected decades later, "Why not really cross the line? We wondered. Why not create a Mau Mau in Mississippi? Each time whites killed a Negro, why not drive to another town, find a bad sheriff or cop, and kill him in a secret hit-and-run raid?"

The Evers brothers did not take the idea of an insurgency—or of retributive violence against whites—any further than speculation. "We bought some bullets [and] made some idle Mau Mau plans," says Charles Evers. "But Medgar never had his heart in it." Myrlie Evers elaborates, "Part of him realized that nothing could be solved by violence but more violence." Evers had been heavily influenced by his mother, Jessie, who was devoutly religious, which partly explains his reluctance to organize and engage in guerrilla warfare. As Medgar Evers himself told *Ebony* magazine interviewer Francis Mitchell, "It didn't take much reading of the bible, though, to convince me that two wrongs would not make the situation any different, and that I couldn't hate the white man and at the same time hope to convert him."

Nonetheless, when Medgar and Myrlie's first son was born in 1953, the couple named him Darrell Kenyatta Evers. The couple was then living in Mound Bayou, and because Kenyatta was their young son's middle name, residents would sometimes ask, "How's the little Mau Mau?" Recalled Myrlie Evers, "They knew the name [from black newspaper reporting] and for them it was a symbol of strength and pride."

Even though the movement struggles of the 1960s have come to be defined in terms of nonviolent tactics and strategies, they can only be fully understood in relation to the deep wells of strength that could be found all across the terrain of black life: the black militias active in self-defense after the Civil War; proud and successful leaders like Theodore Roosevelt Mason Howard, who could have walked away from struggle but chose to stay and fight as long as he could; of men and women like Lou Ella Townsend, Reverend George Lee, Medgar Evers, his father James, and all the "crazy Negroes" who stood their ground time and time again in defense of their families, their property, or themselves. Labels—"nonviolent" or "militant" or "violent"—do not easily describe these men and women. Hartman Turnbow, a black farmer active with the movement in Holmes County, noted as much after driving away night riders by returning their gunfire and, if rumor is true, killing one of them. He explained his action to movement organizers the next morning, declaring, "I wasn't being non-nonviolent; I was just protecting my family."

Significantly, actions such as Turnbow's counterattack did have the effect of reducing violence. But night riders attacked Turnbow's home a second time about a year later. When FBI investigators spoke to Turnbow after that shooting, Turnbow recalled, "They come tellin' me, first words they said to me was, 'Don't kill nobody. Don't kill nobody.'" But Turnbow told the agents that he would not tolerate any more attacks on his home and family and that he wanted the FBI to make sure it was the last time there was one. If not, "it's gonna be some trouble, 'cause I'm gonna git my gun and get busy and see who *I* can shoot." After that, according to Turnbow, violence "cooled off."

———

With one or two exceptions, guns were not much of an issue for the organizers and activists from nonviolent organizations who began working in rural communities. It is the way they accommodated themselves to guns that provides insight into the complexities of the Freedom Movement and, in fact, humanizes it, stripping away the image of noble nonviolent icons prepared for martyrdom to which movement activists have been reduced. Occasionally there was discussion and debate about the possibility of carrying and using weapons, but even that was neither lengthy nor anguished. And in SNCC's somewhat laissez-faire tradition of fieldwork, the question of what to do in regards to guns was pretty much left to those in the field.

No one flashed weapons or carried them openly, but some activists and organizers did possess guns—sometimes they owned them, and sometimes they were given them when people in the communities where they worked thought they needed weapons. When the weapons were accepted—and that was not always the case—a good part of the reason was upbringing. Most movement organizers were not northerners who came "down South" as liberators; rather, they were southerners fighting for change in their own land, and guns—small shotguns, rifles—had been a routine part of their lives, especially if they came from rural communities. "My daddy made sure we knew how to handle a gun," remembers Hollis Watkins. "I could take a .22 rifle and strike a match with it," he boasts. In any case, there was never any discussion of assaulting local bastions of white supremacy with weapons; common sense said that was foolhardy and counterproductive. And although guns did sometimes provide a measure of protection, for the most part it was not organized by movement workers. Many black households already had guns, and they used them when they felt it necessary—a decision SNCC and CORE organizers would not be making and in fact were not qualified to make.

Civil rights workers had virtually no chance of successfully challenging local traditions of keeping guns for protection. Indeed, the issue did not even come up for most organizers, because the work itself—primarily organizing within the black community in rural areas—made the question of nonviolence moot. The ordinary day-to-day interactions of community organizing consisted mainly of attempting to persuade people to try to register to vote, and the question of nonviolence almost never came up. SNCC and CORE organizers were frequently labeled "the nonviolents," but that was because of protests that seemed remote from these rural communities. Occasionally in planning a voter-registration attempt someone might say, "I ain't going down to that courthouse without my pistol." The organizer's response was not a lecture about nonviolence but a conversation about the practicalities of gunplay in that situation. For example, the organizer might ask, Even if you shoot a white man bothering you down there, what's that going to mean for the group? Sometimes guns would then be left behind (Medgar Evers and the group attempting to vote in Decatur in 1946 left their guns in the car), and sometimes a potential registrant would choose not to make the attempt to register.

But such situations were rare. Someone involved enough with "a nonviolent" to seriously consider making a voter-registration attempt was not likely to bring up the subject of guns.

Although organizing for voter registration could put an organizer's life or the lives of others at risk, it usually required no explicit commitment to nonviolence. Sit-ins at lunch counters, Freedom Rides, walking picket lines—these were all direct actions at and inside white-owned facilities, and for tactical and strategic regions, they required an acceptance of nonviolent discipline. Knocking on doors and sitting on porches, attending church, talking over beer at a juke joint, and even walking into cotton fields on white-owned plantations—these all went on entirely within the black community. Movement organizers did not face the necessity of choosing nonviolence because they rarely had direct contact with whites. For the most part, the issue of nonviolence simply did not come up; there was no reason for it to come up. Furthermore, in many ways the young organizers of SNCC and CORE were treated as the community's children, and though for obvious reasons most in the community were not likely to directly challenge white power, movement workers always felt relatively protected in and by the black community. In the final analysis, organizers fit into the patterns of the communities they worked in, and the fact that guns were part of that life simply was not of great concern.

There were times, however, when organizers were faced with choosing whether or not to use a gun. The issue could almost be described as a question of responsibility, or at least of good manners. After all, they had an obligation to the local people who, at great risk, supported the movement. Occasionally a sense of indebtedness led an organizer to participate in armed self-defense in ways that he or she might not normally have done. While working in Holmes County, recalled Hollis Watkins,

> I was living with Dave Howard and his wife. They farmed. I realized after a few days that they had a shift set up to protect me and the house; his wife took a shift and he took a shift. One shift was from dark until midnight; the other from midnight to daybreak. Now here I was living in their house, eating their food and I'm sleeping all night and this man and his wife, *farmers,* are up all night protecting me. At daybreak he's in the field all day until it starts getting dark. When I realized that, I told him I would take a shift. He asked me if I knew how to use a gun. I said, Yes sir, I

do. We don't use them in the movement but I know how. But *will* you use guns? he asked. I said, If necessary I'll use 'em. So he says, Take a look at these and see which one you like the best. I think he was testing me. He shows me a shotgun, a .30-06, and a .30-30 Winchester rifle. As I was checking them out he said I could have them all. Later I told Jim Forman [SNCC's executive director] about this and he said, You can't do that. I said, I'm already doing it.

Although impossible to quantify because such accommodations were not written about in field reports or even much discussed, other organizers had similar encounters with guns—if not picking them up and using them, then at least encouraging their hosts of the need to defend their rights and do so themselves, as in the case of Joe McDonald and his shotgun.

Whether or not they owned guns or had access to guns, activists and organizers knew that nonviolence was generally a much more common-sensical and sustainable tactic—one more likely to succeed—than offensive armed action. But armed self-defense was one thing; armed offense quite another. Recalled Bob Moses:

Black people had organized enclaves which they were prepared to defend. Their self-defense was pretty much around a house or church, a meeting place. "Self-defense" in the white community is surrounding the courthouse. They were going to defend the courthouse in different ways. I think of us going to the courthouse [with potential registrants] as a nonviolent offensive maneuver. It allowed us to take the offensive and actually attack. You couldn't go to the courthouse with guns and attack.

There were tense encounters with the white community of course—bringing people to county courthouses to attempt voter registration is plainly one example—but in the South of those days most of the danger came suddenly (as with Mayor Dorrough's roadside confrontation with myself, Landy, and McLaurin in Ruleville) or from ambush or from being overwhelmed by mob violence—situations in which being armed was often

of little use. CORE's James Chaney, Michael Schwerner, and Andrew Goodman were killed in 1964 after Neshoba County, Mississippi, deputy sheriff
Cecil Price handed them over to a Ku Klux Klan mob. Price had stopped
Chaney, who was black, and arrested him for allegedly driving over the
speed limit. Schwerner and Goodman, both of them white, were with
Chaney in the car, and Price held them in jail along with Chaney "for investigation." Medgar Evers was ambushed and killed in his driveway by a gun-
man hiding behind bushes across the street; he had no chance of reaching
the weapons he always kept in his car and in his house.

And when it came to terrorist attacks on private residences, the decision
of whether or not to respond with defensive gunfire—a decision that had
to be made quickly—was not in the hands of SNCC or CORE organizers.
Men like Hartman Turnbow did not ask movement workers if it was okay
to shoot back. Robert Cooper, another movement supporter and one of
Hartman Turnbow's neighbors, shot it out with Klansmen when they
attacked his home in 1965, and he summed up his and Turnbow's thinking
with absolute clarity: "I felt that you're in your house, ain't botherin'
nobody; the only thang you hunting is equal justice. An' they gonna sneak
by at night, burn your house, or shoot in there. An' you gonna sit there and
take all of it? You got to be a very li'l man with no guts at all."

To be sure, communities reacted differently to the efforts of civil rights
workers. One factor influencing how a community reacted was whether it
was rural or urban. In the city of Greenwood, Mississippi, not too far from
Holmes County, the kind of cooperation between organizers and locals
that occurred in Holmes County never really developed, even at the peak
of movement activity. During a boycott of the downtown area, for example,
a boycott leader noted that participation from city dwellers was spotty,
whereas there was almost 100 percent cooperation from people "out in the
rural," as they say in the South.

And out in the rural, when Mrs. Laura McGhee—who if she thought it
necessary, sat on the porch with her Winchester rifle—permitted movement workers to use her farm outside Greenwood for a rally, the sheriff
came to warn her against holding it. She told him that *he* was on *her* property, that *he* was trespassing and hadn't ever offered her any protection
from the terrorists who kept threatening to shoot up her farm, and that he

therefore had nothing to offer her now and had better leave, get off her land. And the sheriff left.

Yet where individuals or communities fell on a rural–urban scale did not always predict how they would respond to terrorist attack. McComb, Mississippi, for instance, is a small city that had just 12,000 residents in 1961, about a third of them black, yet its dynamic was somewhat different from Greenwood's. This was surely due, at least in part, to the fact that McComb was not part of the plantation tradition. Established as a hub and repair center for the Illinois Central Railroad, McComb had a gritty, rough-and-tumble culture that helped foster Klan recruitment and terrorism but also generated a tough, we-won't-take-it-forever attitude in the black community, even if that attitude was rarely expressed openly. A branch of the NAACP had been established in McComb in 1946, which was relatively early for this part of the South, and some of the city's black workers were unionized, although the unions were racially segregated.

During the summer of 1964, more than a dozen bombings occurred in McComb, earning the city the nickname "bombing capital of the world." In late August, nine unexploded sticks of dynamite wrapped in red tape were found near the front door of Willie and Matti Dillon. Mrs. Dillon was one of the local leaders of the Mississippi Freedom Democratic Party (MFDP), and she had registered to vote. A few seconds earlier, an explosion from another dynamite package had rocked their home. Dillon and his wife were uninjured in the attack, but local white authorities found other ways to punish them. The police chief, the sheriff, *and* the head of the FBI task force in McComb conspired to jail Dillon on charges of operating a garage without a license even though the garage where he occasionally fixed cars was not his. He was finally jailed for stealing electricity. He had attached a wire not registered by the meter to install a floodlight, which he felt he needed to protect his home from sudden attacks by night riders. Dillon was held incommunicado, tried, and convicted without a lawyer.

The Dillons were not the only members of McComb's black community who were targeted by white terrorists. In April 1964, night riders threw dynamite at the home of NAACP president Curtis Conway "C. C." Bryant, the man who had gotten Amzie Moore to send Bob Moses to McComb in 1961. Fortunately, the dynamite fell short. Quickly recovering from the explosion, Bryant grabbed his rifle and fired at the attackers. They fled. In July, Bryant's brother Charlie and his wife, Ora, were awakened by the sound of a car pulling into their driveway. Ora grabbed her shotgun and fired at the attackers just as they tossed sticks of dynamite toward the house. Again the explosives fell short, and again the night riders did not stick around to throw any more dynamite, for C. C. Bryant—who lived across the street—had taken up his rifle and joined his sister-in-law in shooting at the attackers. Others in the neighborhood joined in as well.

By September 1964, McComb's black community had begun to take on some of the characteristics of a military camp, with armed patrols protecting homes, businesses, and churches—although even these patrols could not always stop the violence. The home of Alyene Quin, proprietor of a small café that fed movement workers, was bombed on September 20. Although she and her children survived, the pent-up anger and frustration of McComb's black community erupted in the kind of violence that is born of rage rather than self-defense. In scenes that mirrored the rioting that had occurred in Harlem and Philadelphia that summer, blacks poured into the streets of McComb, some armed with rifles, others with bottles and gasoline—the makings of Molotov cocktails. Teenagers picked up bricks and threw them at police, backing them down and forcing the town to call in state troopers. And C. C. Bryant soon replaced his .22-caliber rifle with a new, high-powered model.

––––––––

This intense period in Mississippi in the summer of 1964 proves a point that was true elsewhere in the South, as well: a clear, sharp line cannot be meaningfully drawn between nonviolence and armed self-defense. Within the framework of black community life and civil rights effort in the South, and in the minds of most who joined the Freedom Movement, the pistol, the rifle, and the shotgun were integrated with the spirit of struggle that has always been a basic feature of black life in America and a critical component of the black experience and of black memory. Nonviolence was an important part of this struggle, too, but it was not the entirety of it; nor was the use of guns the be-all and end-all of black struggle.

"If there is no struggle, there is no progress." These words spoken by Frederick Douglass more than 150 years ago aptly summarized the relationship of black people in America to the largely white nation that surrounded them. "Power concedes nothing without a demand. It never did and it never will. Find out just what a people will submit to, and you have found out the exact amount of injustice and wrong which will be imposed upon them; and these will continue until they are resisted with either words or blows, or both."

Douglass's words describe the basic choice that confronted black people in the 1960s, just as meaningfully as they do the choice that confronted black people in 1857 when he made that speech—or, for that matter, the choice that confronts black people today. Black life in America has always meant struggle to protect and secure black life in America. That struggle has never centered on the question of nonviolence versus violence. Rather, there has always been one fundamental question, a question posed by the civil rights worker to him- or herself in the 1960s, by the rebellious enslaved black person in colonial or antebellum America, by the freedman and freedwoman after the Civil War, and generally by the black community to itself across time: What are you going to do?

The real lesson that emerges from the Mississippi experience, and every Freedom Movement experience across the South, centers on that question. It is what blurs the distinction between nonviolence and armed self-defense. When the night riders attacked his home, Hartman Turnbow had to decide what he was going to do. When Hollis Watkins saw his farmer hosts exhausting themselves staying up all night to protect him and their farm, he felt he had some responsibility for their new burden, and he had to decide how he was going to meet that responsibility. What was he going to do?

Whether the question was one of picking up a gun in response to attack by night riders, or of curling one's body tightly and protectively while being assaulted by a mob during a lunch-counter sit-in, or of shielding an elderly person under attack for trying to register to vote, the decision of what to do centered not on the choice between nonviolence and violence but on the question of what response was best in each situation. Most often, moreover, there was very little time to decide. Sometimes heads of households chose to defend home and family with guns; sometimes it was best to step on the accelerator and speed away or flee on foot. Sometimes ambush eliminated any possibility of choice. What was always at play was the common sense of survival. And flight when necessary was not cowardice, just as shooting it out hopelessly in the name of "manhood" was not always courage.

Black southerners frequently had to make split-second decisions about how best to protect themselves from attack—whether to stand their ground or seek shelter. Although they had a shotgun in their home, Joe and Rebecca McDonald jumped into their iron bathtub when gunfire suddenly struck their home. In Greenwood, Mississippi, when a white mob with guns and chains broke down the door and headed for their upstairs office, SNCC workers Sam Block, Lawrence Guyot, and Luvaugn Brown climbed out the back window, scrambled across the roof of the building next door, slid down a television antenna, and ran into a warren of houses across the street, vanishing into the larger black community. On the other hand, Laura McGhee stayed put and sent the sheriff away.

These choices do not negate each other or diminish each other's value. The decision made by the SNCC workers in their Greenwood office does not conflict with Mrs. McGhee's judgment about how best to deal with the terrorism confronting her and her community. Understanding what shaped Mrs. McGhee's decision, and all decisions about whether or not to respond to attack with gunfire or the threat of gunfire, is only possible by comprehending the complexities of choice, the decision making of life and death. It is not something to be taken lightly, and it is never abstract. Medgar Evers's reasoning and decision not to organize Mau Mau–like retaliation does not define him as nonviolent. The shotguns in Fannie Lou Hamer's bedroom do not make her an armed black militant.

Nor is the sudden expression of anger—a normal human reaction in many instances—an articulation of policy. In 1961, for example, Brenda Travis, a sixteen-year-old McComb high school student, was arrested after leading a protest and sent seventy miles away from home to Oakley reform school in Raymond, Mississippi. One evening, while looking out a window in her room, Travis saw police turn back a bus. It was filled with family and schoolmates who had come to visit her, but she did not know that at the time. She asked the matron about the bus, and soon the reform school superintendent had her brought to his house. He told her whom the bus had been carrying and explained that, because the group had not asked permission to visit her, it had been turned away.

At this point Brenda had been imprisoned for weeks. She had had no trial, had seen no judge. Even more than fifty years later, she almost teared up remembering how angry she had become at hearing that she would not be seeing her friends and family. "I ripped into him," she recalled. "I don't know what all I didn't say to him. He said if I didn't stop talking to him like that he was going to slap my face. I told him that if he did, there was going to be a *war* right then and there. Forget about nonviolence! I didn't care if I lived or died that night."

More famously, in 1965 fifty-four-year-old Annie Cooper slugged a sheriff. She had been standing in line for hours outside the Dallas County courthouse in Selma, Alabama, waiting to register to vote. When Sherriff Jim Clark—Selma's notoriously abusive and bigoted lawman—ordered her to go home, giving her a hard poke in the back of the neck with either a billy club or a cattle prod, Cooper spun around angrily and delivered a right hook to the sheriff's jaw, knocking him to the ground. That night at a mass meeting at Brown's Chapel in Selma, Martin Luther King explained,

> Mrs. Cooper wouldn't have turned around and hit Sheriff Clark just to be hitting. And of course, as you know, we teach a philosophy of not retaliating and not hitting back, but the truth of the situation is that Mrs. Cooper, if she did anything, was provoked by Sheriff Clark. At that moment he was engaging in some very ugly business-as-usual action. This is what brought about that scene there.

Cooper's decision to slug the sheriff and Travis's anger toward her reform school superintendent were emotional reactions lodged in the real-world experiences of ordinary people. Any theoretical or philosophical arguments about their value—at least, any arguments made by people in pulpits and classrooms who do not have to face the human consequences of their thoughts or of the actions they propose—is in the end an intellectual tea party, perhaps momentarily refreshing but only occasionally nourishing.

It may be that "nonviolent" is simply the wrong word for many of the people who participated in the freedom struggle and who were comfortable with both nonviolence and self-defense, assessing what to do primarily on the basis of which seemed the most practical at any given moment. SNCC field secretary Worth Long preferred the term "unviolent." In the thinking of this Durham, North Carolina, native, the notion of "unviolence" offers a way to transcend the fundamentally false distinction between violence and nonviolence that some have tried to impose in their analysis of Freedom Movement work and decision making. "Most people do not see themselves as being 'nonviolent' . . . and most people would not consider themselves 'violent,'" Long noted. "What's the path for those who would participate in the movement and not be nonviolent? I'm not talking about labeling; I'm talking about their actions." Such people would never call themselves "violent" or "nonviolent"; they would treat both choices as potentially viable, and at any given time, which they would choose would depend on what they had concluded about their immediate circumstances.

Whatever one's personal beliefs, grassroots work like organizing for voter registration, mounting a boycott, participating in a cooperative, or building a political party often did not involve any discussion of nonviolence as tactic, strategy, or philosophy. Rather, the day-to-day realities of these organizing efforts always kept discussion centered on a much more basic question: What was best to do?

BLOW FOR BLOW.

A Civil War–era card depicting a rebelling slave. Open resistance to slavery was rarely, if ever, nonviolent. (Library of Congress)

African American troops fighting for the Union in Dutch Gap, Virginia, during the Civil War. The U.S. Army reluctantly organized the U.S. Colored Troops (USCT) in 1863. Its members saw action in every major theater of the war; twenty-five were awarded a Medal of Honor. (Library of Congress)

THE GALLANT CHARGE OF THE FIFTY FOURTH MASSACHUSETTS (COLORED) REGIMENT.
On the Rebel works at Fort Wagner, Morris Island, near Charleston, July 18, 1863, and death of Colonel Robt. G. Shaw.

(top) An illustration of the Fifty-Fourth Massachusetts, an all-black regiment, charging Confederate fortifications near Charleston, South Carolina, on July 18, 1863. Memorialized in the film *Glory,* this and other acts of valor demonstrated to a skeptical nation that blacks were fully capable of effective, organized armed struggle. (Library of Congress)

(bottom) An illustration from an issue of *Harper's Weekly* published shortly after the Civil War showing a man representing the Freedmen's Bureau standing between armed groups of white and black Americans. Reconstruction saw confrontation between budding black power and white power that sought to remain entrenched. At issue: What kind of South would replace the one destroyed by the Civil War? (Library of Congress)

(top) An African American unit of U.S. Army Infantry troops marching north-west of Verdun, France, in World War I. Military service provided a new generation of Afro-Americans with training and self-confidence that would irrevocably change their attitudes—and responses—to white-supremacist power back in the United States. (Library of Congress)

(bottom) Members of an all-black artillery unit during World War II. Their experience fighting fascism abroad would lead men like these to take an active stand against white supremacy at home in the years following the war, thereby laying the foundation for the freedom struggle of the 1960s. (Library of Congress)

(top) A heavily armed white trooper menacing a protest march through Bogalusa, Louisiana, in 1965. Faced with the prospect of overwhelming violence from state and federal authorities, Afro-Americans had to carefully weigh the prerogative of armed self-defense against the brutality that their resistance might elicit. (© 2014 Matt Herron)

(bottom) Guards in front of Birmingham, Alabama's Gaston Motel, which served as the headquarters for Martin Luther King Jr. during his spring 1963 campaign in the city. Confronted with the perennial threat of white-supremacist terrorism, blacks organized self-defense in a variety of ways. (© 2014 Matt Herron)

An elderly resident of Lowndes County, Alabama, with a shotgun. Such weapons were typical of those found in black households of the rural South and were used by both men and women for self-defense. (© 1973, Douglas R. Gilbert, for *LOOK* magazine)

(top) A young man guarding a Black Panther billboard in Lowndes County, Alabama, during the 1966 election for county offices. The year before, only one black person was registered to vote in this majority-black county. Now black registered voters outnumbered white registered voters and had formed the Lowndes County Freedom Organization, a political party whose symbol was a black panther. Both the panther and the young man guarding this sign reflect blacks' willingness to protect both their right to vote and their right to campaign for office. (SNCC Photo: Doug Harris)

(bottom) Charles Sims, president of Bogalusa's Deacons for Defense and Justice, holding Ku Klux Klan clothing at a demonstration. (Corbis)

Two unidentified men keeping a "fire-bomb watch" at a Freedom School's community library in Holmes County, Mississippi, during the 1964 Freedom Summer. (© 2014 Matt Herron)

5

Which Cheek You Gonna Turn?

These are young people armed with a dream.
      —Reverend Kelly Miller Smith, Nashville, Tennessee, 1960

*Wal, in this county, if you turn the other cheek . . . these here peck-
erwoods'll hand you back half of what you sitting on.*
                  —R. L. Strickland to Stokely Carmichael,
                              Lowndes County, Alabama, 1965

After World War II, as black veterans in Monroe and elsewhere began
asserting themselves politically, a relatively new idea began to reshape
southern civil rights struggle: nonviolence. Although the philosophy of
nonviolence was far less familiar than the idea of armed self-defense, it was
not a completely unfamiliar method of political struggle. And as the Freedom Movement evolved and the practice of nonviolent activism began
playing an increasingly important role, it turned out that these two
approaches—so dissimilar on the surface—were in fact quite compatible.
Understanding the southern civil rights movement of the 1960s requires
understanding this counterintuitive but vital compatibility.

Even before the war, Mohandas Gandhi's nonviolent resistance to British
colonialism in India had been attracting attention in black America. Especially important to nonviolent activism's spread into the U.S. civil rights
struggle was theologian Howard Thurman, who in 1936 went on a "Pilgrimage of Friendship" to India with his wife, Sue Baily Thurman, Methodist

minister Edward Carroll, and his wife Phenola Valentine Carroll. At the end of Thurman's visit, Gandhi told him, "It may be through Negroes that the unadulterated message of nonviolence will be delivered to the world." In 1953 Thurman became dean of Boston University's Marsh Chapel (making him the first tenured black dean at any predominately white university), holding the position until 1965. When Thurman became dean, Martin Luther King Jr. was in the last year of his residence at the university for the doctorate he was awarded June 5, 1955, and Thurman was an important influence on him, although the two men seem not to have been very close personally. Thurman had also been a classmate of King's father at Morehouse College in Atlanta and was a family friend. From 1931 to 1944 Thurman had been dean of Howard University's Rankin Chapel. James Farmer, the founder of CORE, had been one of his students there, and it was Thurman who introduced Farmer to the Fellowship of Reconciliation (FOR), an international, inter-faith, interracial organization dedicated since World War I to working for peace and to training activists for nonviolent struggle. FOR would have a formative influence on some of the important figures in the generation of nonviolent activist leaders who preceded the civil rights movement of the 1960s—figures such as Bayard Rustin, organizer of the 1963 March on Washington; Reverend James Lawson, who mentored the Nashville student movement; and Farmer, who found in FOR "a cadre of black and white pacifists primed to act on the race question and examining with close interest the progress of nonviolent direct action in India."

From time to time well before the Montgomery bus boycott and the sit-ins of the 1960s, acts of nonviolent protest had taken place in the United States, often initiated by prominent or rising black intellectuals. In 1935, Charles Hamilton Houston, then dean of Howard University's law school, took a ferry from Norfolk, Virginia, to Washington, D.C. He refused to eat supper behind a screen in the ferry's dining room, so he ordered food to be brought to his cabin. Then he refused to pay the additional service charge that almost doubled what the same meal would have cost him in the dining room. In the same year, Howard University student Kenneth Clark—a budding psychologist and editor of the school newspaper, who years later would convince the Supreme Court of the damaging psychological effects of school segregation on black children—was arrested for picketing the U.S. Capitol to protest the segregation of its restaurants. In 1940, Pauli Murray, an FOR member who would become the first African American woman to earn a doctorate from Yale Law School and the first black woman ordained as an Episcopal priest, was arrested with a friend for violating Virginia's segregation laws by sitting in the whites-only section of a bus. In 1943, Murray, then a law student at Howard University, led female students in a sit-in at a nearby cafeteria that refused to serve blacks.

CORE, founded in March 1942 by James Farmer, was the first organization specifically concerned with the application of nonviolent resistance in the civil rights movement. Its members conducted a few sit-ins in Chicago and St. Louis. In 1947 CORE's "Journey of Reconciliation" through part of the upper South, testing compliance with Supreme Court–ordered desegregation of interstate travel, inspired the Freedom Rides of 1961. Although CORE remained a tiny, mostly northern, and mostly white group until the sit-ins and Freedom Rides of the 1960s, its members actively protested the considerable racial discrimination above the Mason–Dixon Line. When, for example, CORE established a chapter in Columbus, Ohio, its membership was drawn from the 1,500-member interracial and nonviolent Vanguard League, which for several years had been protesting job discrimination.

These examples notwithstanding, for the most part black veterans and other leaders of the black community hardly thought about nonviolence. The 1950s did begin, however, with a widely shared hopeful sense that change was coming. *Things are going to open up for you* was a refrain many young black people heard from their elders, and a spirit of resistance infused these years with purpose on a deeper level as well. Postwar allegiance to ideals of freedom and an accompanying commitment to struggle against white supremacy were the tissue connecting men and women who—apart from their shared Afro-American identity—were very different from one another; people like Robert Williams, the advocate of self-defense, and Martin Luther King Jr., who championed nonviolence. This shared sense that a time for change was at hand explains why the gentle Rosa Parks admired Robert Williams and could give the eulogy at his 1996 funeral, praising "his courage and his commitment to freedom."

Resistance is the touchstone for understanding what drove nonviolent and non-nonviolent or unviolent approaches to the expanding civil rights movement. In Monroe, North Carolina, for example, black citizens first made the decision to resist the Ku Klux Klan's attempt to seize Bennie Montgomery's body; weapons were simply the means of implementing that decision. A similar decision to resist terrorism a decade later resulted in the use of guns to protect Dr. Albert Perry's home from Klan attack. Likewise, what was fundamental to the nonviolent character of the 1955–1956 Montgomery bus boycott had nothing to do with an embrace of nonviolence as either tactic or philosophy; rather, it reflected a decision, indeed, a determination, to fight city bus segregation—that is, to resist.

From the beginning, the line between armed self-defense and the nonviolent assertion of civil rights was blurred. The idea of nonviolence as a way of life in the black freedom struggle only became prominent in the early 1960s, and even then it was embraced mostly by the small group of ministers surrounding Reverend King within SCLC—and, significantly, not even by all of them. Moreover, those who did not subscribe to nonviolence philosophically, along the lines formulated by King, cannot be described as advocates of violence.

To be sure, some of the men and women who did not consider themselves nonviolent sometimes espoused retaliatory violence, as Williams did in that particularly angry moment after the 1959 acquittal of the white man accused of assaulting a pregnant black woman:

> We cannot rely on the law. We can get no justice under the present system. If we feel that injustice is done, we must then and there on the spot be prepared to inflict punishment on these people. Since the federal government will not bring a halt to lynching and since the so-called courts lynch our people legally, if it's necessary to stop lynching with lynching, then we must be willing to resort to that method. We must meet violence with violence.

Although Williams's outrage was understandable, after his outburst any suggestion that the freedom struggle might devolve into acts of retaliatory violence was quickly and forcefully rejected by the civil rights establishment.

Following Williams's statement, a fierce telephone argument between

NAACP executive secretary Roy Wilkins and the Monroe leader brought to a head the long-simmering antagonism between the two men. Differences of class and personality as well as organizational priorities framed much of what kept the two men apart. Williams's local NAACP branch and the NAACP's national office had long clashed over the North Carolina unit's confrontational tactics and rhetoric; this was the last straw. Wilkins was alarmed by the media attention that Williams's outburst had attracted. "N.A.A.C.P. Leader Urges Violence" blared a May 7, 1959, headline in the *New York Times*. Wilkins phoned Williams asking that he not talk to the press.

Williams stood by his statement and told Wilkins that he would continue delivering the same message to television, radio, and newspapers. Wilkins asked Williams to consider the larger goals and needs of the NAACP. In response Williams told him, "That's what I said and that's what I am going to tell them. . . . I am just about sick of this racial injustice down here." Wilkins reiterated that "meeting lynching with lynching" was not NAACP policy—a distinction that, he noted, the news media seemed unable or unwilling to make. But Williams was having none of it. He accused Wilkins of not being interested in ordinary people, of caring for only "a few Negroes, not the masses of Negroes." He added, perhaps in a last-minute effort to mitigate Wilkins's obvious anger and concerns, that he knew his remarks to the media did not represent the views of the NAACP and were his own opinions, and he assured Wilkins that he would try to make that distinction clear in the future. The exchange ended there. Before the day was over, Williams was suspended from the organization.

Williams's anger was certainly legitimate; even Wilkins, who agreed with the right of self-defense, understood that. The regular abuse of black women by white men had been stoking anger in black communities for centuries and was an important part of what fueled Williams's rage. Still, Williams never expressed any belief that his call for retaliatory violence— or, for that matter, for urban rebellion and guerrilla warfare against white supremacists, both of which he would later promote from exile—implied hostility to nonviolent activism. In fact, before his exile, he had sent young Monroe activists to workshops on nonviolence, although he tellingly noted that such workshops only seemed to be for black people: "Nonviolent workshops are springing up throughout black communities. Not a single one has been established in racist white communities to curb the violence of the Ku Klux Klan."

His frequently angry and strident rhetoric notwithstanding, Williams stopped short of calling for an armed insurrection aimed at overthrowing either local or national government. And when he finally returned to the United States in 1969, so-called black militants were extremely disappointed by his lack of interest in leading any revolution. Rather than being labeled "violent," men like Williams and the veterans in his NAACP branch are better described by Hartman Turnbow's term, "non-nonviolent," or Worth Long's word, "unviolent." Violence was always an option for these men, and they sometimes used it, although it was never their first choice.

———

Even though the traditions of armed self-defense and nonviolence coexisted, the southern civil rights movement has come to be defined as a nonviolent movement. This is due in large part to the student sit-ins and protests that were launched from the campuses of historically black colleges and universities—events that captured the imagination of the nation, and young people especially, as soon as they began in 1960. Even large demonstrations such as those in Birmingham and Selma in Alabama and St. Augustine in Florida—protests often identified with Reverend Martin Luther King Jr. and such adult associates as Reverend Fred Shuttlesworth, Reverend Andrew Young, or Reverend Ralph Abernathy—were driven by student energy. But "nonviolent" incompletely describes these student activists. Indeed, because of their evolution from sit-in protesters to community organizers, armed self-defense and nonviolent activism came to be intertwined in unprecedented ways during the 1960s.

The sit-in movement began quietly and unexpectedly. On February 1, 1960, four students from historically black North Carolina Agricultural and Technical College (A&T) walked into the F. W. Woolworth department store in downtown Greensboro, bought a few school supplies, and then walked over to the store's lunch counter. They sat down and tried to order something to eat. They were refused service but remained seated until the store closed. The next day, twenty-seven students—twenty-three from

A&T and four from Bennett College, the historically black women's college just a few blocks away from A&T—went back to the department store and sat in until it closed. And on the next day, sixty-three students returned and sat in, occupying every seat at the lunch counter. On February 6, a date now known as Black Saturday, hundreds of students, including the entire A&T football team, sat in or protested. Crowds of young whites, some waving Confederate flags, heckled the protesters and threatened them with violence. A&T's football team formed a flying wedge, however, aiming to protect protesters and to enter the department store; they charged through the white mob. "Who do you think you are?" one of the whites yelled angrily. "We the Union Army!" a footballer shouted back.

By the end of March, sit-ins had spread from Greensboro to scores of southern cities. Only the 1961 Freedom Rides and the Montgomery bus boycott that thrust Martin Luther King into national prominence in the mid-1950s are as strongly identified with nonviolence as these protests. But nonviolence is of limited use for understanding these student actions. At the time, the protests were less about that new philosophy of action than about addressing a question that had long animated black challenges to white supremacy in America: What is the best way to resist it?

When the four Greensboro students decided to sit in, they were not consciously launching a nonviolent protest; they were simply resisting segregation. One of the four, Ezell Blair (who in 1968 converted to Islam and took the name Jibreel Khazan), recalled that his roommate Joseph McNeil, who also participated in the February 1 sit-in, had been denied service at a Greyhound bus station on his way back to school after Christmas break. Because of this experience, McNeil had proposed the sit-in during a dorm-room conversation about Greensboro segregation. "McNeil said, 'Well, we ought to have something like a boycott,'" Khazan recalled. "And I said a boycott? And he said, 'Yes, we should go in and sit down at the lunch counter,' and he named Woolworth. 'And if they refuse us, then we continue to sit there, and if we're thrown in jail, we go to jail. And then, we ask the people not to buy in the place.'"

The original four protestors did not have to decide how to respond to violence, because neither they nor the students who joined them were met with violence. That was not true in every city. In Jacksonville, Florida, during a

Saturday sit-in, high school students were assaulted by a mob, some of whom were wielding ax handles that had been handed to them by men in a downtown park wearing Confederate Army uniforms. The police were nowhere to be seen and protection was nonexistent, but as word of the assaults spread, a group of young black people known as "the Boomerangs" poured into the street from the nearby Joseph Blodgett public housing project. They began beating back the mob with their fists, and some even snatched ax handles from members of the mob to use as weapons themselves. At that point, recalls Rodney Hurst, who was president of the NAACP youth council and a protest leader, "police came from everywhere, blocking off downtown and making arrests."

The mob's attack on the sit-in led to one of the first instances of angry black retaliation anywhere in the South. The same day, now remembered as "ax-handle Saturday," whites—milkmen, postmen, and others—doing business in the black community were threatened and sometimes attacked. Cars driven by whites using the entrance to the expressway in the black community were stoned. Later that night a rumor spread that the Ku Klux Klan was planning to bomb St. Paul's AME Church—a movement center of planning and support. Armed men guarded the church and shot at the one truck of Klansmen that dared appear on the scene, driving them away.

Events were very different in Nashville, Tennessee. The protesting students had been well trained in nonviolence by Reverend James M. Lawson, who had been imprisoned for fourteen months as a conscientious objector to the Korean War and had studied nonviolence in India as a Methodist missionary. The Nashville protesters were heckled and assaulted, and the home of their attorney was bombed. The students refused to respond with violence, however, and the tactic appeared to work; on April 19, 1960, Nashville mayor Benjamin West agreed that the city's downtown should be desegregated.

The widely televised success in Nashville helped give the sit-in movement an indelible identity as nonviolent, and so did other highly visible student protests in Atlanta, Georgia; Charlotte, North Carolina; and Orangeburg, South Carolina. The quiet dignity of well-dressed students who sat in or picketed, not retaliating even while being attacked, won sympathy for the civil rights movement and inspired other student activists to follow their lead. Thus, the founding document of SNCC—a direct outgrowth of the 1960 sit-in movement—opens with affirmation of "the philo-sophical or religious ideal of nonviolence as the foundation of our purpose, the presupposition of our belief, and the manner of our action."

Very few delegates attending SNCC's 1960 founding conference, which was held on Easter weekend at Shaw College (now University) in Raleigh, North Carolina, actually believed this first sentence. Despite deliberately des-ignating itself a nonviolent organization, SNCC would eventually find itself at the nexus of its nonviolent idealism and armed self-defense, and indeed many in the group were skeptical of nonviolence from the very beginning. All the conference's attendees were engaged in nonviolent direct action, and most greatly admired the Nashville students, who were the largest delegation at the conference. It was also the only delegation philosophically committed to nonviolence. They stood out because of their tangible inner strength, camaraderie, and trust in one another. They carried themselves with unusual confidence, which seemed to forecast how they had achieved a victory in Nashville so quickly, just after the Shaw conference ended.

The students wanted to do more than assemble at one conference or meet occasionally for discussions. They shared a commitment to sit-ins and other forms of nonviolent direct action—even if not to the core philosophy under-lying them—but their main goal in the conference was to build connections with other students and coordinate campus activism going forward. "We knew we wanted to be students and we knew we wanted to be coordinating," recalled Lonnie C. King, who at the time of the Raleigh conference was chair-man of Atlanta's student movement, the Committee on Appeal for Human Rights (COAHR).

According to Charles "Chuck" McDew, another of the conference's atten-dees and a future chairman of SNCC, throughout the conference, the ques-tion of nonviolence had hovered over formal and informal conversations, but "there really wasn't that much debate about it." The name initially selected in Raleigh for what became SNCC was Student Coordinating Com-mittee, he says. "We said we should be able to continue with the movement without having to accept nonviolence as a way of life." The students had already proven themselves pragmatic in their use of nonviolence; they had immediately recognized it as an effective tool for challenging segregation and were of one mind about continuing to use it. As COAHR's Lonnie King explained years later, "In Atlanta we accepted [nonviolence] as a tactic and were using it that way. . . . I didn't believe we could have won with violent confrontation; you would have civil war all over the South."

A key moment in this discussion—and in the birth of SNCC more generally—came when Martin Luther King, who had given the conference's opening keynote address, asked to speak to the attendees a second time. He told the group that he would like them to become a student arm of his organization, SCLC. However, he went on, they would have to commit to nonviolence as a way of life. This all-or-nothing approach held little appeal for the students, who turned down the proposal. "Acceptance of nonviolence as a way of life was not something we could commit to, and I think Dr. King made a mistake asking us to do it," says Chuck McDew. "We probably would have joined SCLC if not for that." However, emphasizes McDew, the students' rejection of King's offer "wasn't an aggressive or belligerent rejection of nonviolence. Speaking against [nonviolence] is like speaking against your mother; it's God and apple pie. How could you disagree with the ideal? But if some redneck cracker tries to shoot me I'm justified trying to defend myself if I can. I'm not going to let him kill me."

Most of the students gathered in Raleigh were unfamiliar with guns; lethal weapons were virtually nonexistent on their college campuses. Lonnie King was chairman of the student movement in Atlanta, a city that boasted it was "too busy to hate." But even so, he and other activists knew that as their activism increased, and with it their visibility, the potential for racist attack was present anywhere and at any time. "When they arrested us they published our addresses; they even published *my apartment number*," Lonnie King mused. "What do you think they're trying to say with that?" He did not feel the need to have a bodyguard, however, and he did not own a gun, but on one occasion, at least, armed protection may have kept him alive. "Charles Johnson, a Korean War veteran, told me this later," said King:

> at the height of the 1960 protests four white men were waiting in their car in the parking lot of my Gordon Road apartment building. I believe they wanted to ambush and shoot me when I got home later that night. As it happened, though, I was in Cleveland, Ohio.

Charles told me that after spotting the four men he contacted three guys he knew who were also Korean War veterans. All of them were living in the same apartment complex as me. They had guns and they formed what might be called a vigilante group. When these white men showed up a second time they approached their car from four different directions. When they reached the car, Charles asked them why they were sitting there. "Oh, we're just waiting for someone upstairs," they told him. Charles clicked his shotgun and told them to wait somewhere else and those guys jetted out of there; they never came back. These war veterans were not talking about "nonviolence." They were saying, "Let's protect this kid from white people who want to ambush him."

Stories of this kind pepper movement history and serve as important reminders that the civil rights movement was driven by individual black communities and actions as well as by national organizations, their leaders, and their policies. And communities, unlike national organizations, did not subscribe to particular schools of philosophy or tactics when they chose how to respond to danger. It is an obvious but often overlooked fact, moreover, that the communities in which the student activists of the 1960s grew up shaped much of their thinking. In the political evolution of Charles Sherrod, for example, it is easy to see how important influences in his and other's background helped process a new idea like nonviolence. Sherrod would become a legendary figure in SNCC and was closely identified with acceptance of nonviolence as a way of life. But although he had been leading nonviolent protests in Richmond, Virginia, he did not label himself nonviolent until the conference at Shaw College. Before then, nonviolence had just been a word to him. "I'd only heard about it because I read about [Martin Luther King] in newspapers," Sherrod recalled later. Before the conference, he had had almost no philosophical concept of what nonviolence might mean as a way of life, but at Shaw he recognized a part of himself that had always been committed to nonviolence "because I was a Christian," he explained, and nonviolence was "Christ in action. [With sit-ins and protest] I'm overcoming evil as the scripture says; scripture I've been nourished with all of my life." The gathering at Shaw brought Sherrod into contact with the idea of nonviolence as a principle for day-to-day living as well as a tactic for social change.

Few in SNCC became more committed to nonviolence as a way of life than Sherrod. Yet even for Sherrod, living it could be challenging. In 1961, as a SNCC field secretary, Sherrod moved to Southwest Georgia, one of the most dangerously antiblack regions of the South, and he found himself accommodating his belief in nonviolence to precautions he felt necessary for his family's safety. "The only thing that ever caused me to question my nonviolence was when I got married," he admitted, "especially when I became a father. What I did was get a dog—actually four big dogs, and I kept a dog until my children were grown."

Like Sherrod, most of the students attending the Shaw conference were surprisingly unfamiliar with the underlying philosophy of nonviolence, even though they were using nonviolence as a tactic and wound up incorporating the word "nonviolent" into their organization's name. The nonviolent challenges to white supremacy they had already mounted were influenced more by the example of their fellow students than by any understanding of, much less commitment to, nonviolence as a way of life. They saw nonviolent direct actions like those in Nashville and Greensboro as demonstrations of effective ways to take on segregation and white supremacy.

Julian Bond, for example, was a Morehouse College student when he took part in the sit-ins and picket lines in Atlanta, and he does not remember receiving any kind of formal training for them. He and other students were just responding to headlines and images of the Greensboro sit-ins that had appeared in their city's black newspaper, the *Atlanta Daily World*. One afternoon a few days after the Greensboro sit-ins, at a student hangout, Lonnie King showed him a headline in the *Daily World* reading, "Greensboro Students Sit-In for Third Day." Years later, Bond still remembered the moment clearly. "And Lonnie said to me, 'Why don't we do this here?'" The two of them and another student, Joe Pierce, began organizing what became the Atlanta student movement. Their "nonviolent" approach to participating in protests did not have great philosophical depth: "It was, 'if somebody hits you, don't hit back,'" recalls Bond. "You said, 'okay I'll do that,' and that was it." Or if a person could not accept that discipline, he or she could decide, "then I won't be on the picket line."

When it came to deciding whether or not to participate in protest, most sit-in participants could see enough of what nonviolence was to reach the same conclusions as Bond and the Atlanta students. And slowly they made their way toward deeper understanding and training. The Atlanta sit-ins began on March 15, 1960, and not until more than a year later—April 1961—was the first nonviolent workshop held at the Spelman College YWCA. In 1962, at Morehouse College, Julian enrolled in a social philosophy class, taught by Martin Luther King Jr. and Atlanta NAACP president Samuel W. Williams, that included considerable discussion of nonviolence. Only seven other students were enrolled.

Although in the beginning the movement was largely made up of college students, it quickly attracted a wider spectrum of young people. In Birmingham, Alabama, Annie Pearl Avery—another one of SNCC's legendary figures—made her way into the movement from a tougher life than that usually found on a college campus. She brought both a knife and a gun to her first Birmingham protest. Her godmother, who was also participating in the protest, told Avery that she couldn't have the weapons with her. So, says Avery,

> I took the gun home. I came back and told [my godmother], "I still have this knife. I've got to take something." "No," she said, and took my knife. . . . I was just hoping that nobody would get me—that's all! I didn't know how I would react. I was hoping that I would be able to restrain myself, but I wanted protection, just in case I couldn't.

Her attitude was not changed by her godmother's confiscation of her weapons. On another occasion Annie Pearl was arrested in Danville, Virginia, and placed in solitary confinement. "One night a policeman came into my cell. Thinking he wanted to mess with me, I took off my shoe and beat him on the head until he left."

Whether one had doubts about nonviolence, as Annie Pearl Avery did, or believed in it fully, as did Diane Nash, who was willing to have her child born in prison, commitment to the movement transcended commitment to any particular tactic. Observes Ivanhoe Donaldson, who in 1962 became one of SNCC's most effective field secretaries, "The civil rights movement was about civil rights, not about nonviolence. Nonviolence was a tool the movement used to create confrontation without hate, without force, without brutality. Yes, all the blood that was shed was ours, [but] we accepted that for the greater good—the mission—and that was not about nonviolence but about change. I didn't go to Mississippi to celebrate nonviolence; I went down there to fight for the right to vote."

———————

Like many youthful activists becoming involved with civil rights struggle, Stokely Carmichael—the charismatic SNCC leader who eventually became controversial for his Black Power speech in 1966—came to nonviolence slowly and skeptically. At first, when sit-ins broke out during his senior year in high school, he dismissed them as "inconsequential and fleeting." He was a New Yorker and thought of himself as hip, smart. He thought the best means for effecting change was organized, ideologically coherent struggle, not spontaneous outbursts—which, to him, was what the sit-ins seemed to be. However, the first time he saw students on television calmly sitting at lunch counters facing racist abuse and sometimes violent assault, "that made a believer out of me. Instantly." In retrospect, Carmichael would come to view sit-ins as "an apprenticeship in struggle."

Soon after entering Howard University in the fall of 1960, Carmichael joined the small group of students who had responded to the February Greensboro protests by forming the Nonviolent Action Group (NAG), which was committed to the practice, though not the philosophical principle, of nonviolence. The nation's capital, itself a southern city, had only begun to desegregate a few years earlier; the bordering states of Virginia and Maryland were still segregated. Despite the city's distance from the Deep South, there was no shortage of work and struggle to engage NAG.

Their organization's name notwithstanding, the Howard students who formed NAG were as skeptical of nonviolence as any of the attendees at the Shaw conference. "I remember my first reaction [to the idea of nonviolence]," says Courtland Cox, who joined NAG because it offered a way to directly fight segregation and white supremacy and not out of any philosophical commitment to nonviolence. "Appeal to a man's *heart?* Might as well appeal to his liver; they're both organs of the body." However, says Cox, "The conditions of your existence did not have any reality to most whites. Nonviolence was the only way they could understand the movement and not be totally afraid."

Whatever their opinions about nonviolence, these student activists shared one thing: they were truly the luminaries of the rising generation of Afro-Americans, although they did not think of themselves in such terms. Stokely Carmichael, Julian Bond, Lonnie King, Courtland Cox (who would later become SNCC program director), Herchelle Sullivan (a Spelman College student who after returning from study in France cochaired COAHR with Lonnie King), Henry "Hank" Thomas (who sat in alone in St. Augustine, Florida, and would become one of the original Freedom Riders in 1961), Charles Sherrod, Chuck McDew, Diane Nash (who led the Nashville movement), Bernice Johnson (a student leader in Albany, Georgia, and later founder of the renowned a cappella singing group Sweet Honey in the Rock), sisters Dorie and Joyce Ladner, Colia Liddell (all three mentored by Medgar Evers in Mississippi and Joyce would briefly be president of Howard University)—these are just a few of the students who represented a prediction made by W. E. B. Du Bois in 1903: "The Negro race, like all races, is going to be saved by its exceptional men. The problem of education, then, must first of all deal with the Talented Tenth. It is the problem of developing the Best of this race that they may guide the masses away from the contamination and death of the Worst in their own and other races."

The students who participated in sit-ins were, by and large, consciously or unconsciously, members of Du Bois's talented tenth, the best and the brightest on their college campuses. Good grades and inquisitiveness had marked them for distinction even before they joined the protests; their intellectual and political energy was evident. They held offices in student government: Carmichael, for example, was a philosophy major but also sat on the Howard University student council. Jean Wheeler, one of the young women active in NAG who would later work with SNCC in Mississippi and Southwest Georgia, was a member of Phi Beta Kappa. Annette Jones White, who as an Albany State College student was one of the young leaders of the Albany Movement, had been voted most likely to succeed when she graduated from Monroe High School in that city (and she was elected Miss Albany State College in 1961). Charles Jones, leader of the sit-in movement in Charlotte, North Carolina, was president of the student body at the Johnson C. Smith College. Marian Wright, another of the Atlanta movement's student leaders, graduated from Spelman College as valedictorian of her class.

Given their promise as students, these young leaders might have found it difficult to rebel against the status quo. School administrators, moreover, sometimes put pressure on them and their fellow students to stop protesting. That they resisted is another important aspect of their characters. Inspired by the Greensboro sit-ins, students at Southern University in Baton Rouge, Louisiana, launched a sit-in movement a little over a month after the Greensboro protests began, much to the dismay of the school's president, Felton Clark. During a school dance on March 27, 1960, the students were excitedly talking about the sit-ins they had planned for the following day. Clark interrupted their partying and told the students, "There will be no more discussion of protest, or no dance. You have one minute to decide!" Immediately, Dr. C. O. Simkins asked to speak. Simkins was a Shreveport dentist who had been important to the founding of SCLC in New Orleans, was an active supporter of the student sit-in movement, and was in Baton Rouge for the pending protest. Because of his prominence, he was given the microphone. He shouted, "You have one minute to decide! Do you want your dance or do you want your freedom?" The students began chanting: "We want our freedom! We want our freedom!"

These students had much to lose, and many were the first in their families to attend college. But students across the South bravely resisted pressure to conform. In Baton Rouge, the day after the dance, seven students sat in at the Kress department store lunch counter downtown and were arrested for disturbing the peace. There were more sit-ins and arrests the next day. And on March 30, three days after the dance, students walked out of their classes en masse and marched on the state capitol.

Throughout the South, young people were pushing back against the established order. Students resisted school authorities and their efforts to slow protests; they chafed at the restraints an older, more cautious civil rights leadership tried to impose. The generation gap would be a source of continuing tension within the movement throughout the 1960s. "I was nervous about being under the leadership of any adult," recalled Lonnie King later. "I was a strong believer in there being an independent student coordinating committee, and I would have been suspicious of us being under Dr. King or anyone else."

But sometimes people in authority responded to student militancy in unexpectedly supportive ways. Lonnie King experienced this at Morehouse College, which Martin Luther King Jr. had also attended and which was part of a consortium of six historically black institutions of higher education contiguous to one another (the others being Spelman College for Women, Morris Brown College, Clark College, Atlanta University, and the Interdenominational Theological Center, or ITC). "Not long after we began sitting-in," he remembers, "the college presidents summoned Julian, myself, and others in the movement into the Council of College Presidents conference room":

> What these powerful men basically told us was, "Go back to class. Your parents did not send you here for protest. Get your education and change the world tomorrow." Four of the presidents took this position, but Dr. Harry Richardson of ITC disagreed and said, "I believe that the students are right." The room got quiet. You could hear—to use an old expression—a rat piss on cotton. Dr. Richardson went on to say, breaking with the other presidents and their desire for a gradual approach to change, "I am a Negro. I'm the president of a university. But I cannot go downtown to Rich's [department store], buy something, then go into the Magnolia Tea Room there and buy something to eat. Something's wrong with that!" Dr. Frank Cunningham, the president of Morris Brown, was sitting next to him, and he said, "I agree with Dr. Richardson." All of a sudden the college presidents were split in front of the students.

This was unprecedented, not something Du Bois would have anticipated in the development of his desired talented tenth, despite his own quarrels with Booker T. Washington's leadership early in the century. But this meeting reveals an important aspect of the southern Freedom Movement of the 1960s: as much as it challenged white supremacy, it was also shaped by the challenges black people made to each other within the black community, challenges most often initiated by young people. Such defiance reflected just how rapidly and radically times were changing. Nonetheless, says Lonnie King, "I don't know what it was in the ether that caused the southern black Negro student revolt." They were certainly fed up with segregation and with the slow pace of change, but in addition, many of the college students were the children of World War II veterans—and that, Lonnie King thinks, might be part of the explanation: "My daddy was a World War II veteran; they changed the climate of the South."

There were certainly sympathetic professors on historically black college and university (HBCU) campuses who supported student protesters, as Lonnie King's anecdote vividly illustrates. But students often found themselves challenging the deference expected of them by the generally conservative school administrators. They soon discovered there were consequences. At Southern University in Baton Rouge, as well as at other HBCUs and high schools, students who participated in sit-ins were expelled. In Mississippi, Jackson State College president Jacob L. Reddix dissolved the student government because of civil rights protests.

The opposition of college authorities like Reddix to student protest was more complex than simple aversion to militant student activism. Almost certainly they had experienced far harsher encounters with white supremacy than most of their students, and in their guts many of them, like Richardson and Cunningham, were sympathetic to the students' impatience. But they considered their primary mission and duty to be the protection of the institutions they headed—and all these institutions, whether state or private schools, were dependent on white patronage, through the allocation of tax money or through financial gifts from white benefactors. "I understood why adults favored gradualism," says Lonnie King. "It was safe. But I felt young people had been waiting long enough and thought, let's organize and bring [segregation] to an end." Franklin McCain, one of the four students to begin the sit-ins in Greensboro, puts it a different way: "We had the confidence of a Mack truck."

With rebellion against their elders and with their movement involvement, many students began thinking differently about themselves, discovering a strength they did not know they had. "Something happened to me as I got more and more involved in the Movement," wrote Anne Moody, a Mississippian active with CORE in that state. "It no longer seemed important to prove anything. I had found something outside myself that gave meaning to my life." For Bernice Johnson in Albany, Georgia, "There was a clarity about everything. I knew where I was; I knew what I was doing. . . . I was where I was supposed to be. My life was being used for a purpose—fighting racism—and it lifted me up. . . . I was free and centered." Like Moody and Johnson, the most committed of these student activists found that their involvement in protests had altered their view of the lives they were expected to lead. Indeed, some of them left school or put off attending college in order to work full time with SNCC or CORE.

The ranks of civil rights organizations swelled with these new student activists, and their commitment to the movement would soon take them into uncharted territory. In June 1961, Charles Sherrod became SNCC's first paid field secretary, earning $9.64 a week after taxes. In less than a year, a handful of students, themselves also SNCC field secretaries, would plunge into the rural Black-Belt South, a wilderness where white supremacy had a tighter grip on black life than anywhere else in the country. CORE too was undergoing a similar process as young southern blacks entered its ranks and transformed the organization. In the violently antiblack terrain of the rural South, the idealism lodged in nonviolent protest at whites-only restaurants met the harsh realities of trying to stay alive in politically hostile and physically murderous counties or parishes. Working there finally settled the argument in SNCC between the advocates of massive nonviolent direct action that would take on every aspect of segregation and the advocates of a more narrowly focused effort to gain voting rights.

This question had sharply divided SNCC. The organization might have been destroyed by its fierce internal debate over this were it not for a suggestion from Ella Baker. Her experience as the NAACP's director of branches in the 1940s and her recognition of the importance of the student sit-in movement had led to the creation of SNCC and had made her the most respected adult voice among the students. At the height of heated argument at the Highlander Folk School in Knoxville, Tennessee, she suggested that SNCC form two wings: a voter-registration wing and a direct-action wing. She knew that this distinction was largely meaningless; voter registration was a form of direct action, as students would soon discover. She also knew that there was a consensus among local black leaders in the South that voter registration was what was most needed, and that to do any sort of organizing would require working within the consensus that existed.

Baker's pragmatic suggestion would also change the student activists' views about the viability of nonviolence. The antiblack, antimovement violence they encountered in rural areas of the Black Belt was unlike anything they had ever experienced. Segregationists and white-supremacists targeted homes, families, and communities, not just picket lines or sit-in protesters. Collective punishment was the rule. Confronted with such indiscriminate terror, the students would have a much harder time practicing nonviolence—never mind subscribing to the demanding philosophy behind it. And they would find, too, that the question of armed self-defense was far more relevant than it had been in their previous activist experience.

The rural black culture that SNCC field secretaries encountered in the Deep South had long accepted armed self-defense as legitimate. Although local black people could be uncertain about when and how to best employ it, the idea itself was not subject to debate. Guns were common in southern households, used not only for hunting but also for protection from white violence. The idea of removing guns from the equation was, for the vast majority of rural southern blacks, simply a nonissue.

The young SNCC and CORE activists now becoming grassroots organizers learned almost immediately that guns were in the political mix in a way they had never been before, on picket lines and at sit-ins. In rural Lee County, Georgia, for example, seventy-year-old Annie "Mama Dolly" Raines was a key movement supporter. Her small farm "was like a stop on the Underground Railroad because so many of us in the Albany Movement came there," recalled Peggy Trotter Dammond Preacely, a student who became involved with the Albany project in the summer of 1962. Mama Dolly was one of Charles Sherrod's earliest and closest confidants in Southwest Georgia, but not because she shared his philosophical commitment to nonviolence; far from it, in fact. Sherrod remembered,

[Mama Dolly] had this big shotgun. I tried to talk her out of guarding me but she said, "Baby, I brought a lot of these white folks into this world, and I'll take 'em out of this world if I have to." Sometimes, no matter what I said, she would sit in my bedroom window, leg propped up with that big ol' gun. She knew how to handle it way better than I did. In fact, I didn't know nothin' about no shotgun.

Preacely would remember the experience of sleeping at Mama Dolly's farmhouse in more general terms. "When we slept at night," she said, "we felt somewhat protected. It was ironic and ambiguous all at the same time."

Developments such as these were indeed ambiguous. The ideal of non-violent struggle had driven Sherrod and most of that first small group of students to leave school to work full-time with SNCC. With one or two exceptions—John Lewis was one, James Bevel another—these students were products of the urban South. They had varying degrees of personal experience in the rural South, but guns, even for hunting, had never been an important part of their lives. Their earliest movement activity centered on protests against segregated public facilities, and the great majority of those protests occurred in urban areas, where guns were rarely a factor in any violence the activists might have experienced—white mobs seemed to prefer fists or clubs. This would all change as they entered the rural Deep South.

———

It was the work of SNCC field secretary Bob Moses that first began to make plain the issue of self-defense for the organization—ironically, because Moses has always been identified with nonviolence and as a college student had worked on Quaker projects overseas. At twenty-six, Moses was slightly older than most SNCC workers, and he already held a master's degree from Harvard. In the summer of 1961, after finishing a teaching contract in New York City, he joined SNCC's staff and wound up in the small city of McComb in Pike County, Mississippi, where he began SNCC's first voter-registration project. About a month after he arrived, he was joined by

Reginald Robinson, a SNCC activist from Baltimore, and John Hardy, a Freedom Rider from Fisk University in Nashville.

Freedom Riders were interracial groups of young men and women who challenged the segregation of interstate transportation by riding together on buses traveling between southern states. They began coursing into Mississippi early in the summer of 1961, and hundreds were arrested. Before he came to McComb, Hardy himself had been imprisoned in the notorious Parchman Farm (Mississippi State Penitentiary) in the Mississippi Delta. By penetrating the rural South on buses, Freedom Riders served as highly visible symbols of resistance to white supremacy for the black people in small towns and hamlets across the region, places that had no Woolworth lunch counters or, indeed, much beyond a gas-station restroom where segregation could be directly challenged. Some of the riders remained in Mississippi after being released from jail. Thus it was that Hardy had joined Moses's work in McComb—just an hour and a half south of Mississippi's capital city and the last major stop on the bus route to New Orleans.

Freedom Riders were not the only ones interested in Moses's work. Shortly after his arrival in McComb, a cadre of young black people emerged to help him. They were mostly too young to vote, and they were impatient. These young people had been admiring the Freedom Riders and sit-in activists from a distance. Now, as some of the riders and SNCC activists began arriving in McComb, the young people of the town welcomed their help in forming a local nonviolent organization. And so, in this small Southwest Mississippi city, we see for the first time the convergence of nonviolent direct-action protest with community organizing focused on voter registration. It was here that SNCC's most militant proponents of nonviolent direct action—who were also the ones most suspicious of voter-registration campaigns—began to get their first close-up view of organizing at the grassroots and began to understand its implications.

It did not take long for word of Moses's work to spread beyond McComb, and a group of residents from neighboring Amite and Walthall Counties sought help in launching similar voter-registration efforts. Curtis Conway "C. C." Bryant, head of the Pike County NAACP branch, brought Moses to Amite County and introduced him to his NAACP counterpart there, Eldridge Willie "E. W." Steptoe. And Steptoe offered to let Moses use the church on his small farm outside of the town of Liberty as a voter-registration school. "I've been expecting you," the farmer told Moses after being introduced to him.

Steptoe was a small, wiry man of renowned toughness, intelligence, and determination. As founder and president of the Amite County NAACP in 1953, he was always in the crosshairs of local white supremacists. In 1954 Amite County sheriff Ira Jenkins and fifteen or twenty other deputies and Klansmen raided an NAACP meeting on Steptoe's farm, confiscating the membership list and other records. Not surprisingly, NAACP membership dropped sharply. But Steptoe kept the branch alive by buying enough memberships himself to meet the quota that the NAACP national headquarters required for a chartered branch.

White supremacists constantly threatened and harassed Steptoe, but they had to be careful. Night riding was not likely to be successful in confronting a man like Steptoe—and in fact, it could be deadly, for it was well known that his farmhouse contained a small arsenal and that he would not hesitate to shoot back. If you stayed overnight with Steptoe, recalled Chuck McDew, "as you went to bed he would open up the night table and there would be a large .45 automatic sitting next to you. . . . [There were] guns all over the house, under pillows, under chairs." Steptoe also traveled as heavily armed as possible. His wife, Sing, was uncomfortable with the idea of her husband carrying weapons on his person, so sometimes before he left to go into town she would pat him down, confiscating any guns she found. Still, he was rarely unarmed. He often carried a derringer in his sock, a firearm that somehow Sing never found, despite the fact that almost everyone in Amite County seemed to know it was there.

Steptoe's grit mirrored the landscape that had produced him. Southwest Mississippi is a hilly, hardscrabble place; most of its residents, black or white, were poor. They had never managed to come together to fight the causes of their poverty, however, for race trumped everything. As tough and racist as McComb was, Amite and Walthall Counties made it seem a haven of moderate, understanding whites. In these counties whites displayed none of the pretense of paternalistic affection that some white planters in the cotton country of the Delta seemed to reserve for blacks. Southwest Mississippi was the most Klan-ridden region in the state, and the Amite County chapter of the Klan was headed by the sheriff's son. Only one black person in Amite County—a majority-black county—was known to be registered to vote, and he had never tried to exercise that right.

Surprisingly, in spite of the ferocious white-supremacist opposition to civil rights in Southwest Mississippi, the NAACP was in some ways stronger in this region than anywhere else in the state. Steptoe's determined protection of his NAACP branch is one example. Although no black person was registered to vote in Walthall County, it had an NAACP chapter, and its residents were the first in Mississippi to file a school-desegregation suit. In McComb, Medgar Evers organized an NAACP youth chapter specifically concerned with police brutality. Pike County members of the NAACP went to Washington, D.C., to testify in support of the 1957 Civil Rights Act.

But overall, Amite, Walthall, and Pike Counties were the stuff of black nightmares. Wrote journalist Jack Newfield, "In the mythology of the Movement Amite County is synonymous with the Ninth Circle of Hell." Some in McComb urged Moses to stay away from Amite and Walthall Counties, fearing that he would never get out alive. However, Moses had been asked for help by the residents of these counties, and he felt that to refuse would defeat the purpose of what he and others from SNCC had begun. "Farmers came over and were very anxious to try and register," Moses explained, "and you couldn't very well turn them down. . . . You can't be in the position of turning down the tough areas because the people, then, I think, would lose confidence in you." By late August Moses was holding regular classes on Steptoe's farm.

As other SNCC organizers joined Moses in Amite, Walthall, and Pike Counties, it quickly became apparent just how dangerous those places were. After Moses brought two people to register in the tiny town of Liberty, the county seat of Amite County, the cousin of Amite County's sheriff accosted him in the street and beat him with the butt end of a knife. Steptoe's neighbor Herbert Lee, an NAACP leader and a key supporter of SNCC's voter-registration efforts in Amite County, was shot and killed in broad daylight at the town's cotton gin. Three weeks later, a crowd of enraged white men beat SNCC organizer Travis Britt into semiconsciousness at the Amite County courthouse. Britt later reported to SNCC that one of his attackers had yelled out, "Brothers! Should we kill him here?" In another incident,

John Hardy brought two potential registrants to the courthouse in Tyler-town, the county seat of Walthall County. The clerk told Hardy he was not registering voters that day, and when Hardy leaned forward to ask why, the clerk pulled a pistol from beneath the counter and smashed the gun into the side of his head. Hardy staggered from the courthouse out into the street, where he was placed under arrest for disturbing the peace.

Violence often works in the short term, and it initially stopped the work of Bob Moses and his SNCC colleagues in Southwest Mississippi. "Can we really keep doing this?" Moses would later recall asking himself after the murder of Herbert Lee, knowing that the price could get higher. He tem-porarily retreated from the region and returned to McComb, where high school students' protests against segregation were heating up. But angry black adults in McComb opposed the protests, for which they blamed him and SNCC. The NAACP leaders, who had initially invited Moses to McComb, were furious about the sit-ins, protest marches, and, especially, the consequent jailing of high school students. They held Moses and SNCC responsible for this unexpected development and felt they had been double-crossed; sit-ins were not why they had invited them to McComb. C. C. Bryant even asked the state NAACP executive committee to condemn the SNCC project in McComb. Although Steptoe, Amzie Moore, and several other local civil rights leaders defended Moses, by December he and SNCC had left McComb, not to return until 1964.

Moses may have felt defeated in the short term, but the experience in Southwest Mississippi contained important lessons. He and others from SNCC had learned that it was possible to dig in and organize, especially for voter registration. They now understood that they were capable of attracting a critical mass of local supporters, young people especially. They found support from existing (if sometimes invisible) local leadership and discovered new leaders who arose as the local movement emerged. As Moses later put it, he and his fellow SNCC organizers "had, to put it mildly, got our feet wet."

These first, uncertain steps in Southwest Mississippi were invaluable, pioneering not only SNCC's future work in Mississippi but also its efforts across the rest of the South. Although organizers like Moses were outsiders to the rural communities they worked in, local blacks embraced them—as family, not just as allies. Indeed, the organizing efforts in Southwest Mississippi confirmed what Ella Baker and Amzie Moore had already stressed in their conversations with Moses and SNCC: that there were people in rural communities, like Steptoe, who had been waiting for—even expecting—them. The nature of the relationship, however, was "totally unexpected," Moses recalled:

> I had become part of something else besides a civil rights organization in Mississippi. Everywhere we went I and other civil rights workers were adopted and nurtured, even protected as though we were family. We were the community's children, and that closeness rendered moot the label of "outside agitator." . . . Importantly, as is always true in close families, our young generation was dynamically linked to a rooted older generation who passed on wisdom, encouragement, and concrete aid when possible. This was empowering, enabling SNCC and CORE field secretaries to move from county to county across a network that provided different levels of support. A network made up of people offering whatever they could within their means.

The experiences of Moses and SNCC in Southwest Mississippi drove home what Ella Baker knew they would learn: that organizing for voter registration *was* direct action. And even if sit-ins seemed counterproductive without the support of local leadership in small towns like McComb and all but impossible in rural areas like Amite County, organizing for voter registration was proving itself as direct a challenge to white supremacy as any sit-in or Freedom Ride. SNCC's Reggie Robinson succinctly described how these first efforts in Mississippi drove home this lesson: "If you went into Mississippi and talked about voter registration they're going to hit you on the side of the head and that's as direct as you can get."

––––––

The voter-registration campaign in the Delta had merely been postponed when Moore sent Moses to McComb. Moses (now living in Jackson) realized that a unified effort was needed in order to tackle voter registration or to make any sort of meaningful stab at community organizing in the state. David Dennis, CORE's Mississippi project director, had reached the same conclusion, and it had long been the view of Aaron Henry, now state president of the NAACP. In January 1962, Henry convened in Clarksdale a meeting of representatives from SNCC, CORE, SCLC, and the NAACP. This meeting gave new life to a statewide organization that had originally been formed to support Freedom Riders: the Council of Federated Organizations (COFO). The attendees decided that a revitalized COFO would launch a voter-registration campaign, to be staffed largely by SNCC and CORE field secretaries. Moses was named COFO's state project director, and Dennis was named assistant director. Partly because of his relationship with Amzie Moore, and partly because of the numbers—Delta counties were roughly two-thirds black—Moses and SNCC targeted the Delta. And now a cadre of young Mississippians had emerged from McComb and Jackson who were prepared to work in the Delta with Moses and SNCC. Dennis began a project staffed by CORE in the center of the state between Canton and Meridian, in what was then Mississippi's Fourth Congressional District.

As voter-registration work expanded, however, attacks by white supremacists intensified, and the federal government refused to provide protection for either the organizers or the communities they worked in. Discussions about self-defense accelerated. One issue was whether or not civil rights workers in the Delta and elsewhere in the Deep South should carry weapons for their own protection. They and their cars were known to hostile whites. Many of the adult leaders they worked with traveled armed and sometimes offered them weapons. "My position," says Moses considering it years later, "was that the SNCC field secretaries themselves should not carry guns. Local people might be carrying guns—that was up to them—but we would all be in danger if the idea went out that SNCC field secretaries were arming themselves."

Although the young Mississippians now working with Moses and SNCC were local people just like the older leaders in their communities, they did not put up much of an argument over Moses's antigun stance, which mirrored SNCC policy. Just as for their parents and grandparents, the practicalities of the day were the determining factor in their attitudes toward armed self-defense. Police commonly stopped, questioned, and searched blacks, so gun possession could indeed put a person at risk by giving police an excuse to gun him or her down. At the very least, it could give weight to whites' claim that blacks were plotting armed insurrections.

Most of the organizers now working with SNCC and CORE realized that carrying a gun would not necessarily save their lives. They were most likely to be accosted by white supremacists on back roads and highways, where they would have little use for guns unless they were trapped. And even then, firing back might only save them if their attackers were civilians, cowards, or both. Shooting back at racist police officers only made matters worse. Activists knew that it was better to try to outrun pursuing vehicles than to engage their occupants. And a tragic fact of the Deep South was that black victims could not always anticipate the attacks that killed them. Herbert Lee, for instance, kept a gun in his truck but was shot down and killed by a white man—a boyhood playmate—who he thought was calling him over for conversation. It admittedly would have been an argumentative conversation, but Lee was expecting to talk to the man, not shoot at him.

The violence only heightened the uncertainty over how much or how little protection weapons provided. In many cases, such as Herbert Lee's, it was clear that the targets never had the chance to use a firearm even if they were carrying one. In 1963 SNCC worker Jimmy Travis was machine-gunned while he was driving from Greenwood to Greenville, Mississippi. He was unarmed, but a pistol would have been of little use in this sudden attack. Medgar Evers, who always traveled armed, was gunned down in the driveway of his Jackson home later the same year, bleeding to death without ever managing to reach the pistol and rifle that were in his car. CORE organizers James Chaney, Michael "Mickey" Schwerner, and Andrew Goodman were killed in 1964 after a Neshoba County deputy sheriff handed them over to a Ku Klux Klan mob.

These and other incidents in the early 1960s were a far cry from the Wild West shoot-outs romanticized by Hollywood cowboy movies. The good guys and the bad guys did not stand at opposite ends of dusty southern streets facing one another *mano a mano*. And the lawmen were not always—or even usually—a force for good. Indeed, state power was almost always willing to step in and ruthlessly reinforce local white violence in the name of law and order.

There is some comfort in carrying a weapon in dangerous situations. And more than a few local movement supporters carried them, though for the most part they did not flash their guns or display their rifles on gun racks in their trucks, as whites were able to do. But local supporters who did carry guns exerted pressure—whether consciously or unconsciously—on organizers and activists to do the same. "Steptoe and other people [in Amite County] chided me a lot for not being willing to carry a gun," recalled Moses, "telling me when they had their guns, 'But you're nonviolent and you're not going to help with the protection, are you?' So on that score you were the odd man out."

Moses resisted the culture of gun ownership and armed self-defense as much as he could. Steptoe's son, E. W. Steptoe Jr., remembered one disagreement over weapons that took place as his father and Moses were preparing to visit Lee's widow. "Daddy wanted to put a gun in the car," E. W. Jr. related later. "[Bob] said 'No, I'm not going with you if you're going to carry a gun.' [Daddy] said, 'You don't know these people around here.'" Eventually, Steptoe reluctantly left the gun at home—although he may well have kept the derringer that he habitually carried in his sock.

The threats that drove local people to carry guns were certainly real, and few organizers were prepared to go as far as Moses did in objecting even to traveling with an armed protector. Indeed, when it came down to a question of survival, most activists' practice of "nonviolence" proved quite flexible.

Although it was not usual for "nonviolent" activists to possess or use guns, they did carry weapons from time to time. Willie (now "Wazir") Peacock illustrated the fluidity of attitude about weapons at a June 10, 1964, SNCC staff meeting in Atlanta. Peacock, a young activist from Tallahatchie County, was organizing in Greenwood, and at the meeting he passionately described some of the complexities that could be involved in balancing the need for self-defense with SNCC's official commitment to nonviolence:

> I asked a local man to fire on anyone who broke into our Freedom
> House, so that neither I nor any other SNCC staff person would
> be compromised by using arms. But he would not agree. So,

instead, I placed guns [in the house] so that we could at least guard the Freedom House at night. We have done this since February. . . . Violence is not being preached about, but the local people all say that the white man thinks it's war and he is preparing to defend his home . . . [and] whites in Greenwood are more convinced than ever that they can kill a Negro and get away with it.

It became clear that Peacock was not alone in challenging the philosophical principles espoused by his organization. All that year, violence against activists and their supporters had been increasing, and the topic of self-defense continued to be the subject of much debate at the meeting. This was SNCC's most intense organizational discussion of the issue to date, and there were myriad questions swirling around it. Should SNCC workers carry guns? Would SNCC defend a field secretary arrested for helping a household that used arms to defend itself from terrorists? Did SNCC even want local people to defend its organizers with arms? Should they seek such protection?

Both sides argued their positions passionately. "Willie said he was concerned about the people around the office who might die," said Prathia Hall, a fellow organizer who was also at the meeting. She was totally committed to nonviolence and opposed to the use of violence, whatever its context. "But at the same time," she argued, "you might shoot a person breaking in to plant a bomb, you might shoot someone who broke in because of hunger." Sam Block, a native of Cleveland, Mississippi, was of the opposite mind-set. He had begun the Greenwood project, and he spent his first days in the city ducking white terrorists determined to kill him, even sleeping in a junkyard in the backseat of a car until he found a family brave enough to put him up. He told the meeting, "Amzie Moore has reported that vigilantes will kill Fannie Lou Hamer, Bob Moses, Aaron Henry, Dave Dennis and me. . . . I'm not going to carry a gun but if someone else is going to protect himself, then let him protect me as well!" Block also succinctly summed up an important sentiment held by many of the activists who were skeptical about the effectiveness of nonviolence: "I would back nonviolence if the whites coming down [as volunteers] for the summer would go into the white community and preach nonviolence."

Just three months earlier, Peacock informed the meeting, someone had shot at him in front of the SNCC office in Greenwood. He then suggested that it would be worthwhile for SNCC to consider organizing defense for its field secretaries and their local supporters. "I think an organization to stop whites should be set up," he told the group. Peacock's fellow activist Lawrence Guyot, however, was having none of it. He insisted that carrying guns put the organizers at greater risk, exclaiming at one point, "Don't you see? They'll shoot us quicker if we're armed!" And so it went, back and forth.

The group finally reached a consensus: SNCC field staff would not carry weapons, and summer volunteers who carried weapons would be sent home. No enforcement mechanism or penalty for staff was discussed, however. In effect, the question of guns and self-defense remained open. Still, at least some of the organizers took this new SNCC policy seriously. When he returned to Greenwood after the meeting, Stokely Carmichael removed weapons from the office.

The meeting in Atlanta reflected a crucial reality about nonviolence and armed self-defense: the choice of which tactic to use in a given situation was, ultimately, up to the organizers in the field. Movement culture granted organizers a great deal of latitude in decision making in the field, which effectively made the 1964 Atlanta consensus moot.

Virtually all the SNCC projects across the Deep South were wrestling with the tension between nonviolence and self-defense, trying to find the balance that would best suit the communities where they were working. Don Harris, who directed a SNCC project in and around Americus, Georgia, told the Atlanta meeting that there had been six shootings in eighteen months in his area and that locals were resistant to the idea of not firing back at terrorists. "At a mass meeting two nights after the last shooting we talked about nonviolence," Harris told the meeting, "but the people walked out angry and frustrated." Later, in discussion among themselves, staff members in Americus questioned "what right they had to stop the local people from whatever they wanted to do." Sherrod would later attest that his Southwest Georgia project had "many discussions" about weapons. His project was headquartered in Albany, the major city in the region, and any volunteer or staff person planning to work with SNCC arrived there first and was oriented.

My instructions were that nobody was to have guns, or buy guns, or take guns into the community, but also to withhold our judgment on the local people who did have guns because *everybody* in Albany had guns. The counties were just as bad. You couldn't look into a room without seeing a gun either on the mantelpiece, above the mantelpiece, or in a corner somewhere. We didn't come to change their local culture.

Nonviolence was an abstract and sometimes impractical idea to many, perhaps most, people in the rural South, where antiblack terrorism was often protected by local law enforcement and treated as customary by many whites. The alternative to self-defense could be a brutal death. In 1965, Hosie Miller, the father of Charles Sherrod's wife Shirley Miller Sherrod, was murdered by a white man in Baker County, Georgia ("bad Baker," as the county was nicknamed), gunned down on his own land following a dispute over some cows. Not long after her father's killing, Shirley, then seventeen years old, and a handful of other young people desegregated the local high school; the Ku Klux Klan burned a cross in the Millers' farmhouse yard in retaliation. More than a dozen Klansmen were there, and the cross burned brightly enough to reveal the faces of several of the night riders. Shirley's mother stood on the porch with a pistol and shouted out, "I know who you are!" as Shirley and her sisters telephoned neighbors. Armed black farmers quickly showed up and surrounded the Klansmen. The night riders were allowed to flee, but only after they had pleaded for the life of one of their number, who was in the rifle sights of an angry young black man. Some of the Millers' defenders might have considered their actions nonviolent, because no shots were fired in response to the Klan raiders.

Although Charles Sherrod retained his commitment to nonviolence even as he immersed himself in Southwest Georgia, most who emerged from nonviolent protests and began working as community organizers did not press the idea in southern black communities. Many organizers saw nonviolence as a tactic and did not think it necessary to raise the issue unless it was tactically necessary—for example, in bringing people to courthouses to register to vote or for a protest march. Many movement activists agree that there was a racial element threaded into attitudes toward nonviolence: white volunteers seemed to be in favor of it; black activists seemed to be skeptical of it. This of course is not absolute; there were strong black proponents of nonviolence—Charles Sherrod, for example—and there were also whites who considered self-defense valid and necessary.

Living and working in southern black communities had a profound effect on organizers. Respect for community life was at the heart of their project and affected their attitudes toward armed self-defense. Organizers who were taken into a community felt an obligation to abide by local values, especially if those values were contributing to the protection of the organizers. Sam Block's sister Margaret understood this when she was organizing in Tallahatchie County in January 1964. She stayed with eighty-six-year-old Janie Brewer, the matriarch of a large black family who lived with some of her children and grandchildren on the family farm about four or five miles outside the tiny village of Glendora. "Mrs. Brewer asked me what did SNCC mean," Block would later recall, "and I told her the Student Nonviolent Coordinating Committee. And she stopped me. [She said] 'You said nonviolent. If somebody come at you, you ain't gonna do nothing.' . . . She pulled up a big ole rifle. . . . She kept a big rifle behind the chair. . . . [Mrs. Brewer said,] 'Shit, we ain't nonviolent.'" Ideas like this shaped Block's own feelings about nonviolence. "Since I was living with [the Brewers]," she later explained, "I had to be what the family was."

The experience of fieldwork changed organizers' actions as well as their attitudes. One night in August 1964, after four of Mrs. Brewer's sons and another local resident tried to register to vote at the county courthouse in Sumner, Mississippi, whites in cars began circling the family's farmhouse. This was not the first time such harassment had occurred; when SNCC staff took local people to attempt to register to vote, whites often followed the groups back home. On this night Janie Brewer had already been warned by her local sources of a possible attack, and she instructed her children, grandchildren, and SNCC guests to arm themselves and hide in the cotton fields. Meanwhile she and Margaret Block began making Molotov cocktails in the kitchen, "spilling gas everywhere," Block remembered. "And I'm like 'Damn if we get burned up in here, everyone was going to swear the Klan did it [and] it's going to be Mrs. Brewer blowing us up." As the sheriff and a "truckload" of Klansmen approached the farmhouse, Brewer family members and some of the SNCC workers were still in the fields with rifles and shotguns. Before the raiders reached the house, someone shone a floodlight on them. Others fired into the air. Brewer stood on the front porch ready to hurl a Molotov cocktail. Everyone, including the sheriff, fled. Night riders never returned to the Brewer farm.

SNCC and CORE field secretaries almost never had to ask for protection, and when protection was needed, their defenders often received signals that the field secretaries did not even know were being transmitted. Bernard Lafayette was one of those in SNCC most committed to nonviolence. In Selma in 1963 he was saved from possible assassination by a neighbor and Korean War veteran whose name he remembers as "Red." Red fired a rifle and drove away two white men who had been assaulting Lafayette in front of his home with their fists and a pistol. Lafayette was understandably relieved, but even in the moment he attempted to reconcile his commitment to nonviolence with the gunfire that saved him. "When I saw Red had a rifle I shouted out, 'Red, don't shoot him!'" he recalled. "Then I placed my body between Red and the big burly white man who had been beating me." Lafayette's attackers were not killed, or even wounded, and they fled. "I stopped Red, that's the point. My position was practical *and* moral. I didn't want to be involved or participate in somebody getting killed." Afterward, "Red kind of assigned himself as my bodyguard because there were four units in the house. Red lived in one of them and if somebody threw a bomb he was gonna get killed too."

Organizers recognized that armed protection was an intrinsic part of life in black communities and accepted it as natural and necessary. One of the places where guns were thoroughly integrated into movement life was Lowndes County, Alabama, a place so notoriously violent that it was known as "Bloody Lowndes." When SNCC organizers led by Stokely Carmichael began working there in 1965, just one black person was registered to vote—this despite the fact that the population of Lowndes was 80 percent black.

The organizers arrived shortly after the Selma-to-Montgomery march, and almost immediately terrorists began targeting the black community. In August students decided to picket stores at the county seat, an action unusual in such a rural area. Accompanying them was a young white Episcopal minister from New Hampshire, Jonathan Daniels, who had first come to Alabama for the Selma-to-Montgomery march and had stayed as a volunteer in Lowndes County. The group was arrested, and released a few days later. Then Daniels and others of the group entered a white-owned store frequented by blacks to buy some soft drinks. A deputy sheriff holding a shotgun ordered them out. Then, suddenly, he opened fire, killing Daniels and wounding a catholic priest, Father Richard Morrisroe. According to Ruby Sales, a Tuskegee student, "Things happened so fast. . . . There was a shotgun blast and then another shotgun blast, and I heard Father Morrisroe moaning for water. And I thought to myself, This is what dead is. I'm dead."

As the violence grew, black people fortified their homes and began to organize protection. Bessie McMeans of Fort Deposit in Lowndes County placed a mattress in her living room and stacked a dozen or so guns on it. People kept shotguns behind their bedroom doors; they oiled their old pistols and placed them on nightstands. Local people carried weapons while canvassing for potential voter registrants. They also organized armed caravans to and from mass meetings. Gun shops stopped selling bullets to black people, but family members and friends who were part of a "Lowndes diaspora" in Detroit and other places outside the state helped smuggle guns and ammunition into the county. The daughter of one local leader who taught school in Georgia began purchasing large quantities of ammunition and some weapons, which she brought home whenever she visited.

The important lesson here is that SNCC staff did not have to organize self-defense in Lowndes. Nor did they automatically reject the idea of grabbing a weapon if necessary to help protect a household under fire from terrorists. R. L. Strickland, a farmer, told Stokely Carmichael, "Wal, in this county, if you turn the other cheek . . . these here peckerwoods'll hand you back half of what you sitting on." Men like Strickland sat on their porches with guns, "and Stokely wasn't inside the house being protected by them," says Ivanhoe Donaldson. "He was right there with them."

Organizers elsewhere in the South also kept open the option of armed self-defense. In Natchez, Mississippi, during the period that became known as the 1964 Freedom Summer, organizers stored guns in a shack near the "freedom house" they rented as their organizing headquarters and living space. Organizers could get away with breaking official SNCC doctrine like this because of their relative autonomy and distance from the core of the organization. In an era before smartphones and social media, movement fieldwork was largely invisible to SNCC headquarters until an organizer wrote a field report and snail-mailed it to the organization's main offices— Atlanta, in the case of SNCC and SCLC, and New York, in the case of CORE. Organizers who carried guns did not put that fact in their field reports.

In the summer of 1964 Chuck McDew, who by then was no longer SNCC's chairman, entered Natchez with two other SNCC workers: Dorie Ladner and George Green, both native Mississippians. But before going to that notoriously Klan-infested river city, says McDew, "I got three guns from Mr. Steptoe down in Amite County—a .32 pistol, a Japanese luger, and a .45 pistol. The .32 was for Dorie." After they settled in the house where they had made arrangements to stay overnight, McDew showed Dorie how to aim and shoot the pistol. "We'd already been stopped by the cops coming into town. They knew where we were staying, which meant the Klan knew we were in town and where we were staying." Dorie was in a bedroom on the third floor. George and Chuck were downstairs in a first floor bedroom, and McDew's instructions to Dorie were explicit. "I explained that if Klansmen tried to get into the house she would probably hear some noise—shooting and stuff," McDew remembered. He told her, "If anybody comes up the stairs, unless it is me or George don't open your door, just shoot. I repeated, Nobody can get in your room without coming through your door. If anybody you don't know tries, just shoot 'em; hit them any-where. Just shoot!"

McDew's fears were justified. Earlier that summer, three CORE workers— James Earl Chaney, Andrew Goodman, and Michael Schwerner—had dis-appeared while attempting to register black voters in central Mississippi; they would later be found shot to death. At the time, says McDew, "there really wasn't any lengthy discussion" about whether or not SNCC workers could participate in armed self-defense if they were attacked, as their three fellow workers presumably had been. McDew noted,

> Chaney, Goodman, and Schwerner were missing and we assumed
> they were dead. We also thought that there was a statewide plan

to get rid of us all, or at least to kill as many of us as they could get away with killing. Now, I was not an advocate of going out and killing white people, but I did know how to use a gun, and when it came down to thee or me, *you* were going to die before me. I didn't think about the effect on the organization [SNCC]— a "nonviolent" organization. It was my feeling that some dumb-ass cracker is not going to catch me and shoot me down here in Natchez, Mississippi, without me taking him and his friends along on that trip to the other side.

Although no formal survey of movement veterans has been done, it is virtually certain that most field workers shared Chuck McDew's attitude toward guns. Most did not carry weapons on their person in their day-to-day work, but there were moments when organizers felt it could be handy to have a gun.

Besides the disappearances of the three CORE workers, a host of other violent events occurred that summer and fall that reinforced organizers' desire for protection. In September, Natchez mayor John Nosser—a native of Lebanon who had immigrated to the United States as a nineteen-year-old—proposed opening discussions with the NAACP; the Klan bombed his home in retaliation. A few weeks earlier a bomb blast had demolished a black-owned tavern almost next door to the house that movement workers in Natchez had rented. "The fire chief said the bomb was meant for us," Dorie Ladner said later, "and the police chief said he was surprised that we hadn't been killed already."

Dorie Ladner was well acquainted with the dangers of being black in Mississippi. As high school students she and her sister Joyce had been mentored by both Medgar Evers and their hometown NAACP leader, Vernon Dahmer, who would be murdered in 1966 when Klansmen firebombed his home. However, said Dorie, "I didn't think about white people and violence when growing up because I wasn't around them that much. Then I jumped into the movement full time and saw how they *really* were." Nonetheless, she said, "It was strange to have a gun. I guess it was sort of like being given a plank to use for walking across the water if necessary." There had been guns in her house when she was growing up; her father kept a shotgun above the front door. But like many grown-up things in a young girl's household, especially things mostly associated with adult males, the shotgun had been unimportant to her. She did not know how to use it and had never tried to learn.

Dorie Ladner never had occasion to use the pistol Chuck McDew gave her, but she might have been willing to do so. "I am not a violent person, but I knew I was going into a very violent territory," she said later. "I didn't anticipate violence because if you did that all of the time, day to day, you couldn't live that way; you might go crazy with fear. But when Chuck gave me the gun, in my own head I thought if somebody I didn't know came up those stairs I was going to shoot them. I didn't think about the ramifications or anything like that; it was save yourself, survive."

6

Standing Our Ground

If you are not afraid, you can make a good leader. If you are scared of white folks you don't make a good leader. That white man will beat your brains out.

—Clarence Chinn Jr. to author

We decided since we didn't have protection from the law, by the law, we should organize a group to protect our peoples in the neighborhood. . . . And we took up the job of self-defense. . . . We never attacked anyone, but we would defend ourself against anybody at any time, anywhere, regardless of the price.

—Charles Sims, president of Deacons for Defense and Justice, to Howell Raines, Bogalusa, Louisiana

Tough men and women and the weapons they sometimes used were essential to the southern Freedom Movement. And it seems remarkable that some of the most defiant survived in parts of the South where even in the mid-twentieth century, some whites thought they had a God-given right to kill any black person showing discontent. One such unlikely survivor was C. O. Chinn. In his early forties and tall, dark, and muscular, Chinn was already a legend in Madison County, Mississippi, because of his unwillingness to bend to white power. David Dennis, then CORE's Mississippi project director, recalls being in the courtroom of the county courthouse in Canton, Mississippi, one morning in 1963, attending a bond hearing for a volunteer who had been arrested on a traffic violation, when C. O. Chinn walked in. Chinn was wearing a holstered pistol on his hip, which probably would not have raised an eyebrow if he had been white.

"Now C. O.," drawled the judge, "You know you can't come in here wearing that gun." Madison County sheriff Billy Noble was also in the courtroom; Chinn looked over at him and responded, "As long as that SOB over there is wearing his, I'm gonna keep mine."

The enmity between Chinn and the sheriff was well-known throughout the county, and half expecting a shootout, Dennis thought to himself, "We're all dead." But the judge spoke coaxingly to both men: "Boys, boys, no. Why don't you put your guns on the table over here in front of the bench. Let's be good boys." Both men walked to the table and—eyeing one another "very carefully," Dennis remembers—set their pistols down.

Chinn stands out among the men and women who were willing to provide armed protection to Freedom Movement workers in Mississippi. As Sheriff Noble himself once said, "There are only two bad sons of bitches in this county; me and that nigger C. O. Chinn." Many whites in notoriously racist Madison County feared Chinn. CORE field secretary Mateo "Flukie" Suarez, who worked in Canton at the time, said of Chinn, "Every white man in that town knew you didn't fuck with C. O. Chinn. He'd kick your natural ass."

Chinn had earned his reputation early in life. He had grown up in a family of small, independent farmers, and although they did not have much money, he did not work for white people. One day a white farmer approached his mother and told her that Chinn needed to find work with a white person or leave the county. When she told her son about it, he went to the farmer, armed with a .38-caliber pistol, and told him to stay out of Chinn family affairs, thereby establishing his reputation as a "crazy Negro," a "dangerous Negro."

Chinn was one of the movement's most unusual stalwarts. He was an entrepreneur, and his business concerns included a 152-acre farm, Canton's Club Desire (one of Mississippi's major rhythm-and-blues nightclubs), a bootlegging operation, and other enterprises that skirted and occasionally crossed the line of legality. Chinn, his daughter-in-law Mamie Chinn explains, "was always fearless." She remembers her mother-in-law, Minnie Lou Chinn, telling her years later, "My husband never been no nonviolent man. He'd fit [fight] the devil out of Hell if he had to." Chinn's son Clarence elaborates, "He was raised to believe that you were supposed to work hard, treat everyone right, respect everybody but take no mess off nobody, regardless of color."

When Dennis first met Chinn (just a few months before the incident in the courthouse), it was also the first time he encountered the reality that guns were inescapably going to be part of his and CORE's grassroots organizing projects. Although Dennis was never committed to nonviolence as a way of life, he had organized nonviolent CORE chapters and protests in his home state of Louisiana. As CORE's project director for Mississippi, he had sent organizers to Canton. On his first visit to Canton, George Raymond, the project director Dennis had sent there, told him that he had a problem with Chinn bringing his guns around movement activities.

Nonviolence was more deeply embedded in CORE than in SNCC. CORE had roots in Christian pacifist activism that went back to World War I through the Fellowship of Reconciliation, and CORE's local chapters were bound more tightly to their national headquarters than were SNCC field secretaries and the community organizations they developed. Commitment to nonviolence was mandatory in CORE chapters. SNCC did not even develop chapters; there was no SNCC membership card and, unlike the NAACP, SNCC required no dues. SNCC had staff who were "field secretaries," not members. As historian Emily Stoper notes, "Nowhere was there a pamphlet stating authoritatively 'this is what you must believe to be a SNCC member.'"

Most of the organizers in Madison County, including Raymond himself, had come over from the very strong CORE chapter in New Orleans at Dave Dennis's request, and they were heavily invested in the idea of nonviolence. As with many other members of southern CORE chapters, key leaders of New Orleans CORE were trying to embrace nonviolence as a way of life. Some members fasted in preparation for nonviolent protest and followed CORE's rules for action, pledging to "meet the anger of any individual or group in the spirit of good will." They also pledged that they would "submit to assault and not retaliate in kind by act or word." Except for the Nashville,

Tennessee, group, this commitment was much stricter than anything found in the campus protest groups associated with SNCC.

Although, as Chinn's wife had noted, he "never been no nonviolent man," he admired the young civil rights organizers who had come to Madison County. As CORE field secretary Suarez remembers,

> [Chinn] believed we were doing the right thing and felt he should be supporting us and providing us with a certain amount of protection. Everything he had was just put at our disposal. There was never a time you needed to go someplace that he didn't assign somebody to go with you. He was his own man in his own mold. I don't think there were many parts [of him] that came from somewhere else.

George Raymond, who was committed to nonviolence as a way of life, was uncomfortable with Chinn's guns. So, as a meeting at a local church got underway during Dave Dennis's first visit to Canton, Raymond asked him to step outside and talk to Chinn. "Whenever we have a meeting," Dennis later remembered Raymond telling him, "C. O. Chinn sits outside with his guns. He won't leave. He says he's here to protect his people. Can you talk to him?" So, Dennis recalled,

> I went outside to talk to him. He's sitting in the back of his truck with a shotgun across his lap and a pistol by his side. I introduced myself; told him about CORE's nonviolent philosophy. He listened. Then, very calmly he told me: "This is my town and these are my people. I'm here to protect my people and even if you don't like this I'm not going anywhere. So maybe *you* better leave." I could tell he wasn't a guy for any bull and I could tell he was there to do what he said he was going to do. I didn't argue. I said, "Yes, sir," and shook his hand then walked back into the church thinking, he's got his job to do and I've got mine.

To Dennis, who had not wholly committed himself to the philosophy of nonviolence, Chinn's insistence on his right to defend himself and his community was reasonable enough. But as more organizers like Raymond encountered local men and women like Chinn, their perspectives on armed self-defense slowly began to change.

Everywhere they worked in the rural South, CORE organizers were finding that black people were not going to abandon the practice of armed self-defense, and thus the same transformations were occurring among CORE members as in SNCC. Unlike the people they met when they were students and leading sit-ins and Freedom Rides, the older people in rural counties and parishes (as they are called in Louisiana) made it clear that they were not going to commit to the nonviolent way of life advocated in the philosophies of Martin Luther King Jr. or Mohandas Gandhi. Most of the local people attracted to the movement were—like Chinn in Madison County, E. W. Steptoe in Amite County, or Janie Brewer in Tallahatchie County—seeking change and justice, which they often summed up in a single word: "freedom." They were willing and even eager to participate in the movement, but they were unwilling to give up their right to make their own decisions about how best to protect themselves and their communities, although they were always willing to consider concerns of "the nonviolents" now living with them.

Consequently, by 1964 CORE—at least its field staff—found itself reconsidering just how applicable nonviolence was to its work in the rural South. And as CORE expanded its work in Louisiana where it was making its biggest effort, the organization's relationship with weapons and self-defense quite unexpectedly took a significant turn.

Most of the CORE organizers in Louisiana had been born in the state. Most had quit school and, like SNCC's organizers, had taken on the challenge of voter registration in rural areas. But in Louisiana they had also begun organizing nonviolent direct actions to test compliance with the 1964 Civil Rights Act, which made it illegal to deny access to public accommodations. Unlike in Mississippi, some of these actions took place in rural Louisiana. These areas were not the Louisiana of Mardi Gras or sophisticated Creole cuisine, nor were they neighborhoods like the New Orleans Garden District. In fact, most of rural Louisiana was a far cry from the relatively comfortable urban campuses that many of the CORE organizers had recently left. As Jack Newfield once wrote of Amite County, Mississippi, rural Louisiana was, in many ways, far removed from the twentieth century itself.

CORE's efforts in these areas were immediately met with coordinated police and Klan violence. In Plaquemine, Louisiana, the seat of Iberville Parish near Baton Rouge, nonviolent protesters found themselves attacked by mounted state policemen, who hurled tear-gas canisters and then charged their horses into the ranks of demonstrators approaching the parish courthouse. In this parish the Ku Klux Klan literally hunted CORE national director James Farmer, who had to be smuggled out of the area in a hearse. Farmer's terrifying experience in Plaquemine seems to have caused him to question his own beliefs and to begin seriously, if privately, reconsidering the place of nonviolence and self-defense in the southern movement. The driver of the hearse and his companion were both armed and had been given explicit orders by community leaders: "Don't stop for anything and, if forced to stop, shoot."

Officially, Farmer and CORE remained firmly committed to nonviolence. Increasingly, however, many local blacks involved with the organization were arming themselves in response to violent onslaughts by white supremacists. In a January 1964 field report, one CORE organizer—who was still committed to nonviolence—wrote, "[Education] was needed to cement the relation between CORE and the people of West Feliciana Parish. The idea of nonviolence is a new one, and will require much discussion and training, especially for the older people." CORE began nonviolence-training workshops in the area, but they had no more success in persuading older residents to that seismic change in attitude than Dave Dennis had with Chinn in Canton or that Bob Moses had with Steptoe in Amite County. For instance, Reverend Joseph Carter made several attempts to register to vote in West Feliciana Parish. When he finally succeeded, he kept a shotgun nearby at night to protect himself and his neighbors. "I value my life even more since I became a registered voter," Carter explained. "If they want a fight, we'll fight."

In Louisiana gun use was more thoroughly integrated into the civil rights struggle than in most places in the South. This was due in part to the influence of a highly organized armed self-defense group: the Deacons for Defense and Justice. Nowadays, the Deacons barely appear in study and discussion of the southern Freedom Movement, but they were heavily armed and defiantly outspoken about their willingness to shoot back when fired upon. They were committed to protecting the nonviolent movement, but their involvement caused some contention in the movement. Some in the movement felt there was a practical rationale for opposing such groups: namely, that they invited swift, brutal, and overwhelming retaliation by all levels of government. Yet CORE's Louisiana experience seems to refute that assumption, as well as the argument that organized armed self-defense was incompatible with nonviolence; in fact, CORE organizers helped create the Deacons.

The emergence of a group like the Deacons was also due in part to Louisiana's uniqueness among the southern states. So-called racial purity, and the segregation and white supremacy intended to preserve it, was more distorted by the state's history than was the case elsewhere. Latin and Catholic influences made the southernmost part of the state unlike any other area in the South. Most of those enslaved in Louisiana came directly from Africa, and strong African retentions helped cultivate a Creole culture of unique racial intermixture and interaction. Even the racist and demagogic Huey Long, who served as governor from 1928 to 1932, once cracked with more truth than untruth that it would take only "a nickel's worth of red beans and a dime's worth of rice" to feed all of the "pure whites" in Louisiana. Discovery of oil, and with it the establishment of oil refineries and petrochemical plants, contributed to the state's difference by making Louisiana more urban than any other southern state. That led to unions and union agitation. In some places, music, ranging from jazz and New Orleans rhythm and blues to zydeco, and the New Orleans Carnival tradition of masquerading, parading, and street culture made it less difficult or dangerous to cross racial lines than in other parts of the South. There is certainly no shortage of antiblack violence in the state's history, and large areas of the state were exactly like neighboring Mississippi in attitude: the Florida Parishes east of the Mississippi River and south of the Mississippi state line, the Red River Valley where Colfax is located, and especially North Louisiana, the "top of the boot" where virtually all of the early-twentieth-century lynching in the state took place. But there is also no shortage of examples of black resistance to the vicious and violent white supremacy that continued to prevail in Louisiana as CORE organizers began their work.

———

Organized armed resistance began in the 1960s in the small North Louisiana town of Jonesboro, lying about fifty miles southwest of Monroe. The Deacons for Defense originated there within the context of CORE organizing. Jonesboro, the seat of Jackson Parish, was a demographically complex town whose population had been shaped by two large migrations. One was an exodus by poor whites seeking opportunity and an escape from drought and the depleted soil of southeastern Louisiana after the Civil War. The sandy soil in this part of North Louisiana was not much good for farming either, and the best land in the area was already owned by well-off farmers, but these impoverished whites somehow scratched out a subsistence living. The other was the relocation of large numbers of Black people fleeing plantations, the memory of chattel slavery, and the plantation-based debt peonage that had become a new form of slavery. Poor as the soil was, there were no plantations on it, and many of these Afro-Americans were enticed by the prospect of finding a piece of land here—little, perhaps, and barely farmable, but well out of the sight of white people. Indeed, one of the characteristics that came to define the black people living in and around Jonesboro was an independence of spirit.

At the opening of the twentieth century, Jonesboro's surrounding pine forests had also attracted timber companies and paper mills. The Continental Can Company paper mill and the Olin Mathieson Chemical Company were the main employers, hiring many of the town's residents, but most people nevertheless lived in abject poverty. In every respect, Jonesboro was a poorly serviced company town. By 1964, it had a population of about 4,000 people out of Jackson Parish's total population of about 16,000. Roughly a third of Jonesboro's inhabitants were black; they held only the most menial jobs. There was a strong Ku Klux Klan presence throughout the parish, and Jonesboro was strictly segregated.

But segregation also meant that there were a handful of black-owned businesses servicing Jonesboro's black community and a small black entrepreneurial class that lived a few notches above poverty. Some black enterprise even developed in contact with the town's white community, mostly through the use of rigs to haul pulpwood to paper mills. A black political leadership also developed and grew in influence. There were also black social networks—churches, teachers' associations, Prince Hall Masons, and the Benevolent and Protective Order of Elks (BPOE) among them. An NAACP chapter had been organized in Jackson Parish in the 1940s. In the 1950s, when Louisiana passed a law requiring the disclosure of NAACP membership, the chapter changed its name to the Jackson Parish Progressive Voters League. In 1956, when Jackson Parish's Citizens' Council conspired with the local voting registrar to remove black registrants from the voting rolls, the Voters League and the U.S. Department of Justice initiated and won a suit blocking the action and requiring the parish's registrar to make registration records available for review by a federal judge. And nearly a decade after the Voters League won its suit, a self-defense group sprouted up within Jonesboro's black community as well.

In late July 1964, just a few weeks after the passage of the 1964 Civil Rights Act, Ernest "Chilly Willy" Thomas and Frederick Douglass Kirkpatrick brought together a group of African American men in Jonesboro. Many were veterans of World War II or of the Korean War. Thomas and Kirkpatrick had assembled them to initiate a discussion of how best to meet increasing violence from the Ku Klux Klan. CORE had recently come to Jonesboro, and white supremacists had been launching attacks against the organizers and against black townsfolk.

CORE had been invited to Jonesboro by the Pleasant Grove Baptist Church, a more independent black church that was not overly concerned about the financial and physical dangers of supporting the growing civil rights movement. In early 1964, two organizers operating out of CORE's regional office in Monroe, Louisiana, began regularly visiting Jonesboro to assist the Voters League. One of the organizers, Mike Lesser, was northern, white, and inexperienced. The other was Ronnie Moore, a black native of New Orleans; in 1962 he had been expelled from Southern University for protesting segregation in Baton Rouge. By the time he made his first visit to Jonesboro, Moore had already been jailed eighteen times.

At the beginning of summer 1964, the first CORE volunteers began arriving in Jonesboro as part of the organization's 1964 Louisiana Summer Task Force. This effort was quite unlike Mississippi's 1964 Freedom Summer, in which antisegregation direct-action protests were discouraged and the focus was entirely on voter registration, "Freedom Schools" aimed at addressing the poor education found in public schools, and the development of the

Mississippi Freedom Democratic Party (MFDP). In Louisiana CORE also promoted nonviolent direct action against segregation and began testing the newly passed Civil Rights Act. Jonesboro student protesters regularly targeted the public library and the municipal swimming pool.

At first the CORE summer volunteers stayed with local black families, as was customary in the southern organizing tradition. Soon, however, a local supporter fixed up an empty dilapidated house so that CORE's young organizers could have a place of their own as their "freedom house"—their living quarters and operational headquarters. Jonesboro's black community "was unbelievably supportive," remembered Fred Brooks, a CORE volunteer who arrived in the town after finishing the spring semester at Tennessee A&I College in Nashville.

But as welcoming as their reception from Jonesboro's black community was, CORE organizers found themselves the target of white terrorism almost as soon as they arrived. Although they suffered minimal police harassment, recalled Brooks, the freedom house, with its nonviolent inhabitants, was more vulnerable than a private home, most of which were protected with guns. The Ku Klux Klan brazenly threatened the freedom house and its occupants. Klansmen regularly fired into the air around the house, shot through its windows, or drove by shouting threats. Picket lines and other protests also endured Klan harassment.

But Jonesboro's black community wanted the CORE activists in their town and had no intention of letting Klansmen run them off. So, a few men—Ernest "Chilly Willy" Thomas, then twenty-nine years old, among them—began to quietly guard the freedom house and its occupants. At first, they simply sat unarmed on the porch watching the street, shadowed CORE workers as they canvassed for voter registration, or placed themselves near picket-line protests. Their presence meant that no one was going to walk up to the civil rights workers and beat them up. But the efforts of Thomas and his companions also represented a middle ground. Thomas wanted to work with the CORE organizers, but he could not commit to nonviolence. And for their part, the CORE activists were reluctant to compromise their commitment to nonviolence. But the two groups were not as incompatible as they might seem. Thomas and his guardians simply found a way to assist the CORE activists short of the use of armed self-defense, at least temporarily.

Though at first Thomas and his guardians provided unarmed protection, before long they were watching over the CORE workers with concealed weapons. "What happened," Brooks related, "is that Chilly Willy and others told us that they understood the nonviolent method that we were using. And they said, 'O.K., you guys can be nonviolent, but we are *not* nonviolent and we are *not* going to allow these people to beat up on you or kill you.'" But Thomas and his group of local defenders did not join the CORE activists in nonviolent direct action. The discipline was impossible for them to accept. If they were spat upon or physically attacked in any way, they were not going to turn the other cheek, and they understood that *their* response would cause problems for CORE. Yet they saw no problem with standing on the sidelines and stepping in if someone threatened to harm the nonviolent activists. As Fred Brooks explained,

> If we had a picket line, these guys were standing on the corner, on both sides of the street. Any time we were having a demonstration these guys would be standing there on both sides of the street. Wherever we went it was like a caravan; these guys in their pickup trucks with those high-powered rifles up in the back. White people didn't mess with us. . . . They [the defenders] would come by at night and want to know what the next day's agenda was. Different ones of them took different patrols. They told us we were not to leave the black community without security.

Their protectiveness made quite an impression on Brooks, who was just eighteen years old when he went to Jonesboro and considered himself on the militant, cutting edge of the movement. "Many of these guys were older people! Old people!" he marveled later. "You couldn't be telling these people *anything* about security, self-defense, or protection. They were our parents." Still, among themselves, Brooks and his fellow CORE organizers argued heatedly about the armed protection they were receiving. Could it coexist with CORE's commitment to nonviolence? If so how? Adding urgency to this question was the steady growth of the Ku Klux Klan and Klan violence in 1963 and 1964. Louisiana's Original Knights of the Ku Klux Klan was closely related to Mississippi's White Knights of the Ku Klux

Klan; the Louisiana organization had, in fact, been born in Natchez, Mississippi. Samuel Bowers, the leader of the Klan group that had murdered CORE workers James Chaney, Michael Schwerner, and Andrew Goodman in Philadelphia, Mississippi, was from a prominent Louisiana family and had studied engineering at Tulane University in New Orleans.

The ranks of CORE's armed defenders were growing as white violence undermined the philosophy of nonviolence. Even some idealistic northern volunteers within CORE thought it unrealistic. "The concept that we are going to go South and through love and patience change the hearts and minds of Southern whites should be totally discarded," concluded one CORE activist in a discussion paper.

Some black leaders in Jonesboro sought official parish approval for organized self-defense, and for a moment they seemed to have gotten it. After discussion and negotiations with Jonesboro's police chief Adrian Peevy, Jackson Parish high school teacher and football coach Frederick Douglass Kirkpatrick organized a five-man, all-volunteer black "auxiliary" police squad to protect both the black community and the CORE activists. The police chief (and some of the town's more conservative blacks) may have hoped that Kirkpatrick's group would help prevent antisegregation protests. Chief Peevy even provided Kirkpatrick's group with an old police car, handcuffs, and a few other supplies.

Ernest Thomas, for his part, was suspicious of these new defenders, despite the fact that a couple of the men in his group were also part of Kirkpatrick's "police" squad. "They were looking for some black policemen to do their dirty work," he said later of the white authorities in Jonesboro. It did not take long, however, before continuing Ku Klux Klan violence and the black community's worsening relations with official law enforcement pushed Thomas's group and Kirkpatrick's group closer to each other.

One night in the summer of 1964, while driving back to Monroe from Jonesboro, Mike Lesser and CORE's regional director Ronnie Moore found themselves being chased by three cars filled with Klansmen. One of the cars passed Lesser and Moore and blocked the way forward. They made a sudden U-turn and headed back toward Jonesboro—and toward the other Klansmen, whose cars were now blocking the way back. Lesser, who was driving, pressed the accelerator to the floor, forcing the remaining Klansmen to veer away at the last minute, and Lesser and Moore narrowly escaped.

When they made it back to the CORE freedom house in Jonesboro, Lesser and Moore discovered that their ambushers had already filed a complaint with the local police. Jackson Parish sheriff Newt Loe ordered one of Kirkpatrick's black deputies to arrest the two CORE organizers, but the deputy refused. Instead, his fellow black deputies provided an armed escort for Moore and Lesser as they drove back to Monroe later that night.

The campaign against CORE intensified. Police and Klan harassment of CORE workers became routine. But something had changed. Jonesboro's blacks were proving themselves unwilling to stand idly by while whites threatened them and their guests—and now Thomas and his small crew were just the tip of the iceberg. One night later that summer, when whites came to the freedom house to harass and frighten CORE workers, Kirkpatrick and two of his black deputies scared the men off. Word spread throughout the black community that the retreating whites had threatened to come back with reinforcements. Soon dozens of armed men from Jonesboro's black community were in the streets. The threatened counterattack never came.

But Kirkpatrick was reaching the end of his patience with the white police force. The day after the incident at the freedom house, he became further alienated from them when, after refusing an order from Chief Peevy to arrest fifteen young black people protesting at Jonesboro's white-only municipal swimming pool, he watched white policemen arrest the youths anyway. The police chief also ordered two of the protesters' mothers arrested for "contributing to the delinquency of minors."

The tipping point came one night late in July 1964, when Jonesboro's assistant police chief led a fifty-car Ku Klux Klan caravan through the town's black neighborhood. Instead of firing from their car windows, the Klansmen threw leaflets denouncing the "outside agitators" and desegregation efforts in Jonesboro. Although they could have done far worse, Thomas still sped to Chief Peevy's house and demanded to know why the police had escorted Klansmen through the neighborhood. The chief said that sometimes the department escorted funerals and that he considered the Klan caravan to be the same thing. Thomas later claimed to have bluntly told the chief that if another Klan convoy ever came through the black community, "there was going to be some killing going on."

Elsewhere in the parish on the same night, white night riders burned crosses and an armed white mob converged on the parish jail where local protesters and CORE organizers were being held. The evening seems to have pushed Kirkpatrick over the edge, convincing him that his black auxiliary police unit was at best a useless tool and at worst a pawn in the hands of white power.

A few days later, some twenty men from both Thomas's and Kirkpatrick's groups met to discuss the best ways to protect Jonesboro's black community. Kirkpatrick himself chaired the meeting. Its attendees vowed to never again be caught unprepared, as they had been when the Klan caravan rode through their neighborhood. They resolved to protect the CORE freedom house, and—most important—to supplement Kirkpatrick's black police auxiliary with an organized group independent of local police authority, a group that would provide security to the black community without any association with the police.

The group had no name or formal organization at this point, but the galvanizing effect on the black community of even its immature presence became apparent shortly after this meeting when Klansmen attempted to burn a cross in the yard of Reverend Y. D. Jackson's rural home. When the Klansmen put a torch to the wooden cross, shots rang out and drove them away. Jackson's wife had opened fire on them. And before the end of 1964 Jonesboro's emerging defensive movement would coalesce even further— urged on, ironically, by the local CORE group, and particularly by a white organizer named Charlie Fenton.

Fenton's life experiences had already marked him as a fervent advocate of nonviolence. At seventeen he had joined the navy, where he became a medical corpsman on the assumption that he would not have to carry a weapon. When he was informed that navy regulations required him to be armed, he refused, earning himself two weeks in the brig. He became an activist in San Francisco, then joined CORE in Louisiana. In 1964, after a month's training in Plaquemine, Fenton was assigned to the CORE project in Monroe. He wound up spending most of that summer in jail. In November he joined the CORE project in Jonesboro. It was there that he first encountered guns in the local movement.

Fenton had become a part of CORE in order to engage in nonviolent struggle, so the presence of guns alongside—and sometimes on the persons of—civil rights workers was a complete surprise. When he arrived at the Jonesboro freedom house, he later recalled, "I got out of the car and realized that I was surrounded, *absolutely surrounded* in an armed camp. They were on top of roofs, they were under the building . . . they were all around the building." Although he was impressed, Fenton later remembered, "I was not very happy." Like most CORE workers who had come from outside the South (and especially those who were white), Fenton was utterly committed to nonviolence, and he could not conceive of compromising his ideals for the sake of mere safety.

It did not take Fenton long, however, to realize that the armed men were a necessary part of the project in Jonesboro and that people like himself had little or no influence over their decisions to possess and use weapons. As if to drive that point home, local black CORE supporters assigned a bodyguard to protect Fenton, and there was little he could do about it.

Although he remained committed to the goal of building a nonviolent civic organization in Jonesboro, Fenton also began to suggest that the men protecting him and his fellow CORE workers formally organize themselves. "Fenton was the one who sat down and said, 'We need to provide some structure—president, secretary, treasurer—some organization,'" Fred Brooks recalled. "And that's what they did, although nothing really changed in terms of what they were doing to protect us."

Although others from CORE were involved in the organization of Jonesboro's black defenders, it was Fenton who primarily encouraged and arranged the November 1964 meeting at Jonesboro's Masonic Hall that led to formation of a "protective association"—which in practical terms meant a merger between Thomas's group and Kirkpatrick's auxiliary police. The participants were nervous and uncertain, fretting over the possibility of police spies, organizational issues like whether or not there should be dues, and the dangers inherent in being a visible organization. But they did agree to meet again to talk some more, and a series of Tuesday-night meetings followed.

On January 5, 1965, the organization that would call themselves the Deacons for Defense and Justice was formally incorporated. For the first time anywhere in the South, representatives of a national civil rights organization had played a role in creating a group for the express purpose of providing armed self-defense. The CORE organizers, predictably, were still torn; as Fenton told the *New York Times* in February, he still believed in nonviolence, and he acknowledged that Jonesboro's Deacons had difficulty understanding why he did not want them bringing weapons into the office. "I hope that they will become a civic organization," he told *Times* reporter Fred Powledge, "bettering the community and eventually making the defense part of it obsolete . . . but still no one can tell what would have happened here if the Deacons hadn't formed their own ideas of protection."

The national civil rights establishment was rattled by this development in Jonesboro. Before the formation of the Deacons for Defense and Justice, CORE, SNCC, and SCLC had consciously steered clear of any public show of support for the idea of using arms, defensively or otherwise. Only Robert Williams had organized an armed group, and he had done so against the wishes of his national headquarters; moreover, no outside organizers had helped create Williams's rifle club. CORE's national office was hostile to the practice of armed self-defense in its project areas, even when organized by local people. Now in Jonesboro an organized armed group had taken shape with the assistance of some of its staff.

The tension between the national CORE office and organizers in the field increased markedly as news spread of the Deacons' formation. As Dave Dennis recounted later, "We were telling [CORE's national leadership] that we were committed to these people and you take people where they are." Richard Haley, CORE's southern regional director, was even more explicit in his support for the armed defenders. "The Deacons have the effect of lowering the minimum potential for danger," he told *New York Times* reporter Roy Reed. "That is a valuable function that CORE can't perform." The Deacons, Haley further explained, actually helped secure the place of nonviolence in the southern movement. "Protected nonviolence," he observed, "is apt to be more popular with the participants than unprotected."

Some people at CORE's national headquarters in New York were more tolerant of organizers' alignment with the Deacons than was apparent on the surface. There was growing internal tension around race in both CORE and SNCC, as nonviolence and the achievement of integration and even desegregation became less important goals than the development of a strong black consciousness or self-awareness and self-reliance in black communities. Many in CORE's younger black leadership appreciated the challenges of organizing in some of the most violent areas of the South, and as a result, they were increasingly sympathetic to the idea of self-defense and accepting of its legitimacy. More and more, nonviolence seemed like a luxurious abstraction, an idea remote from the harsh reality in which organizers lived. They faced threats and attacks on a daily basis and were under pressure from black people in the communities where they worked to support the practice—if not the underlying principle—of armed self-defense absent any other reliable source of protection.

Protection was not forthcoming from any of the local or national agencies with the power to provide it. As late as the summer of 1964, when the projects of both SNCC and CORE in Mississippi and Louisiana were under constant violent attack, Attorney General Robert Kennedy and the Johnson administration were insisting that they had no authority to intercede and no way to protect organizers, their local allies, or local black communities from violence.

By the time of CORE's July 1965 convention in Durham, North Carolina, the organization's Resolutions and Constitution Committee seemed prepared to rescind its commitment to nonviolence. Ernest Thomas from Jonesboro addressed the meeting and emphasized that the Deacons recognized the use—even the necessity—of nonviolence in demonstrations and tests of the 1964 Civil Rights Act ordering desegregation. CORE's traditional rules, he thought, were appropriate for such demonstrations. However, Thomas told the conference, even at these demonstrations the Deacons were willing and prepared to use their guns for self-defense and to protect protesters if necessary. Earlier in the convention, James Farmer had acknowledged the right to self-defense, citing its value in Louisiana though still arguing that guns should not be used at protests.

The convention did not abandon its commitment to nonviolence, but the organization clearly was in a state of transition. One resolution would have required that a majority of the leadership of CORE chapters be black; it was not passed, but it was discussed seriously. A year later, at the 1966 convention, attendees repealed the nonviolent clause from the organization's constitution. Representatives of the Nation of Islam had been invited to speak at that convention.

SNCC was evolving, too. In 1966 Stokely Carmichael was elected chairman, replacing John Lewis, who had been committed to nonviolence as a way of life ever since his college days in Nashville. Carmichael, on the other hand, had long argued for the legitimacy and necessity of self-defense. During the June 1964 meeting in Atlanta called to discuss remaining preparations for the soon-to-begin Freedom Summer in Mississippi, the question arose of whether SNCC would support a staff worker who picked up a gun to help defend the family with whom he or she was staying. The attendees quickly decided that SNCC would indeed provide support, although carrying weapons would still be out-of-bounds. "I think it's best to discuss the controllable things," said Bob Moses, apparently trying to swing the discussion back toward the practicalities of organizing for the pending Freedom Summer. "I don't know if anyone in Mississippi preached to local Negroes that they shouldn't defend themselves," he added. "Probably the closest is when I asked Mr. E. W. Steptoe not to carry guns when we go together at night. So, instead he just hides his gun, and then I find out later."

SNCC workers, it soon became clear, were not handling firearms just when their host families were under attack. Following the Atlanta meeting, SNCC's Mississippi staff met in Holly Springs, Mississippi, and the conversation once again turned to the question of carrying guns. The attendees reaffirmed the Atlanta decision not to carry guns, but when Stokely Carmichael asked who was carrying a gun at that moment, about a dozen were produced.

These discussions about SNCC workers' need and right to armed self-defense were relatively minor compared to the larger and more serious debate about the group's purpose, political direction, and relationships with other civil rights organizations. Few outside SNCC even knew of the group's internal discussions about armed self-defense. Much the same can be said about CORE.

CORE's shift in attitude on self-defense was more noticeable than SNCC's, perhaps because CORE's deeper roots in the philosophy of nonviolence made the shift more apparent—and perhaps also because newspaper coverage brought national attention to the Deacons and their involvement with the civil rights group. In 1968, when he was no longer CORE's national director, Farmer reflected on CORE's transformation in his introduction to Inge Powell Bell's book *CORE and the Strategy of Non-*

violence. Farmer wrote of his terrifying 1963 experience when he had been forced to flee Plaquemine because the Ku Klux Klan was hunting him to kill him. That moment, Farmer claimed, had altered CORE's history: "CORE nonviolence—never a way of life, but only a strategy—ended on a balmy night, September 1, 1963, in a sleepy town on the Mississippi [River]," he wrote, "when a uniformed mob screamed for my blood. . . . The casket-less hearse in which I escaped, became for CORE a symbol of the burial of peace." The same year Farmer wrote those words, CORE limited partici-pation by whites in the group, adopted a new constitution, and declared itself a Black Nationalist organization.

The Deacons, however, had as profound an influence on CORE's think-ing as did white-supremacist violence. In Jonesboro, the Deacons settled on their officers and structure before reaching a firm decision about their name. Percy Lee Bradford, a paper-mill worker and cab owner who had also been one of Kirkpatrick's auxiliary policemen, was elected president. Henry Amos, who had also been an auxiliary policeman, was elected vice president. Ernest Thomas was employed as an organizer. All members had to be U.S. citizens at least twenty-one years old, of good moral character, and preferably registered to vote. The group decided on a membership fee of ten dollars and monthly dues of two dollars. Members would supply their own rifles, but the organization would provide ammunition, bought in bulk. Most of the founding members possessed shotguns and pistols, not rifles. Thomas thought the group's firearms should be standardized, and he favored .30 M1 carbines and .38 Special revolvers.

How individual Deacons participated varied. There were "four tiers of membership in the Jonesboro Deacons," writes Lance Hill,

> a structure that would be reproduced in other chapters. The first tier, the "activist core," comprised approximately 20 members who paid dues and regularly attended meetings and participated in patrols. The second tier, "active members," consisted of about 100 men who occasionally paid dues and attended meetings but usu-ally took part in activities only when necessary. The third tier, the "reinforcements," comprised roughly 100–200 men who did not pay dues or attend meetings but agreed with the Deacons' strategy and could be depended on to volunteer if needed. The fourth, and

most amorphous, tier contained the "self-proclaimed" Deacons: those individuals who, without official sanction, declared themselves to be Deacons. Though lacking formal ties to the organization, this fourth tier helped popularize the Deacons and their self-defense strategy. In Jonesboro, total dues-paying members never exceeded 150.

The Deacons were overwhelmingly male, although there does not seem to have been a formal ban on women members. Women had not participated in the armed patrols, but they had been active participants in Jonesboro and Jackson Parish's civil rights struggle. Several women, among them Ruth Amos, the wife of the Deacons' vice president, Henry Amos, participated in some of the new group's meetings; there were also rumors that some women engaged in target practice. And there was some discussion—which eventually came to naught—of forming a women's auxiliary—"Deaconettes." This gender distinction was more the result of cultural habit than of any explicit organizational decision to prohibit the involvement of women, and it began to erode as female CORE workers became more involved in the group. And after CORE left Jonesboro, women were central to the local base of movement activists who continued to fight for change in the region.

The Deacons incorporated on March 5, 1965, as the "Deacons for Defense and Justice"—the precise reason for that choice of name is unclear. Some of the founding members may have actually been church deacons. When asked, Dave Dennis noted, "A number of these men were church-going folk, so people may have just begun calling them 'the Deacons'" as a result. Kirkpatrick, who later in his life launched a folk-singing career, wrote and recorded "The Deacons," a song in which he offers a more calculated explanation:

> Let's call ourselves the Deacons and never have no fear
> They will think we are from the church
> Which has never done much
> And gee, to our surprise it really worked.

Kirkpatrick lost his job at the local high school because of his involvement with the Jonesboro movement. He had used his influence as a football coach to encourage students to get involved in protests, but his role in establishing the Deacons was the final straw. His dismissal, as it turned out, would trigger one of the earliest confrontations between the Deacons and Jonesboro authorities.

On March 8 students organized a boycott of the high school to protest Kirkpatrick's dismissal, as well as other inequities. One of their demands was for black control of black schools—an unusual request at that time, given the national civil rights establishment's calls for desegregation and integration. It was yet another illustration that the Jonesboro movement was very much a local one, guided by local concerns.

Students began to picket the school daily. One cold day, as they were picketing, police on the scene called in a fire truck. Ernest Thomas and four Deacons had also shown up, as they did every day the students picketed. They stepped out of their car and immediately began loading their shotguns. When firemen began walking to the school with hoses, apparently planning to break up the protest, Thomas—as much the Deacons' field commander as their organizer—barked out orders: "Men, take firing positions and prepare to open fire!" One of the Deacons, deadly serious, told one of the policemen, "If you turn those water hoses on these kids there's gonna be some blood out here today." The Deacons' show of force seems to have worked, for the firemen soon departed.

Such armed resistance did not go unpunished, however. After the face-off at the high school, police blocked the roads into and out of Jonesboro's black neighborhood. On one occasion, Thomas was arrested at gunpoint for attempting to pass a roadblock to reach protesters picketing the school. He was held incommunicado for twenty-four hours before being released. But the Deacons had made their point. They had stood up to Jonesboro's white authorities with their guns. And they had won the battle—if not yet the war.

———

The Deacons began to reach outside Jonesboro and even beyond Jackson Parish. They first extended their efforts into other parts of Louisiana, and then into a few other parts of the South, mainly Mississippi.

Organizing people and communities for voter registration and nonviolent protest was one thing, but organizing to provide self-defense was something else entirely. The Deacons were unprecedented. Although there were other local self-defense groups (often taking the form of neighborhood or community watches) and although individual acts of protection and self-defense, like those of C. O. Chinn, Hartman Turnbow, and E. W. Steptoe, were not uncommon, there was no *incorporated* self-defense organization before the Jonesboro Deacons. Furthermore, the Deacons were a formally organized *political* movement that by its very existence directly challenged the civil rights establishment's approach of nonviolently appealing to sympathy and goodwill, both of people and of the government. The Deacons were not beholden to any other organization, not even CORE. Their willingness to strategically use weapons sharply differentiated them from the black middle-class institutions and liberal institutional funders who dominated national civil rights organizations—and this helped them to appeal to an entirely new segment of the black population in the South.

The Deacons' first major outreach took place in the city of Bogalusa in Washington Parish, Louisiana. Bogalusa differed from Jonesboro in almost every respect. Almost 250 miles southeast of Jonesboro and about 60 miles north of New Orleans, it sits on the Mississippi–Louisiana border and had three times the population of Jackson Parish. A tough sawmill town, Bogalusa was dominated by the Crown Zellerbach paper mill. It was an ugly, violent place that, like the steel city of Birmingham, Alabama, dubbed itself "Magic City." It was also one of the South's staunchest bastions of white supremacy. Author Howell Raines characterized Bogalusa as having "no redeeming touch of grace, beauty, or elegance to surprise the eye or rest the spirit." In the 1960s the city had more Ku Klux Klan members per capita than any city or town in Louisiana. Klansmen held offices in city government. Klan headquarters were at the fire station across from city hall. They assaulted and terrorized blacks and any whites who did not share their bigotry. Bogalusa's sawmill and a logging pond separated the black and white communities. The city was, as one local judge put it, "segregated from cradle to coffin."

In 1965, when Brooks Hays—former Arkansas congressman and former president of the Southern Baptist Convention, but at the time a special assistant to President Lyndon Johnson troubleshooting racial problems—was preparing to come to Bogalusa to address a group of white and black community leaders, the Ku Klux Klan went door-to-door handing out leaflets that threatened retaliation against any white person who attended the proposed meeting with Hays. The leaflets said in part that those attending the meeting would be "tagged as integrationists and . . . dealt with accordingly by the Knights of the Ku Klux Klan." Half a dozen crosses were burned on the lawn of the proposed meeting place, St. Matthews Episcopal Church. The church canceled the meeting, and Bogalusa's mayor, Jesse H. Cutrer Jr., turned down a request for Hays to speak at city hall. Bogalusa's white-supremacist terrorism would die a slow death.

Although Bogalusa seemed an unlikely place for the emergence of one the South's most militant movements, what appeared to be black submission to white supremacy hid surprising strength. Black farmers owned their own land and were largely self-sufficient. There was a black farmers' league. In 1950, with NAACP help, blacks had opened up voter-registration rolls, and in 1960, with NAACP help again, they beat back an attempt to purge black voters. The Crown Zellerbach plant was unionized, and workers, black and white alike, belonged to one of two unions: the United Papermakers and Paperworkers Union or the International Pulp, Sulfite, and Paper Union. Both maintained segregated locals, but the all-black locals, though small in membership, were seedbeds for the growth of organizing skills. In 1956, when the Louisiana legislature passed legislation aimed at destroying the NAACP, the Bogalusa Civic and Voters League (BCVL) was formed.

Local activists in Bogalusa began testing compliance with the 1964 Civil Rights Act. They were dissatisfied with the quiet, accommodating negotiations of the BCVL's cautious leadership. CORE, which was most active in Louisiana, could not ignore Bogalusa, and it began investigating the possibility of working in Bogalusa. On February 1, 1965, two CORE organizers based in New Orleans attended a meeting in Bogalusa during which the older BCVL leadership was replaced by a new, younger group of local blacks. A. Z. Young, a World War II veteran and a leader in the segregated union at the paper mill, became president. Robert Hicks, another union leader, became vice president. After the meeting, Hicks invited the two workers to spend the night at his home.

Dinner and sleep should have been the program for the rest of the night. Instead, Bogalusa's police chief, Claxton Knight, and one of his deputies visited the Hickses' home. The chief told the Hickses that the Klan was angry that the CORE workers—both of whom were white—were staying in a black home. A Klan mob, he warned, was gathering and intended to attack Hickses' house unless their two guests were immediately escorted out of town by police. Mrs. Hicks, Valeria "Jackie" Hicks, was adamant, however; the CORE workers were going to stay with them. The chief left, refusing to provide protection. "We have better things to do than protect people who aren't wanted here."

Robert Hicks told his daughter Barbara to telephone for help, and soon men with rifles and shotguns began filling the house; the Klan attack never took place. A few weeks later, Hicks invited leaders of the Jonesboro Deacons to Bogalusa. By that time, he had his own bodyguard. "My husband could never go out without someone protecting him," recalled Valeria years later.

> They would carry him to work and pick him up at the end of the day. There was always someone in the house. It was the only form of protection we had. At one point [the police] tried to take the guns away from us, but they couldn't. We had the right to bear arms; we had the right to protect ourselves. But it was so unusual for Black men to stand up for their rights.

The men guarding Hicks and his wife were not yet a formally organized group, but they were committed, and they extended their protection to the Hickses' guests. The two CORE workers realized this for themselves a few days after their arrival. Returning to New Orleans from Bogalusa, they noticed that they were being followed. They turned into one of Bogalusa's black communities to try to make a phone call, but the men who had been following them—a carful of white supremacists, almost certainly Klansmen—attacked. The CORE workers finally escaped into a small, black-owned café, where they made frantic calls as whites circled the block in their cars. Soon, armed black men began slipping in through the café's back door. Perhaps aware that the two men they were chasing now had armed protection, the pursuers disappeared as the sun set. Both CORE activists were pacifists, but the experience left them uncertain about their own convictions. "Up to that point I embraced nonviolence," one of them, Steve Miller, said later. "[But] at the point [that armed protection came] I guess I said, 'Oh, I guess I'm not nonviolent anymore.'" Concealed in the backseat of a car, the two rode back to the Hicks home protected by an armed convoy.

The defense of the Hicks and their white guests marked the beginning of the Deacons in Bogalusa. These new black voices would attract the attention of like-minded individuals and would strengthen the relationship between Bogalusa's burgeoning self-defense organization and CORE's expanding organizing in the state.

CORE's field secretaries encouraged self-defense-minded blacks to meet with the Jonesboro Deacons. On February 21, Thomas and Kirkpatrick drove to Bogalusa, where that night at the Negro Union Hall they met with fourteen local men, including Hicks, who had been the primary local organizer of the meeting. Kirkpatrick and Thomas had come with pistols in their waistbands, and when they sat down, they placed their guns on the table. It turned out that everyone in attendance had brought pistols, and they too placed their guns on the table, where they remained in a large heap throughout discussion. It was a tense meeting. Kirkpatrick and Thomas continually challenged the group, stressing the need for secrecy, loyalty, and discipline. They described the way they used two-way radios and secret codes in Jonesboro and Jackson Parish, and they presented their vision of a statewide network of Deacons linked via two-way radio. Cheap, small-caliber weapons, such as .22-caliber pistols, were inadequate, they insisted, and the Bogalusa men would be better off with .30-06 rifles, shotguns, and other large weapons instead. They also urged the Bogalusa group to initiate discussions with middle-class black leaders, who, they said, could be helpful so long as they weren't shouted down and berated as "Uncle Toms." And lastly, Thomas and Kirkpatrick proposed that if a self-defense group was organized, it affiliate with the Jonesboro Deacons. Around midnight the Bogalusa men formed a Deacons chapter and agreed to an organizational meeting the following week. At that meeting, the group elected as its president Charles Sims, an insurance salesman and a legendary brawler.

It was natural for black people in Bogalusa to take into account the experience and expertise of the Jonesboro Deacons in considering how best to organize for their own protection. Articles about the Deacons had been appearing in such national newspapers as the *New York Times*, and in Louisiana's black communities—and probably in white communities too— word of mouth spread news about the Deacons even faster than the press coverage. Bogalusa, bigger and economically more important than Jones- boro, became a highly visible stage for the group.

With the Ku Klux Klan as powerful as it was in Bogalusa, the creation of a new chapter of the Deacons fueled further white-supremacist violence. But there is little doubt that the sight of openly armed black men frightened and confused many whites. The language the Deacons used was terrifying too— deliberately so. "It takes violent blacks to combat these violent whites," Thomas said. "It takes nonviolent whites and nonviolent Negroes to sit down and bargain whenever the thing is over—and iron it out. I ain't going to."

On May 23, 1965, Mayor Cutrer announced that all Bogalusa segrega- tion ordinances would be repealed; a remarkable if limited victory. It had been made possible by a movement that combined nonviolent struggle and armed self-defense to protect that struggle. The mayor was forced to take the business-sensitive, law-and-order middle ground; he was not renounc- ing his belief in white supremacy. He was not a changed man. "We must obey the law," Cutrer told Bogalusa's white townsfolk, "no matter how bitter the taste." Business, after all, was business. Income and image, important to attracting needed new businesses to the state, were at stake in Bogalusa, and Cutrer was under pressure from both corporate powers and Louisiana's state government to get Bogalusa and the Deacons off the front page.

Such sentiments and necessities did not sit well with some locals. Deadly antiblack danger had not been eliminated. On June 2, 1965, O'Neal Moore, who the year before had made local history by becoming the first black deputy sheriff in Washington Parish, was shot and killed while parked on the edge of Bogalusa in his patrol car—a crime that remains unsolved. His partner, Creed Rogers, the second black deputy hired by the parish, was also wounded and lost the sight of one eye.

CORE national director James Farmer traveled to Bogalusa for Moore's funeral, and he chose to accept protection from Bogalusa's Deacons for Defense rather than from local police, dramatically signaling CORE's sup- port for the Deacons. Sims, leader of the Bogalusa Deacons, picked Farmer up from New Orleans and drove him back to Bogalusa along with three other Deacons. All were armed.

"CORE is nonviolent," Farmer said later, explaining the organization's support for men like Sims and the Deacons. "But we have no right to tell Negroes in Bogalusa or anywhere else that they do not have the right to defend their homes. It is a constitutional right." But men like the Bogalusa Deacons were protecting more than just their own homes and more than national civil rights bigwigs like Farmer. "CORE had projects throughout this part of Louisiana," recalled Dave Dennis, who in 1965 became CORE's director of southern projects. "And the Deacons would tell us, 'Let us know when you're coming. We'll meet you.' When we met them, they would put two trucks in front and two behind. In those trucks were armed men. And you rode right through town into the black community." CORE field secretary Mateo Suarez remembers riding with the Jonesboro Deacons' leader Chilly Willy Thomas and another Deacon. "They were telling me how dangerous it was, wherever it was we were, but assuring me that they had guns. 'You don't need one,' they said."

SNCC, too, felt connected to the Deacons, although most of its organizers were never deeply involved with the group. James Forman, for one, considered the Deacons an outgrowth of his and other organizations' practice of nonviolent direct action. Student protesters who would form SNCC and those who would become the heart of CORE as well "were the forerunners of the Deacons for Defense," he wrote. Activism aimed at challenging white supremacy was going to trigger violent white reaction resulting in greater black militancy and thus greater need for protection; history showed that, Forman felt. "Given a nonviolent movement, the Deacons had to spring up."

———

CORE and SNCC were sympathetic to groups like the Deacons for Defense and Justice, though they were not organizationally bound to them. However, SCLC, led by Martin Luther King Jr., never came close to endorsing armed self-defense, even though as a black, southern organization it was impossible for King and his group of ministers to escape the currents that led to the formation of a group like the Deacons.

King had long been ambivalent about the idea of self-defense. After the 1956 bombing of his Montgomery, Alabama, home, he had persuaded his enraged neighbors to go home with their guns, even though he was then hardly committed to nonviolence and had guns in his home. If his wife, Coretta, or their daughter, Yolanda—both of whom had been in the house when the bomb went off—had been injured or worse in the explosion, who knows how he would have responded or who he might have become? Neither mother nor daughter was harmed, however, and soon King completely embraced nonviolence. He would eventually denounce the Deacons for what he called their "aggressive violence."

It may not be an overstatement to suggest that King was behind the curve of history on the question of self-defense. Across the South in the summer of 1964—the year the Jonesboro Deacons formed—groups and individuals were organizing for armed self-defense. Many of these groups took shape within the formally nonviolent civil rights movement. The passage of the Civil Rights Act that summer, like the 1954 Supreme Court *Brown* decision before it, had fueled the growth of the Ku Klux Klan, and the climate in the South was particularly hostile to the movement and to black people in general.

White-supremacist violence and black anger seemed to be erupting everywhere during the summer of 1964. On July 2, nine days after the Civil Rights Act was signed into law, U.S. Army Reserve officer Lieutenant Colonel Lemuel Penn was murdered by a three-man Ku Klux Klan "security patrol" while driving through Madison County, Georgia, on the way back home to Washington, D.C. He had just completed a training exercise at Fort Benning, Georgia. Earlier, one of the Klansmen had told his two accomplices, "I'm gonna kill me a nigger tonight."

Mississippi was particularly violent that summer. A month before Penn's murder, CORE workers Chaney, Schwerner, and Goodman had been murdered in Neshoba County. Their murders had a profound impact in Louisiana and may partly explain the involvement of Louisiana CORE workers with the Deacons. Two new station wagons had been donated to CORE that summer, one for Louisiana and one for Mississippi. The car carrying Chaney, Schwerner, and Goodman was one of them. Louisiana CORE workers could not help but feel especially connected to their murdered colleagues in Mississippi, says Fred Brooks.

Far from Louisiana and Mississippi, as early as 1963, the city of Cambridge on Maryland's Eastern Shore was occupied by the National Guard following violent clashes between blacks and whites during a summer of protest. Gloria Richardson, leader of the Cambridge Nonviolent Action Committee (CNAC), told *Ebony* magazine that her small city *and* the nation now faced a choice "between witnessing change or experiencing destruction. . . . The status quo is now intolerable to the majority of Negroes and may soon be intolerable to the majority of whites." The magazine dubbed her "the lady general of civil rights." After a dozen of his men were wounded, General George C. Geltson, commander of the guardsmen occupying Cambridge, considered replacing the blanks in their weapons with live ammunition. Of Richardson, he declared, "She's the only real leader in town." A spokesman for the Citizens' Council despaired, "We can't deal with her and we can't deal without her."

Meanwhile, in that same summer of 1964, St. Augustine, Florida—America's oldest city—was the scene of the most violent response to an SCLC campaign ever experienced by the organization, according to Andrew Young. During a night protest, Young was slugged, hit across the head with a blackjack, then kicked and stomped after he fell to the ground. Police did nothing. It was the first time Young had ever been beaten during a civil rights demonstration. By the time SCLC became involved in St. Augustine, its black community had weathered arrests, several bombings, and the Ku Klux Klan kidnapping of local movement leader Dr. Robert Hayling and three other local activists. It was Hayling who had invited King and SCLC to come into the city.

Despite the extreme violence that confronted them in St. Augustine, SCLC workers stuck to their nonviolent principles. Although tough black teenagers would sometimes place themselves at the end of protest marches, prepared to both defend marchers and retaliate against any violence by whites, nonviolence prevailed in St. Augustine, and there was no serious discussion of organizing the kind of self-defense group that existed in Louisiana. But sentiment in favor of armed self-defense was not far beneath the surface. SCLC staffer Dorothy Cotton noted, "This was about the roughest city we've had—45 straight nights of beatings and intimidation. In church every night we'd see people sitting there with bandages on. Some would sit with shotguns between their legs." Hayling had no problem with these gun-toting men and women, although he had taught methods of non-violent activism to students at his dental office. When a reporter asked him how he planned to respond to the continuing threats against his life and the lives of others, he replied, "I and the others have armed. We will shoot first and answer questions later. We are not going to die like Medgar Evers."

King's active, direct involvement in St. Augustine's movement undoubt-edly helped keep the protests there on a nonviolent course, but the story was different in Tuscaloosa, Alabama, that summer. In January 1964, Rev-erend T. Y. Rogers—who had been an assistant pastor at King's church in Montgomery—began pastoring the First African Baptist Church in Tuscaloosa. It was the city's oldest, largest, and most prestigious black church, and King had recommended Rogers to the church's search com-mittee. Rogers's admiration of King had led him to embrace nonviolence. He even imitated King's preaching style. But in Tuscaloosa, he found him-self having to reconcile his commitment to nonviolence with self-defense as never before.

Like Bogalusa, Tuscaloosa was a notorious Ku Klux Klan city. Located about fifty miles southwest of Birmingham, the city was then about one-third black, and it was also home to the University of Alabama. In 1956, after a three-year court battle, Autherine Lucy had become the first black person to enroll there. The white-supremacist violence that her bravery elicited and the response by Tuscaloosa's black community would set a precedent for the clashes of the following decade.

On Lucy's third day at the university, a mob of hundreds had jeered and pelted her with eggs as she walked to class. They might have killed her, but state policemen rescued her and took her to the nearby offices of a black newspaper, the *Alabama Citizen*. From there, the frightened, egg-splattered student was taken next door to Howard and Linton's Barbershop, where, in its back room, two beauticians consoled her while washing the egg out of her hair. She wanted to go home, but before she could leave the shop a carload of white hoodlums pulled up and continued taunting her from out-side the barbershop. Reverend T. W. Linton, one of Rogers's predecessors among the Tuscaloosa clergy and a co-owner of the barbershop, called the police, but no help came. Somehow he was able to get a shotgun from a friend across the street. His business partner, Nathaniel Howard, made a series of phone calls and arranged for a six-car caravan of armed black men to escort Lucy to the relative safety of nearby Birmingham. When the defenders arrived at the barbershop, the hoodlums fled. In a perverse irony, shortly thereafter Lucy was expelled from the University of Alabama because the school claimed—and successfully argued in court—that it could not guarantee her safety. Neither police nor university officials seem to have given much thought to how to actually do so.

This episode in 1956 marked the beginning of an armed network of black men in Tuscaloosa. For the rest of the decade, they would provide informal protection to the city's black community. But it also foreshadowed the armed protection that enabled the activism, especially student activism, that would shatter segregation in Tuscaloosa with unanticipated speed in the subsequent decade.

In the early 1960s students at Stillman College in Tuscaloosa, like the young people at most other historically black colleges and universities at the time, were caught up in the fervor of the sit-in movement and were mounting protests against white supremacy and segregation. By then the Ministers Alliance—a small group of young, socially conscious black ministers that had formed at First African Baptist Church in the mid-1950s—had evolved into the city's first civil rights organization, the Tuscaloosa Citizens for Action Committee (TCAC). The organization's president was Reverend Willie Herzfeld, who before coming to Tuscaloosa had advised the Greensboro students after their February 1960 sit-in. TCAC quickly affiliated with SCLC and, officially anyway, shared its commitment to nonviolence. But TCAC had received little support from the city's black community. When Rogers, who was deeply influenced by SCLC, arrived to pastor First African and almost immediately expressed his desire to press for civil rights, Herzfeld told him, "I'm tired. I have worked and they have not accepted me. . . . Maybe you are not tired and you can do something. Whatever you want to do, I'm with you in it."

Rogers breathed new life into the organization, and in April 1964 TCAC began a direct-action campaign in Tuscaloosa, first targeting segregation at the new county courthouse. On April 23 hundreds of protestors—most of them Stillman students—gathered at First African and marched downtown carrying signs that read, "Segregation Must Go." Rogers mounted the courthouse steps to read a statement, but police forced him off. However, he was not arrested—a sign, perhaps, that authorities in Tuscaloosa, having watched national reaction to the dogs and fire hoses used against protesters led by Martin Luther King in Birmingham the year before, were beginning to realize that a hard-line, abusive response to civil rights activism was counterproductive.

The TCAC campaign intensified over the next two months, launching a voter-registration drive and a boycott of downtown Tuscaloosa. Activists also established so-called Citizenship Schools to help potential voter registrants cope with Alabama's difficult and unfairly applied literacy requirements. Both King and his closest SCLC colleague, Ralph Abernathy, visited Tuscaloosa to meet with activists there, strengthening the connection between Tuscaloosa's protest movement and SCLC's nonviolent approach to struggle.

White resistance to the movement was growing, but among Tuscaloosa's black residents, there was growing unwillingness to back down in the face of intimidation. There were, of course, consequences. As the leader of the movement in Tuscaloosa, Rogers became the main target of white harassment, but he remained committed to nonviolence. His wife, LaPelzia Rogers, stood in sharp contrast to her soft-spoken husband. She gave as good as she and her husband got. "To tell you the truth," she said later, "I wasn't too nonviolent. I had a temper and I had a big mouth." Sometimes, when racist whites telephoned the Rogers household to berate or threaten her husband, LaPelzia would silence them with a harangue of her own. Her husband admitted later, "I felt sorrier for the people who called than I did for her. If she got a chance to talk to them, she talked to them worse than they talked to her. It stemmed some of the tide," he acknowledged, "because they finally reached the point, I guess, when they said, 'Well that lady's crazy, anyway, so there's no point in calling so much.'"

LaPelzia Rogers did not participate in demonstrations because her husband demanded strict adherence to nonviolence, to which she just could not agree. Thus, she was not present on June 9, 1964, when hundreds of demonstrators, the bulk of them students, gathered at First African, intending to march to the courthouse in defiance of Police Chief William Marable's prohibition on marches. Rogers began to lead the long column of marchers away from the church and toward the courthouse; Marable and a large number of policemen wearing blue helmets almost immediately stopped them. "Do you intend to continue marching?" the chief asked. "Yes," replied Rogers. The policemen promptly arrested him and the other TCAC leaders in the march.

Much worse soon followed. Police now blocked the marchers' way to the courthouse. A fire truck with high-pressure hoses sat nearby, awaiting orders, but was not used. The policemen suddenly assaulted the demonstrators with cattle prods, nightsticks, and their fists, pushing them back into the church. A group of teenagers allegedly threw some rocks; one of Marable's men fired a tear-gas canister into the church. Protesters broke church windows to let in air, so the police fired more tear gas into the building. Finally, the students poured out of the church; police arrested some of them and beat others in the street.

Tuscaloosa's black community was outraged. Although local blacks had not shown much support for the protests or even for the civil rights movement in general, they felt the police had crossed a line, desecrating their most prominent church and unfairly, brutally, and unnecessarily attacking their best and brightest young people. The response of many local blacks was telling: expecting more violence, they brought out their guns in order to protect themselves and their homes. Many of them were expecting the Ku Klux Klan to conduct drive-by shootings and did not intend to be caught unprepared. Moreover, the fact that most of the TCAC leadership was in jail did little to convince locals that nonviolent protest was sensible. In a revealing comment, one man—a factory worker who had brought his shotgun to First African after the police assault—explained later, "At that time, I wasn't a civil rights man . . . cause if anybody hit me I [was] gonna hit him back."

One particularly outraged Tuscaloosan was Joseph Mallisham, a native of the city and a Korean War veteran who was also a union organizer at Tuscaloosa's Ziegler meatpacking plant. Mallisham had been one of the men who rushed to the defense of Autherine Lucy at Howard and Linton's Barbershop. Later he helped establish the SCLC chapter in Tuscaloosa. Now, in this explosive atmosphere, Mallisham resolved to do something to focus and organize the community's anger.

He called together a small group of men—almost all of them World War II or Korean War veterans—to discuss armed self-defense, telling them, "If we're going to do this thing, let's do it right." He emphasized that the community needed organization and planning, not inchoate anger. The group discussed the possibility of retaliating against the police, but backed away from the idea in favor of a more constructive plan. Mallisham felt that if the police failed to perform their duties, someone else would have to do them; that if the police were going to let the Klan run rampant, someone else would have to stand up to it; that if men, women, and children were being beaten, someone else would have to stop it. The group all felt that these things required an organized group of black defenders.

The following night, another meeting was held. This one was much larger and involved a wider range of participants: factory workers, teachers, businessmen, and even young gang leaders. These diverse attendees resolved to create a new organization to safeguard Tuscaloosa's black residents. As far as is known, they chose no name for the group. It was not a mass movement; rather, it was limited to about a hundred members and was roughly structured like a military combat unit: a commander chaired a small executive board that determined strategy, lieutenants, and troops. Mallisham was elected chairman, and one of the requirements for membership in the group was active combat experience in World War II or the Korean War.

If aspiring members of Tuscaloosa's new defensive group passed a background check and were accepted into the organization, they had to pledge to protect the black community, even at the cost of their own lives. Members were required to be married; they were drawn from a wide range of occupations and had varied educational backgrounds, social standing, and economic class. Personal responsibility counted more than any other factor; a heavy drinker whom the others in the group thought of as "a talker" was excluded, according to University of Alabama historian Harold A. Nelson. "The organization functions in a semi-secret manner. . . . It operates on the principle that those who need to know of its existence do know or will be informed of it. It sees no value in general publicity, and consciously avoids it."

Rogers was now receiving constant death threats, so his safety became one of the group's first priorities. Almost immediately, members set up a round-the-clock guard at Rogers's home. Armed guards demanded identification from anyone approaching the house. On more than one occasion guards fired at white drivers who did not stop when ordered to do so. But the group also extended their support to other at-risk individuals.

Shortly after the group was formed, it began protecting TCAC president Willie Herzfeld and T. W. Linton, the barbershop owner who had provided refuge for Autherine Lucy nearly a decade earlier. It also protected some whites who had assisted movement efforts, and the group's efforts in this regard were even more covert, because there were limits on how easily and how safely a black man, especially one carrying arms, could move around a white person. Nonetheless, Mallisham's group surreptitiously guarded Alberta Murray, a white attorney, teacher, and founder of the Council for Human Relations, as she moved throughout the county encouraging voter registration. She did not even know about their protection until much later.

Mallisham and his men were not quite a secret organization, but very few of the area's white residents could have known how sophisticated their group was. When the group conducted inquiries, it did so as secretively as possible. "As soon as [Mallisham] is informed of an incident with which the Defenders might become involved, he dispatches investigators to interview witnesses and to gather any other pertinent information," notes Nelson. "Seldom do investigators make public their duties. Rather, interviewing and data gathering are carried on without revealing that an investigation is under way or that the organization is in any way involved in the situation." Tuscaloosa's newspapers never reported on them, and except for the Klansmen who came up against them, most whites were probably unaware of the group's existence. Furthermore, although police were surely alert to the fact that some sort of organized black armed protection was at play in Tuscaloosa, they found themselves unable to stop such determined black protection.

To be sure, the group often operated in full view of the white community—as it did on July 8, 1964. A group of black teenagers went to the Druid movie theater in downtown Tuscaloosa to test its compliance with the recently passed Civil Rights Act. A mob of about two hundred whites greeted them by throwing stones and bottles. The teens telephoned Mallisham. He sent two cars filled with armed men who picked up the teenagers and sped back to the black community. When they arrived they found Klansmen lying in wait. The hidden terrorists opened fire, but Mallisham's group fired back, and the astonished Klansmen fled. Klan violence in Tuscaloosa's black community ended when Klansmen discovered that attack would be met by an organized armed response. Police violence also slowed.

The fact that Mallisham's group existed at all is remarkable. That they achieved a balance between secrecy and easy accessibility to the black community is even more remarkable. Before their founding, it had been the practice of Tuscaloosa's Ku Klux Klan leader to show up where TCAC meetings were being held, sometimes "patrolling" the area by car and sometimes simply planting himself and others in front of the meeting place. One night members of Mallisham's group showed up too; when the Klansmen watching the meeting place saw that these new arrivals were prepared to fire on them, they raced away. Klansmen never again appeared at TCAC meetings.

The effectiveness of Mallisham's group cannot be underestimated. Although their existence did not in and of itself lead to new civil rights legislation, they played an essential role in liberating the black community from fear, which certainly helped support other black Tuscaloosans' struggle for new laws. The greater significance of Mallisham's group lies in its integration into the nonviolent civil rights movement. Although for a variety of reasons Mallisham's group was not as visible as the Deacons, in Tuscaloosa the two strands of activism, armed and nonviolent, were even more entwined than in Louisiana.

Despite Rogers's deep commitment to nonviolence, he welcomed the protection of Mallisham's group; his wife certainly did, as well. And despite the obvious differences between Rogers's philosophies and Mallisham's, the two men's efforts and organizations were tightly linked. Some members of Mallisham's group were on the TCAC executive board. And Mallisham insisted that his group be made aware of movement plans so they could decide how best to protect activists, so Mallisham and Rogers met regularly. The effect was to embed Mallisham's group deeply into the activities of the nonviolent movement.

It is unclear whether or not SCLC's leadership in Atlanta knew that an armed group was protecting Tuscaloosa's black community—and specifically protecting the SCLC affiliate there. And if the larger organization did know of the group, their attitude toward it does not seem to have been recorded. Nonetheless, at least some of SCLC's field staff in Tuscaloosa seemed well aware of gun-packing protectors. "I'm here to see that the struggle remains nonviolent," said one SCLC field worker, adding that it was going to be "quite a task."

Rogers had been mentored by Martin Luther King Jr., and SCLC leaders like James Bevel, Ralph Abernathy, and King himself visited Tuscaloosa more than once. Biographers of King, autobiographies by SCLC leaders such as Abernathy or Andrew Young, and studies of SCLC make no mention of the group, despite the fact that Tuscaloosa's decision to desegregate was a significant victory by an SCLC affiliate. By late January 1965 most downtown restaurants had desegregated; in September there were black students enrolled in formerly all-white high schools. The people in King's shop may not have known how important Mallisham's group was to this success, or they may have chosen not to speak publically about it in deference to Mallisham's desire for relative anonymity—or perhaps even out of embarrassment that their nonviolent affiliate in Tuscaloosa was enduring with the assistance of armed defenders. One important mission of SCLC's ministers had always been to protect King's public image; if any associates were involved in armed defensive action, the SCLC leadership would not have wanted to broadcast that fact to the world.

In any case, it would not be long before King had to confront the reality that groups like Mallisham's existed and were becoming increasingly prominent—and were increasingly entangled with the nonviolent movement he was trying to create. And he would be forced to acknowledge that the movement had reached a watershed moment.

———

On June 6, 1966, James Meredith, the first African American to be enrolled at the University of Mississippi, was shot by a sniper on a Mississippi highway while engaged in a solitary 220-mile March Against Fear from Memphis, Tennessee, to Jackson, Mississippi. Meredith's wound was not fatal, but the shooting would reverberate throughout the civil rights movement and help shake apart the fragile consensus built around nonviolent actions, a consensus designed to win popular support and federal backing for the civil rights movement.

Meredith's march, which had initially generated little interest from the major civil rights organizations, now commanded their attention. Leaders from the organizations gathered in Memphis to plan for its continuation. SNCC had already concluded that protest marches were not particularly useful, but it decided that the attack on Meredith required some response, even if that response ended up being a protest march. The group had made a similar compromise the year before. SNCC's executive committee had voted against participating in the Selma-to-Montgomery protest. But during the march, SNCC chairman John Lewis, who had made a personal decision to participate, and scores of other marchers were beaten and tear-gassed by Alabama state troopers and a sheriff's posse on the Edmund Pettus Bridge. SNCC sent a full complement of organizers to Selma. As Stokely Carmichael phrased it, that decision—and SNCC's resolution to participate in a resumption of the Meredith march in 1966—reflected a "violence-cannot-be-allowed-to-stop-the-movement reflex."

But even as SNCC joined other national civil rights organizations to respond to this latest act of violence, the old days of relatively easy agreement and common cause despite political and tactical tensions had clearly ended. This relative harmony had begun disintegrating in 1964, and the fragmentation accelerated with passage of the 1965 Voting Rights Act. Most of the reasons can be traced to disagreements between the young people radicalized by their southern experience and the more conservative members of civil rights organizations; these differences ranged from positions for or against the growing war in Vietnam, alienation from or accommodation with the Democratic Party, and even stances on the Palestinian cause.

When the national civil rights leadership gathered in Memphis in response to the Meredith shooting, these divisions were on full display. Among the assembled leaders were the NAACP's Roy Wilkins; Whitney Young, head of the National Urban League; Martin Luther King Jr. of SCLC; Floyd McKissick, who had become national director of CORE, replacing James Farmer in January; and Stokely Carmichael, SNCC's new chairman, who had defeated John Lewis in an election only a month earlier. It did not take long for them to fall out with one another. SNCC program secretary Cleveland Sellers participated in the meeting and later remembered how difficult it was for the attendees to reach any sort of consensus about resuming Meredith's march: "It was obvious to me from the beginning that the possibilities of unity were almost nil."

One issue in particular divided the leaders: *guns*. If Meredith's march was resumed, Carmichael said he wanted to invite the Deacons for Defense to protect the marchers. McKissick favored the idea, but Wilkins and Young were adamantly opposed. King seems not to have contributed much to this particular discussion, although at one point he did note that there was a difference between carrying guns in self-defense and bringing them to a protest; the latter carried a risk of police retaliation that the former did not. But King does not seem to have put up very much resistance to Stokely's proposal of using the Deacons, and that—in the eyes of some of the meeting's attendees, at least—amounted to assent.

King's tacit assent to Carmichael's proposal about the Deacons was more or less the result of an unstated deal between the two men. Stokely had also argued for the exclusion of whites from any resumed march. King could not possibly agree to such a demand, and Stokely knew it, but he also knew that backing away from that position—a position he himself did not strongly hold—would help persuade King to support him on other issues. And when King did not fight Stokely over the presence of the Deacons, Wilkins and Young angrily stormed out of the meeting—which Carmichael had wanted in the first place. "We did not want the march to lose its militancy," he said years later.

This dispute over the Deacons concerned a larger political issue than simply a debate over whether and how best to resume James Meredith's march. The Deacons had become a growing presence in the South, expanding not only in Louisiana but in Mississippi and Alabama as well. Bogalusa's chapter had commanded much press attention, and its leader, Charles Sims, claimed that there were fifty-five Deacons chapters across the South. The Deacons' secretiveness about their organization's strength makes it almost impossible to verify Sims's claim, and he was known to exaggerate. But his claim could not be disproven, and the Deacons' spread across the South, even if more limited than they claimed, had made them a force to be reckoned with both within the civil rights movement and outside it.

In the end, the Deacons did accompany the Meredith march when it resumed later in June 1966. Although there were multiple confrontations between them, the marchers they were protecting, and Mississippi police, all the confrontations stopped far short of shoot-outs. The Deacons had always been pragmatic in deciding when to use their weapons, and they may also have discovered a difference between the potential for armed self-defense in Louisiana and in Mississippi. Mississippi police were far worse perpetrators of white-supremacist violence than were Louisiana police, and the Deacons had to be restrained in their use of defensive force lest they find themselves in an unwinnable fight against the white authorities. As SNCC's Hollis Watkins later explained, "Tactically and strategically the Deacons knew they couldn't maintain their usual posture. The Deacons usual posture wasn't toward law enforcement."

The Deacons' tactics were not the only things that changed on this march. Whether because of their presence or because of the clear ruptures within the civil rights establishment that were so evident during the march, it had become apparent that none of the old formulas that white power used to stifle black aspirations or to predict black activism were likely to work anymore. This was an issue not of guns or of armed self-defense but, rather, of consciousness. Black consciousness had become "blacker" by the mid-1960s, and Afro-Americans had learned to dig deeper into their shared black experience for political purpose. This change would have enormous consequences, both in the days, weeks, and months following the Meredith march and also in the decades to come. And by linking militant black political expression with violence, it would have the unfortunate side effects of letting white hysteria distort what guns had meant in the earlier phases of blacks' struggle for freedom and of twisting into unrecognizability the vital and laudable legacy of armed self-defense in black history.

EPILOGUE

"The King of Love Is Dead"

I don't grieve for James Chaney. He lived a fuller life than most of us. He's got his freedom, and we're still fighting for ours. I'm sick and tired of going to the funerals of black men who have been murdered by white men. I've got vengeance in my heart tonight, and I ask you to feel angry with me.

—David Dennis at James Chaney's funeral service,
August 7, 1964

When Stokely Carmichael called for "Black Power" during the 1966 Meredith March Against Fear through Mississippi, he did not so much launch a new, more militant era of civil rights and freedom struggle as reflect an evolution of the movement—an evolution that was inevitable and that had begun long before his statement. Many of history's most influential interpreters have treated Stokely's words poorly, associating them with violence and an incoherent, antiwhite black nationalist rage. Even within the Freedom Movement, several prominent figures denounced Carmichael: at the NAACP's annual convention a month after Stokely's declaration, Roy Wilkins charged that black power "can mean in the end only black death." Martin Luther King Jr. called the slogan "unfortunate." And years later James Lawson told an interviewer that he thought Stokely's cry had "betrayed the movement." Many observers and much Freedom Movement historiography identify his Black Power speech as the moment when the "good" nonviolent civil rights movement of love ended and was replaced by the "bad" violent Black Power movement of hate.

In retrospect, the political hysteria that greeted Carmichael's call was predictable, although its intensity could not have been completely anticipated by Carmichael or anyone else who applauded and echoed his stance at the time. The tones of Stokely's words were certainly different, in that we do not hear in them the poignant, almost comforting sound of "We Shall Overcome." His was not an appeal to the heart, and it presumed a black self-interest that involved more than ending segregation and gaining voting rights. So it is not difficult to understand the puzzlement and fright that many onlookers—especially whites—felt at the sharper notes coming from Carmichael and SNCC on that Mississippi march. For despite the passage of new Civil Rights Acts, fear and resentment still governed the way powerful and influential whites reacted to assertive blacks; the "uppity" Negro was still considered way out of line and dangerous.

Some of the fear and resentment that Carmichael's call for Black Power elicited from whites across the country amounted to a backhanded recognition of their own hypocrisy and racism. For to be sure, northern whites bore their share of responsibility for racism's entrenchment in U.S. culture. There had been violent white reaction outside the South to even modest attempts at desegregating schools and housing, as in Los Angeles at Fremont High School, or as on Detroit's Belle Isle during World War II, where residents rioted when the new Sojourner Truth federal housing project built in their all-white community was opened to blacks. In November 1963, CORE's James Farmer and Floyd McKissick were not allowed to speak at the University of Southern California because the school considered them "too controversial." And just a few months after the Meredith March, Martin Luther King and SCLC discovered just how violently segregationist Cicero, Illinois, was when they protested housing discrimination and other inequities. For the first half of the twentieth century, urban rioting was typically white antiblack rioting, and it mostly occurred in the North. As the *Saturday Evening Post* warned in an editorial reacting to the Black Power idea: "We are all, let us face it, Mississippians." The "we" was definitely not meant to express common cause with black sharecroppers in Mississippi, or any other black person in the state or nation.

Fear seemed to underlie much of the media reaction to Carmichael's words. His call, many commentators asserted, reflected his violent intentions. Reporters constantly insisted that Carmichael explain what he meant by Black Power, and no explanation was deemed satisfactory. Many mid-twentieth-century whites, seeing signs of black dissatisfaction, echoed the question Thomas Jefferson had asked in the country's earliest years: "Are our [Negroes] to be presented with freedom and a dagger?" From this apprehensive perspective, the signs—and Stokely's words were but one sign in 1966—did not seem encouraging. Inexplicably to many whites, blacks continued to express dissatisfaction.

The debate about self-defense that took place during the Meredith March lent an additional and ominous dimension to white perceptions of what Carmichael might have meant by Black Power. Some participants in the march—especially northerners—considered the presence of the Deacons for Defense and Justice inappropriate. "The movement's no place for guns," said Reverend Theodore Seamons, a white minister from the North, when he saw a .45-caliber pistol in a car being driven by one of the Deacons. Most organizers, however, felt differently. The police protection the marchers were originally promised had been cut back, and whites harassed them as they marched toward Jackson. Civil rights workers who had spent time in the South knew that these were signs of danger, and many of them appreciated the presence of armed protectors along the march route.

Argument among the march leaders mirrored larger disagreements within the civil rights movement and in the nation's black community. Ironically, many in the black political establishment—those leaders who by now had gained access to the corridors of power and exercised some influence on the nation's politics, however limited—now had to deal with the dissatisfaction of many of their black constituents. Even before the Meredith March, during a May 1966 White House conference on civil rights titled "To Fulfill These Rights," protesting picketers carried signs that read, "Save Us from Our Negro Leaders."

SNCC did not participate in the White House conference. "Regardless of the proposals which stem from this conference," SNCC said in a statement, "we know that the Executive Department and the President are not serious about insuring constitutional rights to black Americans." In a press conference elaborating on SNCC's misgivings about the conference, Ruby Doris Smith Robinson, the organization's new executive director, publicly used the phrase "Black Power" for the first time: "We been head-lifted and upstarted in white societies all our lives and we're tired of that. And what we need is black power." Unlike Carmichael's June debut of the phrase, however, Robinson's remarks attracted little attention.

The first half of the 1960s had seen dramatic changes in the civil rights movement, changes that challenged many of the old guard—and old ideas—that had propelled the movement in its earlier phases. Especially significant changes occurred in 1964: Blacks locally organized armed self-defense and protection much more publicly than at any point in the history of black struggle except the aftermath of the Civil War, and both SNCC and CORE reached a historic turning point as organizations, beginning to move away from any further commitment to nonviolence.

SNCC and CORE both felt they had been betrayed by longtime political allies in the Democratic Party. Despite the power that Dixiecrats wielded within the party, SNCC, CORE, and the rest of the civil rights establishment had more or less considered the Democratic Party an ally because of the considerable northern liberal forces concentrated in it. For SNCC, CORE, and many young people, this alliance effectively dissolved at the party's national convention in Atlantic City, New Jersey, in late August 1964.

The break with the Democratic Party was triggered by the Democrats' rejection of a black Mississippi delegation to the national convention. Although discrimination was widespread in southern states, Mississippi was the most blatant in resisting political participation by black people. The state's whole political apparatus was dedicated to this denial, and that apparatus belonged to the Democratic Party. So one result of Freedom Movement work in the state (a development greatly aided by SNCC and CORE staff working as staff for the Council of Federated Organizations, or COFO) was the emergence in April 1964 of the Mississippi Freedom Democratic Party (MFDP). This new party began planning to challenge the legitimacy of Mississippi's all-white "regular" delegation at the national convention and to claim the right to be seated as the legitimate delegation from the state. Success seemed almost a sure thing; virtually no one denied Mississippi's blatant and brutal discrimination against black people.

At the heart of the MFDP's challenge to the "regular" Mississippi delegation was the charge that the state's official Democratic Party had not even followed its own rules when selecting delegates to the national convention, essentially choosing delegates through what might be called a good ol' boy network that deliberately excluded blacks *and* most whites in Mississippi. The first step in the MFDP challenge, therefore, was to attempt to participate in the delegate selection process of the established "regular" party.

On paper, the rules for delegate selection required much transparency in order to assure maximum participation. For example, precinct meetings were the first step in delegate selection, and the dates and times of those meetings were supposed to be advertised in media accessible to the general public. The rules were usually not followed, however. Even most white people did not know when the meetings were to be held. Even if black people knew when the meetings were to be held, attempting to enter and participate in one of the gatherings could be dangerous for them; in regions like southwest Mississippi, it could be akin to attempting a sit-in at a Ku Klux Klan hangout.

It did not take much for the MFDP to validate their charge of discrimination and exclusion; all their members had to do was show up at an official Democratic Party precinct meeting, if they could find out where one was being held. White men with guns might be in the doorway of a meeting place, the meeting may have been moved, or the door might be locked. When Aaron Henry showed up at a precinct meeting in Clarksdale, he met no violence, and the twenty people he brought outnumbered the five whites participating in the meeting. The white chairman, however, immediately adjourned the session until he could round up enough additional participants to create a white majority.

Ultimately, the MFDP failed to gain access to the regular process of delegate selection, leading them to create—following party rules—their own delegation to attend the convention. The delegation was not all-black; it also included four white members. Still, at the convention, the MFDP's efforts to be seated as the official Mississippi delegation were immediately met with ruthless resistance from the Lyndon Johnson White House and its allies. Liberal Minnesota senator Hubert Humphrey, aspiring to the vice-presidential candidacy, was Johnson's primary hatchet man. He and others threatened some convention delegates sympathetic to the MFDP that they might lose their potential federal appointments. Black leaders seeking favors from the White House were also used to pressure MFDP delegates. United Auto Workers head Walter Reuther even threatened Martin Luther King Jr., promising to cut off union contributions if he did not use his prestige and influence with the MFDP to convince them to back off. To King's credit, he did not do so.

Suddenly, a "compromise" was announced on television by then Minnesota attorney general Walter Mondale. There had been no discussion with the MFDP about it. As Mondale outlined the compromise, the MFDP was to be given two at-large seats to be occupied by two men already chosen by the White House: state NAACP head Aaron Henry and Tougaloo College chaplain Edwin King, both members of the MFDP delegation.

An assortment of black leaders put intense pressure on the MFDP, urging them to accept the offer, but the MFDP turned it down. "We didn't come all this way for no two seats since all of us is tired," said the MFDP vice chair, Mrs. Fannie Lou Hamer, in a now-legendary retort. And the angry but more philosophical Bob Moses commented, "We were trying in part to bring morality into politics, not politics into our morality."

The MFDP delegation returned to Mississippi, angry and disappointed. The young COFO organizers who had invested so much time and energy in the birthing of the MFDP and who had assisted the new party in taking its first uncertain steps were perhaps even more bitter.

The all-white Mississippi delegation who Johnson and his allies had decided were the legitimate representatives of the Democratic Party in the state were not even good Democrats. The white delegates came to the convention supporting Republican Barry Goldwater's presidential candidacy, refused to pledge loyalty to their own party's nominee at the convention, and left still committed to Goldwater. (In the November election, Goldwater received over 87 percent of the Mississippi vote.)

Despite the ignominy of being rejected and the contempt reflected in the seating of the all-white Mississippi delegation, the MFDP decided to campaign for the Johnson–Humphrey ticket. This would prove to be more than some in the civil rights community could stomach. "The national Democratic Party's rejection of the MFDP at the 1964 convention was to the civil rights movement what the Civil War was to American history; afterward things could never be the same again," wrote Cleveland Sellers,

who soon would become SNCC's program secretary. "Never again were we lulled into believing that our task was exposing injustices so that the 'good' people of America could eliminate them. After Atlantic City our struggle was not for civil rights, but for liberation."

In complete disagreement with the MFDP's decision to support the Democratic Party despite their rejection in Atlantic City, but unwilling to fight that decision, Stokely Carmichael and a small group of SNCC organizers traveled to Lowndes County, Alabama, intending to encourage the development of an independent black political party there. This party—and the ideals it espoused and political movement it engendered—would completely refashion SNCC's understanding of where Black Power and armed self-defense fit in its work. On this SNCC project, in one of the most violent regions of Alabama, guns were as routine as leaflets announcing a mass meeting.

The new party that resulted from the work of Carmichael and the SNCC organizers working with him was called the Lowndes County Freedom Organization (LCFO). Because of the high rate of illiteracy in the state, Alabama law required political parties to have a visual symbol. The LCFO selected a black panther and became known as the Black Panther Party. Reflecting on the party's choice of a symbol, LCFO chair John Hulett recalled years later,

> The black panther . . . said that we would fight back if we had to. When we chose that symbol many of the peoples in our county started saying we were a violent group who is going to start killing white folks. But it wasn't that, it was a political symbol that we was here to stay and we were going to do whatever needed to be done to survive. . . . White peoples carried guns in this county and the law didn't do anything to them, so we started carrying our guns too . . . but we wasn't violent. We wasn't violent people. But we were just some people who was going to protect ourselves in case we were attacked.

By the time of the November 1966 elections in Lowndes County, black registered voters outnumbered white registered voters. The LCFO ran a slate of seven candidates seeking the offices of sheriff, coroner, and tax assessor and several seats on the Board of Education. All the candidates lost. Ironically, they lost not because blacks were prevented from voting but, rather, because black sharecroppers and other blacks who were vulnerable to white power were pressured to vote for white candidates. Fear—as well as chicanery, such as selecting polling places that were inconvenient for blacks—kept about 20 percent of black registered voters at home.

The new party also faced great hostility from much of Alabama's middle-class black political establishment, which was now positioning itself to broker the black vote, which had been greatly increased because of the new Voting Rights Act. An independent political party of any kind was the last thing the black political elite wanted. In a diatribe surprising for its contempt, Hosea Williams, the project director for SCLC in Alabama, attacked SNCC while declaring black people politically incompetent: "There ain't no Negro in Alabama including ourselves that knows one iota about politics. Politics is a science. . . . This is why I think SNCC is taking advantage of the Negroes."

Although the LCFO had revealed—and perhaps widened—long-hidden divisions within the civil rights movement and the black community, it had an outsized effect on black self-determination in the areas where it was active. Despite accusations of "reverse racism," SNCC workers did not urge blacks to support "moderate" whites seeking election to office. In Lowndes County, "We just told folks to pull the lever for the Black Panther and then go home," recalls Courtland Cox. "What you have in this country is that Negroes are always told to vote for someone who is less of a racist instead of more for Negroes," said Stokely Carmichael. Although no LCFO candidate won in the 1966 elections, Lowndes County witnessed an increase in black voters from just one at the start of 1965 to almost 2,000 a year later. This alone was a remarkable success story, and so too is the fact that the county's original lone black voter—John Hulett—was elected sheriff of Lowndes County in 1970. Other blacks would soon be elected to a range of county offices.

The LCFO had another significant effect: its success in Lowndes County, combined with the MFDP's experience in Atlantic City, triggered Stokely Carmichael's call for Black Power in Mississippi. Although the idea of black empowerment had underlain SNCC's organizing work throughout the South, the LCFO was crucial in making this political goal explicit.

Not since Martin Luther King had a leader as charismatic as Stokely Carmichael emerged from the southern freedom struggle and exerted such a powerful influence on black people above the Mason–Dixon Line. But it was the times themselves, as much as Carmichael's personal dynamism, that determined his impact.

Before Carmichael called for Black Power, many young blacks in the North had been almost disdainful of the southern movement because of its identification with nonviolence. Stokely himself had been largely unknown outside the places where he worked as an organizer. But his call suggested that a shift was underway in SNCC, that after years of so-called passive resistance, the organization was now open to what they considered more militant and revolutionary struggle.

This new perception of SNCC—as an organization calling for revolutionary change and as one open to armed struggle—resonated in urban inner cities especially, attracting a range of angry young black people. The northern-based Revolutionary Action Movement (RAM), which defined itself as a revolutionary Black Nationalist organization, placed operatives inside SNCC in order to convince the organization of the necessity of armed struggle. Although RAM's idea of a "liberation army" was greeted skeptically within SNCC, RAM operatives' emphasis on black leadership and black consciousness struck a chord with field staff, many of whom had opposed the 1964 summer project that had brought hundreds of white volunteers to Mississippi. Other new forces acting on SNCC included the Black Panther Party, which had just been formed in Oakland, California, and which had borrowed the black panther symbol of the LCFO. There was a brief formal alliance between the two organizations. More broadly, the cultural and political currents of black consciousness washed over SNCC and CORE.

These new forces within and around SNCC had the effect of complicating the group's own internal discussions about its direction and identity. And Stokely's charisma meant that outside the South, for the first time SNCC became defined by what its chairman said instead of by its organizing program. One consequence of this shift was also that SNCC did less organizing.

By the mid-1960s, a generational exchange of ideas was well underway within the black community. Black art, especially in poetry, music, and drama, blossomed and reflected a more political black consciousness. Political excitement and commitment was being generated not only by the southern Freedom Movement but also by liberation struggles in southern Africa and in Africa's newly emerging nations. The 1961 protests in the U.N. gallery following the murder of the Congolese prime minister Patrice Lumumba is a dramatic early illustration of this. Black political activists in the United States interacted with armed African liberation movements. And quite separate from his religious identity, the political words of Malcolm X, perhaps the most influential voice among young black political activists in the North, resonated in the hearts and minds of young black people. Political expression and debate seemed to be everywhere, breaking down what had been the biggest barrier blocking meaningful black North–South political discourse: nonviolence.

The idea of nonviolent struggle had prevented northern and southern activists from truly understanding each other's strategies, tactics, and goals. By 1966, many above the Mason–Dixon Line saw southern struggle as finished and—insofar as it had been defined by gaining voting rights and desegregation—won. "Mrs. Hamer is no longer relevant," is the way one northern activist described the direction of Freedom Movement activism. This statement was not so much a dismissal of southern struggle as a sign of a shift away from grassroots organizing in favor of ideological top-down leadership. Northern activists never fully grasped the nature of southern struggle, so they did not feel it contained many useful lessons. Desegregation was viewed as being the same as integration, nonviolence was considered "passive," and the future was seen as lying in the urban North. Consequently, although northern activists admired the courage of southern activists, actual political conversation between them was limited, and this limitation—and the misconceptions about southern efforts from which it sprung—stunted the development of organized national struggle. In the late 1960s and into the '70s, the Black Panther Party and a handful of small black organizations notwithstanding, national black leadership mainly appealed for money from white people holding various positions of power and organized loud "black" conferences and caucuses that seemed more boast than commitment.

Carmichael bridged these differences for a short while, then left the

United States for a political life in Africa. "We were all tired, exhausted [and] I fought with him over going to Africa," says Cleveland Sellers, who was not in disagreement with Stokely's interest in pan-Africanism. "But SNCC was dying, the FBI was tracking him everywhere, and we had all gone through 10 years with no break and though nobody likes to admit it, you had to take your behind somewhere just to think." SNCC's charismatic leader effectively disappeared from the American political scene, and the vibrant movement Carmichael had helped foster seemed to have arrived at an impasse.

The way forward remained unclear, as it does today. The freedom struggle continues, in ways at once more subtle and more urgent than the efforts of activists in the 1960s. And although the questions of nonviolence and armed self-defense may seem to have receded into the past, they endure in our conceptions of both the civil rights movement and the activism that followed Carmichael's call for Black Power. Today, gun rights are remembered as an unfortunate addition to the story of black struggle, one that helped radicalize and ultimately defeat the greatest ambitions of the luminaries who propelled blacks' age-old freedom struggle to new heights at midcentury. Furthermore, today the issue of gun rights has largely come to be associated with the conservative white Right, and far too often the concept of "standing one's ground" is invoked to defend the murder of a black person. But there was a time when people on both sides of America's racial divide embraced their right to self-protection, and when rights were won because of it. We would do well to remember that fact today.

AFTERWORD
Understanding History

We who believe in freedom cannot rest until it comes.
—Ella Baker

I have never subscribed to nonviolence as a way of life, simply because I have never felt strong enough or courageous enough, even though as a young activist and organizer in the South I was committed to the tactic. "I tried to aim my gun, wondering what it would feel like to kill a man," Walter White wrote of his father's instruction to shoot and "don't . . . miss" if a white mob set foot on their property. If I had been in a similar situation in 1960s Mississippi, I would have wrestled with the same doubts that weighed on the young White. But in the final analysis, whatever ethical or moral difficulty I might have had would not have made me unwilling or unable to fire a weapon if necessary. I would have been able to live with the burden of having killed a man to save my own life or those of my friends and coworkers.

It has been a challenge to reconcile this fact with nonviolence, the chosen tactic of the southern civil rights movement of which I was a part. Yet in some circumstances, as seen in the pages of this book, guns proved their usefulness in nonviolent struggle. That's life, which is always about living within its contradictions.

More than ever, an exploration of this contradiction is needed. The subjects of guns and of armed self-defense have never been more politicized or more hotly debated than they are today. Although it may seem peculiar for a book largely about armed self-defense, I hope these pages have pushed forward discussion of both the philosophy and the practicalities of nonviolence, particularly as it pertains to black history and struggle. The larger point, of course, is that nonviolence and armed resistance are part of the same cloth; both are thoroughly woven into the fabric of black life and struggle. And that struggle no more ended with the passage of the Civil Rights Acts of 1964 and 1965 than it began with the Montgomery bus boycott, Martin Luther King Jr., and the student sit-ins.

In some respects, black struggle took on a new character, as with legislative victory over segregation and new law protecting voting rights the main battleground shifted from the South to the politically more complicated North. SCLC's efforts in Chicago failed. SNCC dropped "Nonviolent" from its name, called for "full retaliation from the black community across America," and then faded into increasing irrelevancy. The Black Panther Party became dramatically visible on the steps of the California State Capitol in Sacramento, where they suddenly appeared strapped in bandoliers, wearing black leather, and carrying weapons. In a manner reminiscent of the 1960 student sit-ins, chapters and some groups just calling themselves "black panthers" spread rapidly across the United States. Before the end of the decade, CORE officially declared itself a Black Nationalist organization, and across the country a dubious black political spontaneity mainly took the form of urban rioting.

Southern struggle had become romanticized—rugged, ragged SNCC and CORE shock troops bravely confronting white supremacy, especially police and mad-dog sheriffs. After the Selma-to-Montgomery march and passage of the 1965 Voting Rights Act, many thought that southern struggle was over, its mission accomplished, civil rights gained. Even that story, however, has barely been told; many of the southern Freedom Movement's dimensions remain unexplored. That is one reason this book has focused on armed self-defense and its place within a nonviolent movement. My aim has been to force a reappraisal of the movement and to open the door to new ways of understanding what happened in the South in the 1950s and '60s.

One oft-repeated assertion about weapons in the 1960s was that their organized use increased the chances of massive retaliation by local, state, and even federal authority. That just did not happen, not even in Louisiana where the Deacons for Defense and Justice came closest to armed confrontation with police. There was no meaningful difference between white responses to armed resistance by blacks and white responses to nonviolent resistance by blacks. Where massive police force or state power was exercised, as in Birmingham and Selma, Alabama, or in Jackson, Mississippi, police violence was not a response to either the use of guns or the practice of nonviolence; rather, it was exercised for the sole purpose of crushing black protest and demands in any shape. The Freedom Rider bus in Anniston, Alabama, for instance, was not firebombed because anyone thought it was smuggling weapons; hate and fear alone drove that attack, as they did the police-backed mob attacks against Freedom Riders in Birmingham and Montgomery.

Almost nowhere in the postwar South was there any significant confrontation between armed black groups and police, especially in the 1960s. Incidents like the one in Columbia, Tennessee, in 1946 were the exception, not the rule. But even there, despite the price paid for the veteran-led armed self-defense, most in the black community thought the decision to take up arms in the face of potential mob violence helped the community rather than hurt it.

Moreover, remarkably few shootouts of any kind involved organized groups, and those that did take place did not last long. Fear explains this fact. Few if any white terrorists were prepared to die for the cause of white supremacy; bullets, after all, do not fall into any racial category and are indiscriminately lethal. Wisely, I think, black defenders who could have opened up with killing gunfire usually refrained. In place after place, a few rounds fired into the air were enough to cause terrorists to flee.

Black defenders also knew when and where to abstain from using their guns. The key distinction made was between police violence and civilian violence. Violent police mobs, like the one that rioted on the Edmund Pettus Bridge in Selma, found it easier—or at least less risky—to target unprotected, nonviolent protesters. Protests like that on Bloody Sunday in Selma and the Selma-to-Montgomery march that followed were always tactically nonviolent. The very practical and disciplined black self-defense groups did not interfere with the violent, hate-fueled actions of uniformed authority in these instances. And although defensive groups were sometimes present at the scenes of such protests, as with the 1966 Meredith March Against Fear in Mississippi, they did not violate the commitment to nonviolence of such leaders as Martin Luther King (although in many communities young people reacted to white violence during nonviolent protests by hurling rocks and bottles).

It is indisputable that nonviolent direct action in the mid-twentieth century brought thousands into the southern civil rights struggle. And it is incontestable that this eruption of protest was a huge factor in securing the Civil Rights Acts of 1964 and 1965. Because nonviolence so often worked as a tactic, it is somewhat surprising that so few participants in the Freedom Movement embraced it as a way of life. But nonviolence has always been much more demanding and difficult than violence—and although it is a beautiful idea, perhaps in the end, it is not one that can be realistically expected to be widely embraced. Yet the notion of nonviolence is certainly relevant in an increasingly coarse society that today is spiraling into violence to such a degree that carrying concealed weapons, including guns, has become acceptable in many parts of the country, as has the right to kill an unarmed person deemed "threatening" in manner or clothing. Furthermore, although the country more or less celebrates the nonviolent southern civil rights movement—whether according to Mohandas Gandhi's strict tenets or in Martin Luther King Jr.'s somewhat less stringent manner—nonviolence itself has yet to find a path into U.S. culture in any significant way; for the most part it has had no impact on the current conversation about what America should be.

What amounts to abandonment or walking away from nonviolence's demonstrable history of success is especially noticeable in the many beleaguered inner-city neighborhoods blighted by unprecedented levels of violence—especially gun violence. Although nonviolence was crucial to black struggle in the twentieth century, it can be argued that violence on a scale much larger than Ku Klux Klan terrorism is the greatest problem facing many black American communities today.

Part of this problem is the relative silence and inaction of black leadership when it comes to addressing the nightmare of violence in so many black and minority communities. Many of the most prominent black leaders live in upper-class neighborhoods—some black, some white—that are largely free of the pressures found in public housing projects and working-class communities. That these leaders now enjoy the comfort and pleasures their elevated status gains them is normal—welcome progress, in one sense. But if there is any place where voices committed to nonviolence need to be continually raised, surely it is in the poorest black and minority communities, where violence and the values surrounding violence—most disturbingly retaliation—are a routine part of everyday life.

In a February 2012 *New York University Law Review* article, James Forman Jr. (son of SNCC leader Jim Forman) has drawn our attention to one important way violence in these communities wreaks long-term havoc and needs attention. "The same low-income young people of color who disproportionately enter prisons are disproportionately victimized by crime. And the two phenomena are mutually reinforcing." Mandatory sentencing and the disproportionate imprisonment of African Americans and Latinos for low-level drug crimes is outrageous and is rightly protested. But what needs much more focus is the fact that in state prisons especially, many are jailed for violent crimes—people of color killing or trying to kill people of color.

We have also become more warlike as a nation, and as individuals. Regardless of race or social status, we are now more likely than we once were to settle arguments or react to frustration with violence. Yet despite the sobering and alarming implications of this growth in violence, public discourse about nonviolence, and thus discourse about effectively confronting violence, has lessened since the 1960s. Despite the very good work of groups like the Cure Violence partnerships, which treat violence like a disease, we do not see much nonviolent grassroots effort in America's most violence-wracked communities.

To be fair, there is more under way than is recognized. Notes Maria Varela, who was part of SNCC's field staff in the 1960s and whose later work organizing in rural communities in New Mexico and the Southwest gained her a MacArthur Fellowship Genius Grant, "There are many inner-city communities where individuals work to keep the peace on the block. There is work going on in rural communities and within Native Nations to defuse violence and suicide. But these people and these organizations aren't considered 'newsworthy.'"

Over the years, former SNCC field secretary Ivanhoe Donaldson, like most of us who were deeply involved in the southern struggles, has given a great deal of thought to violence and nonviolence:

> We are a very violent culture. In fact, human beings are violent by nature—they are born into violence and they live in violence all their lives, either running from it, hiding from it, or participating in it. . . . The reality though, is that violence never changes anything. It does cause realignments of power and authority. [And] it's always unclear as to how [violence will] shape the future. Here in America we have all of these nuclear weapons, and in China they have all of these nuclear weapons. So do other nations. We all have the capacity to blow each other to kingdom come. One day somebody is going to do just that. It's the nature of the beast.

Economist and social theorist Thomas Sowell is not someone I often agree with, but an observation he made in 2013 during the height of Egyptian violence resonates with Ivanhoe Donaldson's gloomy outlook:

> It would certainly be a lot nicer if everyone laid down their guns and just sat down together and worked things out peacefully. But has anyone forgotten that, for centuries, Protestants and Catholics slaughtered each other and tried to wipe each other out? Only after the impossibility of achieving that goal became clear did they finally give it up and decide to live and let live.

Some groups have succeeded in chipping away at urban violence— organizations like the Gathering for Justice, a group of young people from around the nation brought together by Harry Belafonte; the Center for Nonviolence and Peace Studies, founded by Bernard Lafayette, who travels the United States and the world conducting nonviolence workshops; Teny Gross's Institute for the Study and Practice of Nonviolence, which works on the ground in Providence, Rhode Island; the Latino Dream Act activists; Los Barrios Unidos, working with street gangs in western states; and two groups most interesting to me because of their similarity to SNCC in its early days: the young Dream Defenders, who in the summer of 2013 sat in at the Florida governor's office for thirty-one days protesting that state's stand-your-ground law; and Moral Mondays—young people in North Carolina who engage in weekly protests and civil disobedience challenging that state legislature's attacks on voter registration, Medicaid, and cuts to social programs.

However, for the most part, nonviolence has never been the center of the discussion, neither during the 1960s nor since. As Donaldson notes, "It's still always about the mission. We have never seriously taken on nonviolence itself as a concept of life. We talk instead about getting people job training, employment, higher minimum wage, education—all important, but there is no *value* training. We've never had *a movement* against violence." And Donaldson is quick to add that he is not nonviolent himself. Like me, he finds that committing to that way of life requires a special strength, which he acknowledges he does not have either and was not brought up to have. But then again, he points out that a true commitment to nonviolence is uncommon indeed. "SNCC was very rare in even having a conversation about nonviolence as a way of life, but we survived because local folks stayed up all night protecting us."

———

And finally, all of these issues are lodged in a history we need to face squarely. This brings us to Ella Josephine Baker, whose ideals infuse this book and who was one of the great figures of twentieth-century social change. In 1960, she made her way to the young people like myself who were teething as political activists on sit-ins challenging segregation. She was fifty-seven years old then; we were mostly in our late teens and early twenties. Yet despite our differences in age, Miss Baker—as many of us usually addressed her—recognized that the youth-led movement springing from black colleges, universities, and high schools was a significant and creative development in the civil rights struggle. In truth, we ourselves barely realized this at the time; in fact, we did not know very much at all. She was patient with us, however, and among the many valuable things she taught us was that understanding history is essential and liberating:

In order for us as poor and oppressed people to become a part of
a society that is meaningful, the system under which we now exist
has to be radically changed. That means we are going to have to
learn to think in radical terms. I use the term radical in its original meaning—getting down to and understanding the root
cause. It means facing a system that does not lend itself to your
needs and devising means by which you change that system. That
is easier said than done. But one of the things that has to be faced
is, in the process of wanting to change that system, how much
have we got to do to find out who we are, where we have come
from and where we are going. . . . I am saying as you must say
too, that in order to see where we are going, we not only must
remember where we have been, but we must *understand* where
we have been.

In writing this book, I have attempted to record a history as Miss Baker
spoke of history. In order for it to be as useful as possible, I have tried to
present something more than a personal narration of my experiences. An
understanding of history is what I hope to have imparted to readers, and
that is more than understanding Charlie Cobb's experiences.

Nowhere is the need to embrace Ella Baker's instruction on the necessity
of understanding history more evident than with the mid-twentieth-century
Freedom Movement that spread across the South. Many aspects of that
movement are neglected and misconstrued and are thus in need of much
more thorough examination. It is especially critical to understand, as I hope
readers do by now, that the southern Freedom Movement was not simply a
movement of dramatic, mass protests led by charismatic leaders but a movement of grassroots organizing in rural communities—barely visible work
in southern backcountry, dangerous work punctuated by awful violence
that included murder. But this work gained significant ground nonetheless,
not only securing civil rights long denied to black people but also affecting
the entire United States in some importantly progressive ways.

Conventional scholarship has emphasized the national dimension of the
freedom struggle; it defines the southern movement primarily as a story of
prominent leaders whose main objective was to obtain federal civil rights

legislation. Although national legislation was undeniably important, such scholarship—as well as typical media depictions of the civil rights movement—has focused popular memory on iconic figures and moments at the expense of the thought and structures of day-to-day Freedom Movement actions at the grassroots level. And this narrow focus has contributed to much misunderstanding, as well as to considerable distortion of what took place and why. Martin Luther King Jr., for example, has largely been reduced in the public mind to the "I Have a Dream" speech; Stokely Carmichael has been simplified into an angry "militant" whose June 1966 Black Power speech suddenly came out of nowhere and destroyed the "good" movement of love and nonviolence.

Central to much of this mainstream narrative is that the moral splendor of long-suffering blacks persuaded the nation's leaders to sympathize with civil rights legislation. Although black people sometimes manifested impatience or exerted political pressure on these leaders, the conventional narrative goes, they rarely evinced anger at Jim Crow or white-supremacist dominance. NAACP chairman emeritus Julian Bond, who in the 1960s was communications director for SNCC, summarizes this narrative with ironic simplicity: "Rosa sat down, Martin stood up; and then the white folks saw the light and saved the day." This simplistic and conventional understanding of the civil rights movement, however, neglects the many complexities and tensions that defined the movement and that ultimately contributed to its success. One example of this can be found in Bernice Johnson Reagon's criticism of the scholarship that has come to define what took place in her hometown of Albany, Georgia. As a student at Albany State College in 1961, she was active in the freedom struggle. Yet, she says, "When I read about the Albany Movement, as people have written about it, I don't recognize it. They add up stuff that was not central to what happened." Most scholars have declared the Albany Movement a failure and see the city's black activists as having been outwitted by a smart, sophisticated police chief. This version of that city's movement history stems from Reverend King and his SCLC associates, who declared that movement efforts in Albany had failed. They saw the Albany Movement as *their* movement. "The mistake I made there was to protest against segregation generally rather than against a single and distinct facet of it," King reflected in a January 1965 interview. "Our protest was so vague we got nothing and the people were left very depressed and in despair."

To Reagon and many others in Albany, however, this interpretation suggests an almost complete misunderstanding of what happened there. There was nothing vague about the changes they wanted, and there is nothing vague about what they feel they gained. After all, it was *their* movement, not Reverend King's or SCLC's movement. What defines the movement that the people of Albany fashioned cannot be reduced to protest and —notwithstanding whatever King may have thought constituted "victory"— Albany was significantly changed by their struggle. It "gave me the power to challenge *any* line that limits me," Bernice Reagon says. "[It] really gave me a real chance to fight and to struggle and not respect boundaries that put me down." Or, as A. C. Searles, editor of the *Southwest Georgian,* a weekly black newspaper, put it in 1970: "What did we win? We won our self-respect. It changed my attitudes. This movement made me demand a semblance of first-class citizenship."

A central determinant of how we understand history is whether it is framed from the bottom up or the top down. History framed from the bottom up tends to be viewed suspiciously by the academy, and it is more difficult to grasp because of the relative invisibility of its main actors and their thinking. Fortunately, this is slowly changing. A growing body of work is challenging the traditional top-down approach to the history of the Freedom Movement and making us better able to recognize the thinking that shaped the movement's decision making, actions, and events. Significant scholarship of this depth began emerging late in the twentieth century, pioneered by several important books: Richard Kluger's 1975 book *Simple Justice,* which portrayed the ordinary people whose challenge to school segregation forced the Supreme Court's 1954 *Brown* decision; William H. Chafe's 1980 work on the Greensboro, North Carolina, sit-ins, *Civilities and Civil Rights;* Clayborne Carson's 1981 work, *In Struggle: SNCC and the Black Awakening in America*; Taylor Branch's trilogy on the King years; and the books by John Dittmer and Charles M. Payne—*Local People* and *I've Got the Light of Freedom,* respectively—on Mississippi's movement. And as a guide for negotiating the post–Civil War currents of black history in the United States, Vincent

Harding's thorough and beautifully written 1981 book *There Is a River* is essential text.

Such scholarship is being continued in the current work of such scholars as Emilye Crosby, Hasan Kwame Jeffries, Wesley Hogan, François Hamlin, and Akinyele Umoja. What they have written helps us see with greater clarity the various levels of local leadership that gave the southern movement its power and authority, what Charles Payne has described as "sustained courage" at the grassroots. Their works also help us see how what can be considered Freedom Movement culture continuously and creatively generated ideas that mainly bubbled from the bottom up.

Freedom Movement voices and analyses nevertheless remain noticeably damped in the canon. Although the activists and organizers whose ideas informed the movement's work are quite capable of presenting the critical thinking underlying their actions, it is extremely difficult for most of them to get access to the avenues that could make their thoughts and analysis widely available. Far too often and in far too many places, movement veterans are considered insufficiently credentialed to merit academic appointment, or they are thought incapable of writing credible works that go beyond memoir in presenting for public consumption and understanding what they envisioned, launched, and sustained. Even worse, there is no appreciation of their sense of history—of how their understanding of the historical circumstances surrounding black life influenced the choices they made. Their "stories" are sometimes sought out, but rarely their thinking.

This is an old problem. In his 1855 autobiography, *My Bondage and My Freedom*, Frederick Douglass complained that William Lloyd Garrison and other influential white abolitionists thought that his intellectual growth weakened their cause. They only wanted him to "narrate wrongs," bemoaned Douglass, although after escaping from slavery "I was now reading and thinking." However, if he did not have "the plantation manner of speech," John A. Collins, general agent of the Massachusetts Anti-Slavery Society once counseled Douglass, "People won't ever believe you was a slave. 'Tis not best that you seem too learned." The abolitionist went on to tell Douglass with no small degree of arrogance, "Give us the facts; we will take care of the philosophy." Historian, attorney, and activist Staughton Lynd, who was coordinator of the Freedom School program during the 1964 Mississippi Freedom Summer, believes that what is needed is "guerilla history":

> In the practice of guerilla history the insights of non-academic protagonists are considered to be potentially as valuable as those of the historian. Thus guerilla history is not a process wherein the poor and oppressed provide poignant facts and a radical academic interprets them. Historical agent and professor of history are understood to be co-workers, together mapping out the terrain traveled and the possibility of openings in the mountain ridges ahead.

As a journalist, professional writer, and sometime college professor, as well as a veteran of the civil rights movement, I have the advantage of having my feet in scholarship as well as in activist experience and sensibility. And so, although in the preceding pages I have paid attention to and used the works of historians based in the academy, much of the "scholarly" material drawn on by this book is the thinking articulated by people whose minds and actions generated social challenge and social change. These activists rarely wrote down their thoughts and analyses of the movement they fashioned, nor are their thoughts and analyses given much respectful prominence in academic and mainstream media discussions. But their reflections are as authoritative as the interpretive assumptions found in refereed or peer-reviewed scholarship.

Although the words of these men and women need not—and indeed should not—be taken as gospel, my many conversations with Freedom Movement veterans have formed the *intellectual* spine of this book. I have diligently sought out their thinking, and not simply their narration of events; their minds and memory have been my primary archives. Full disclosure requires me to state here that many are friends and former comrades from my years as a SNCC field secretary. We are remarkably diverse, but we share a common language and sensibility whose roots lie in the Freedom Movement that nurtured us. The thinking and the work of that movement reflect what from generation to generation has been the common denominator of black life: struggle—disciplined, thoughtful, creative struggle.

ACKNOWLEDGMENTS

Many hands have helped this book along its way. There are, of course, the Freedom Movement people who were willing to talk to me and were willing to share their thinking—far too many to list here, but without the movement that embraced me, the movement they fashioned, this book would not exist.

More specifically however, I must thank Myrna Colley-Lee and her colleagues at SonEdna in Charleston, Mississippi, for providing the quiet and space to get this book started. Thanks also to Karen Baxter of Brown University's Africana Studies Department for introducing me to Myrna and the retreat for writers and artists she has developed in the Magnolia State. And thanks, of course, to my wife Ann Chinn, for all that she put up with during the writing of this book. Her own work as director of the Middle Passage Ceremonies and Port Markers Project helped greatly with my research into slavery.

I am also indebted to a set of people who gave serious reading to portions of the book, chapters of the book, and even the book in its entirety, offering much useful advice: Maria Varela, John Dittmer, Wesley Hogan, Vincent Harding, Judy Richardson, and Emilye Crosby especially. Errors in the text are mine not theirs. And disagreement with anything needs to be directed at me.

Thanks also to literary agent Deirdre Mullane for her faith in this book, and to Alex Littlefield, my editor at Basic Books for his great patience and invaluable suggestions as my writing wound its way to publication. Thanks also to Robert Kimzey for his diligent work as project manager for Basic in bringing together the various components of this book. Thanks are also due to Kathy Delfosse for her attentive and excellent copy editing of these pages. Errors are mine not theirs.

And finally, as the great theologian Howard Thurman said in his eulogy for educator and political activist Juliette Derricotte, who died far sooner than she should have when, after being critically injured in a 1931 traffic accident, a whites-only hospital near Dalton, Georgia, refused to admit her: "There is work to be done . . . and ghosts will drive us on. . . . This is an unfinished world, and she has left an unfinished task. Who will take it up?"

NOTES

Introduction

1   **scores of Afro-Americans:** The older term "Afro-American" may seem puzzling here. I use it to designate people who, after hundreds of years, are now an Africa-descended ethnic group in the United States. I recognize that the term "African American" is more widespread today and I use it myself if it feels right in the writing. This is admittedly a fairly loose, intangible approach to usage, but in the final analysis, choosing one or the other is relatively unimportant.

2–3   **"Framing the civil rights movement":** Hasan Kwame Jeffries, *Bloody Lowndes, Civil Rights, and Black Power in Alabama's Black Belt* (New York and London: New York University Press, 2009), 4.

3   **"It's not contradictory":** Bob Moses, quoted in Mary King, *Freedom Song: A Personal Story of the 1960s Civil Rights Movement* (New York: William Morrow, 1987), 318.

3   **"She had to be 80 years old":** Stokely Carmichael, *Ready for Revolution: The Life and Struggles of Stokely Carmichael [Kwame Ture],* with Ekwueme Michael Thelwell (New York: Scribner, 2005), 471.

3   **"No normal human being":** W. E. B. Du Bois, "Will the Great Gandhi Live Again?" *National Guardian,* February 11, 1957, repr., *W. E. B. Du Bois: A Reader,* ed. David Levering Lewis (New York: Henry Holt, 1995), 358.

4   **"to teach the Negroes to be defenseless":** Malcolm X, in "A Summing Up: Louis Lomax Interviews Malcolm X" (1963), *TeachingAmericanHistory.org,* www.teachingamerican history.org/library/document/a-summing-up-louis-lomax-interviews-malcolm-x/.

4   **"[It] gave our generation":** Carmichael, *Ready for Revolution,* 166.

4   **"Our struggle was not just against something":** Dr. Vincent G. Harding, conversation with the author, July 20, 2013.

6   **"Self-defense is so deeply ingrained":** Moses, quoted in King, *Freedom Song,* 318.

6   **"I'm alive today":** John R. Salter Jr., "Guns Kept the Klan Enemies at Bay in Deep South," *Grand Forks Herald,* October 9, 1994, www.saf.org/pub/rkba/general/GunsVersusKKK. htm.

7   **"This nonviolent stuff ain't no good":** Turnbow, quoted in Taylor Branch, *Parting the*

Waters: America in the King Years, 1954–63 (New York: Simon and Schuster Touchstone Edition, 1988), 781; see also Emilye J. Crosby, "You Got a Right to Defend Yourself: Self-Defense and the Claiborne County, Mississippi Civil Rights Movement," *International Journal of Africana Studies* 9, no. 1 (Spring 2003): 133.

7   **"Bill, wait, wait!":** John D'Emilio, *Lost Prophet: The Life and Times of Bayard Rustin* (Chicago: University of Chicago Press, 2004), 230; see also David J. Garrow, *Bearing the Cross: Martin Luther King, Jr., and the Southern Christian Leadership Conference* (New York: William Morrow Quill Edition, 1999), 72–73.

7   **"an arsenal":** Smiley, quoted in Adam Winkler, "MLK and His Guns," *HuffPost Politics,* November 22, 2013, www.huffingtonpost.com/adam-winkler/mlk-and-hisguns_b_810 132.html; see also Clayborne Carson, "The Unexpected Emergence of Martin Luther King, Jr.," King Papers Project, Martin Luther King, Jr., Research and Education Institute at Stanford University, Campus Report, 17 January 1996, www.mlkkpp01.stanford.edu/ kingweb/additional_resources/articles/unexpected_emergence.htm.

8   **to protect the Bates home and the surrounding neighborhood:** David B. Kopel, "Civil Rights and Gun Sights," *Reason.com,* February 22, 2005, www.reason.com/archives/ 2005/02/22/civil-rights-and-gun-sights/2.

8   **"watched over us like babies":** Mateo Suarez, interviewed by Harriet Tanzman, March 26 and 30, 2000, for the Civil Rights Documentation Project of the University of Southern Mississippi (USM), USM and the Tougaloo College Archives.

8   **"The first public expression of disenchantment with nonviolence":** Martin Luther King Jr., *Where Do We Go from Here: Chaos or Community?* (New York: Harper and Row, 1967), 57.

10   **"I had a wife":** Turnbow, quoted in Howell Raines, *My Soul Is Rested: Movement Days in the Deep South Remembered* (New York: G. P. Putnam's Sons, 1977), 266.

10   **"Violence is as American as cherry pie":** H. "Rap" Brown, in a press conference at the Washington, D.C., headquarters of SNCC, quoted in the *Evening Star,* Washington, D.C., July 27, 1967, 1.

14   **"the Great Tradition of black protest":** Vincent Harding, *There Is a River: The Black Struggle for Freedom in America* (New York: Harcourt Brace Jovanovich, 1981), xx; see also Eric Foner, "The Long Black Movement toward Justice," *New York Times,* November 1, 1981, www.nytimes.com/1981/11/01/books/the-long-black-movement-toward-justice.html.

16   **continuation of white violence:** On February 8, 1968, in Orangeburg, South Carolina, highway patrolmen raided the campus of South Carolina State College and attacked students protesting segregation at a nearby bowling alley, killing three of them. On May 15, 1970, police in Jackson, Mississippi, opened fire on a dormitory housing students who had been protesting segregation (as well as the Vietnam War), killing two of them.

Chapter One: "Over My Head I See Freedom in the Air"

19 The title quotation is from Bernice Johnson Reagon's spontaneous updating of the traditional black spiritual "Over My Head I See Trouble in the Air" while singing at a mass meeting following a protest in Albany, Georgia. It is now a traditional Freedom Movement song. Charles E. Cobb Jr., *On the Road to Freedom: A Guided Tour of the Civil Rights Trail* (Chapel Hill, NC: Algonquin Books, 2008), 184.

28 **a fact that undermines our understanding of both subjects:** And that sometimes devolves into what can only be called stupidity, as reflected in radio commentator Rush Limbaugh's January 18, 2013 question: "If John Lewis had had a gun, would he have been beat upside the head on the [Selma] bridge?" Limbaugh would still be berating Lewis as a terrorist if, with a gun, he had opened fire on the *policemen* who were beating him. Lewis himself would undoubtedly be dead.

29 **designed to prevent the possession of weapons by black people:** Clayton E. Cramer, "The Racist Roots of Gun Control," *Kansas Journal of Law and Public Policy*, Winter 1995, www.constitution.org/cmt/cramer/racist_roots.htm.

29 **indentured servitude for the rest of his life:** A. Leon Higginbotham Jr., *In the Matter of Color: Race, and the American Legal Process: The Colonial Period* (New York: Oxford University Press, 1978), 28. Interestingly, in 2012 Ancestry.com issued a press release claiming its genealogists had discovered that President Barack Obama is the eleventh great-grandson of John Punch. And this connection is through his mother! Sheryl Gay Stolberg, "Obama Has Ties to Slavery Not by His Father but His Mother, Research Suggests," *New York Times,* July 30, 2012.

29 **import duties on slaves brought into the colony:** March 1659/60-ACT XVI. An Act for the Dutch and all other Strangers for Tradeing to this Place.

30 **bonded together regardless of race:** Bacon himself was a wealthy landowner and a member of the Colony Council, a cousin to the governor by marriage, in fact. But he thought that Native Americans should be exterminated, as did many of the Virginia Colony's freemen and small farmers; the colony's rulers wanted to continue trading with Indians. Indentured servants, black or white, wanted freedom from servitude, which Bacon promised.

30 **driving the colonial governor from the colony:** Edmund S. Morgan, *American Slavery, American Freedom* (New York: W. W. Norton, 1974), 267–268; Theodore W. Allen, *The Invention of the White Race,* vol. 2, *The Origin of Racial Oppression in Anglo-America* (London: Verso, 2012), 205–212.

30 **nonracial unity that had powered the revolt:** "That was the great danger, for in the words of Governor Berkeley himself, 'The very being of the Collony doth consist in the Care and faithfulness as well as in the number of our servants.'" Allen, *The Invention of the White Race,* 212.

31 **"common, for example, for servants and slaves to run away together":** Morgan, *American Slavery, American Freedom,* 327.

32 **"And it is hereby further enacted":** Richard Halpern and Enrico Dal Lago, *Slavery and Emancipation* (Malden, MA: Blackwell Publishers, 2002), 15.

32 **"Freedom," the governor said, "wears a cap":** Spotswood, quoted in Allen, *The Invention of the White Race,* 245.

32 **"any gun, powder, shot, or any club":** Allen, *The Origin of Racial Oppression in Anglo-America,* 250.

32 **"We have already at least 10,000":** Howard Zinn, *A People's History of the United States* (New York: HarperCollins, 2010), 35.

33 **That Jefferson's earliest childhood memory:** Roger Wilkins, *Jefferson's Pillow: The Founding Fathers and the Dilemma of Black Patriotism* (Boston: Beacon Press, 2001), 4.

33 **"Are our slaves to be presented with freedom and a dagger?":** Jefferson to Adams, January 22, 1821, in "Quotations on Slavery and Emancipation," Jefferson Monticello website, www.monticello.org/site/jefferson/quotations-slavery-and-emancipation.

34 **"It would give to persons of the negro race":** A. Leon Higginbotham Jr., *Shades of Freedom: Racial Politics and Presumptions of the American Legal Process* (New York: Oxford University Press, 1996), 65.

34 **"To be a Negro in this country":** "The Negro in American Culture," WBAI radio panel, 1961, moderated by Nat Hentoff, held on the occasion of the Civil War centennial and published in the summer 1961 issue of *Cross-Currents* magazine. In addition to James Baldwin, participants were Lorraine Hansberry, Langston Hughes, Emile Capouya, and Alfred Kazin.

34 **"endangering the peace and safety of the state":** Chief Justice Taney also declared in his ruling that blacks "had no rights which the white man was bound to respect."

34 **"If I was as drunk with enthusiasm as Swedenborg and Wesley":** Adams, quoted in Merton L. Dillon, *Slavery Attacked: Southern Slaves and Their Allies, 1619–1865* (Baton Rouge: Louisiana State University Press, 1990), 128.

35 **"this assemblage of horrors":** Wilkins, *Jefferson's Pillow,* 48.

36 **"I have nothing more to offer":** Robert A. Ferguson, *Reading the Early Republic* (Cambridge, MA: Harvard University Press, 2006), 208; see also a more detailed discussion of the rebellion and trial in Herbert Aptheker, *American Negro Slave Revolts* (New York: International Publishers, 1974), 219–226.

36 **"[My] child will be a black child born in Mississippi":** Lynn Olson, *Freedom's Daughters: The Unsung Heroines of the Civil Rights Movement from 1830 to 1970* (New York: Scribner, 2001), 212.

37 **an all-black military company called the Bucks of America:** Leonid Kondratiuk, "The Bucks of America: Massachusetts' First African American Unit," February 17, 2010, Massachusetts National Guard website, www.states.ng.mil/sites/MA/News/Pages/The%20Bucks%20of%20America.aspx.

37 **between 1619 and 1865 more than 250 rebellions:** Herbert Aptheker, *Herbert Aptheker on Race and Democracy: A Reader,* ed. Eric Foner and Manning Marable (Champaign: University of Illinois Press, 2006), xi.

38 **One escaped slave attempted to marry:** James Oliver Horton and Lois E. Horton, *Slavery and the Making of America* (New York: Oxford University Press, 2005), 140–141.

38   **Historian Corey D. B. Walker notes:** Corey D. B. Walker, *A Noble Fight: African American Freemasonry and the Struggle for Democracy in America* (Urbana and Chicago: University of Illinois Press, 2008), 89; also interview with author, May 1, 2013.

39   **"I can die":** Sam Livingston, "An African Life of Resistance: Moses Dickson, the Knights of Liberty, and Militant Abolitionism, 1824–1857," paper, August 12, 2008, www.academia.edu/1600054/_Moses_Dickson_Militant_Abolitionist_1824-1865, 15; also see Jasper Wilcox, "Secret Societies and Social Justice: Knights of Tabor," www.partofthesolutionvanguard.wordpress.com/2013/01/28/secret-societies-social-justice-knights-of-tabor/.

40   **"In the Darkest hours":** Reverend Moses Dickson, *A Manual of the Knights of Tabor and Daughters of the Tabernacle Containing General Laws, Regulations, Ceremonies, Drill, and a Taborian Lexicon* (St. Louis: A. R. Fleming, 1891), 14. Although early in the manual Dickson describes some of the Knights of Liberty's activities, he is cautious, making it clear after a brief and oblique reference to "the failure of Nat. Turner and others" that he does not intend to reveal much: "The Underground Railroad was in good running order and the Knights of Liberty sent many passengers over the road to freedom. We feel we have said enough on this subject. If the War of the Rebellion had not occurred just at the time it did the Knights of Liberty would have made public history. Let the past sleep; enough has been said." Ibid., 16–17. Dickson would go on to become one of the founders of Lincoln University in Jefferson City, Missouri. Livingston, *An African Life of Resistance*, 17–20.

40   **"Gentlemen, the question is settled":** James M. McPherson, *The Negro's Civil War: How American Blacks Felt and Acted During the War for the Union* (New York: Vintage, 2003).

41   **"The slave pleaded":** Du Bois, quoted in Carole Emberton, "'Only Murder Makes Men': Reconsidering the Black Military Experience," *Journal of the Civil War Era* 2, no. 3 (September 2012): 369, www.muse.jhu.edu/journals/journal_of_the_civil_war_era/summary/v002/2.3.emberton.html.

41   **By the end of the Civil War:** William Loren Katz, "*Lincoln*, the Movie," *Indian Voices*, n.d., www.indianvoices.net/latest-editorials/249-lincoln-the-movie-by-william-loren-katz.

41   **shot and bayoneted the garrison's soldiers:** Eric Foner and Manning Marable, eds., *Herbert Aptheker on Race and Democracy: A Reader* (Champaign: University of Illinois Press, 2006), 160; "The Fort Pillow Massacre: Report of the Committee on the Conduct of the War. All Previous Reports Fully Confirmed. The Horrors and Cruelties of the Scene Intensified. "Report of the Sub-Committee," *New York Times*, May 6, 1864, www.nytimes.com/1864/05/06/news/fort-pillow-massacre-report-committee-conduct-war-all-previous-reports-fully.html.

41   **for the express purpose of teaching the soldiers to read and write:** James G. Hollandsworth, *Pretense of Glory: The Life of General Nathaniel P. Banks* (Baton Rouge: Louisiana State University Press, 1998), 211.

41   **"Knowledge unfits a child to be a slave":** Douglass, quoted in Wilma King, *Stolen Childhood* (Bloomington: Indiana University Press, 1995), 187.

43   **"You never saw a people more excited on the subject of politics":** Quoted in Eric Foner, *Reconstruction: America's Unfinished Revolution, 1863–1877*, Francis Parkman Prize ed. (New York: History Book Club, 1988), 283.

44   **even military titles for the commanding "officers":** Ibid., 283–285.

45   **"No freedman, free Negro or mulatto":** "The Mississippi Black Code, (1865)," in Longman American History Demo site, www.wps.ablongman.com/long_longman_lahdemo_ 1/0,8259,1546454-,00.html. Reading Mississippi's black codes gives one the strong sense that for all practical purposes, they reinstalled slavery.

46   **"virtually re-enacted slavery":** W. E. B. Du Bois, *Black Reconstruction in America: Toward a History of the Part Which Black Folk Played in the Attempt to Reconstruct Democracy in America, 1860–1880* (New Brunswick, NJ: Transaction Publishers, 2013), 405.

46   **One delegate, Reverend Jotham W. Horton:** James Oliver Horton and Lois E. Horton, *Slavery and the Making of America* (New York: Oxford University Press, 2005), 218; see also Donald E. Reynolds, "The New Orleans Riot of 1866, Reconsidered," *Journal of the Louisiana Historical Association* 5, no. 1 (Winter 1964): 12–13.

47   **"Nothing short of the disenfranchisement of the negro race":** Roberts, quoted in Foner, *Reconstruction,* 341.

47   **"the ballot-box, the jury-box, and the cartridge-box":** Frederick Douglass, *The Complete Autobiographies of Fredrick Douglass* (Radford, VA: Wilder Publications, 2008), 291.

47   **"A Winchester rifle should have a place of honor":** Ida B. Wells-Barnett, *Southern Horrors: Lynch Law in All Its Phases* (Surry Hills, Australia: Accessible Publishing Systems, 2008), 33.

47   **In Lowndes County, Alabama:** Hasan Kwame Jefferies, *Bloody Lowndes: Civil Rights and Black Power in Alabama's Black Belt* (New York and London: New York University Press, 2009), 14.

47   **a group of black men threatened to burn down the city:** Edmund L. Drago, *Black Politicians and Reconstruction in Georgia: A Splendid Failure* (Athens: University of Georgia Press, 1992), 90.

47   **an armed guard of 150 men:** Ibid., 90.

47   **there would be "burning":** Harrison, quoted in ibid., 90.

48   **"Let no man or set of men think":** Simms, quoted in ibid., 90.

49   **"The bullets of the assassin":** "Powell Clayton: A Litany of Horrors" (Arkansas), Old State House Museum website, www.oldstatehouse.com/exhibits/virtual/governors/civil_war_ and_reconstruction/clayton2.aspx.

50   **Hidden Hill plantation just outside of Colfax:** Nicholas Lehmann, *Redemption: The Last Battle of the Civil War* (New York: Farrar, Strauss and Giroux, 2006), 4.

50   **extreme violence aimed at intimidating blacks:** Leeanna Keith, *The Colfax Massacre: The Untold Story of Black Power, White Terror, and the Death of Reconstruction* (New York: Oxford University Press, 2008), 59.

51   **"Damn the court," Ward said:** Ibid., 72–75.

52   **"the Mecca of bad and desperate negroes":** Ibid., 78.

52   **"was not altogether certain":** Ibid., 82.

52   **Both appointed a set of local officials for Grant Parish:** This dispute and power struggle resulted in Pinckney Benton Stewart "P. B. S." Pinchback, an African American, becoming governor for thirty-five days, from December 9, 1872, to January 13, 1873. He was the first African American to become a governor of a state.

53   **"We want that courthouse":** Keith, *The Colfax Massacre,* 97.

53   **estimates of the number of blacks killed:** James K. Hogue, "The 1873 Battle of Colfax—Paramilitarism and Counterrevolution in Louisiana" (paper June 7, 2006), 13–19. Hogue's paper is based on a lecture presented at the Southern Historical Association Conference in Atlanta, Georgia, November 6, 1997. Historian Eric Foner has called the Colfax massacre "the bloodiest single instance of racial carnage in the Reconstruction era." Foner, *Reconstruction,* 437. See also Keith, *The Colfax Massacre,* 109. A partial list of names and some eyewitness accounts can be found on the Colfax Massacre 1873 page of the Black Holocaust Society website, www.blackwallstreet.freeservers.com/colfax%201873.htm.

54   **"Practically, so-called Reconstruction":** Du Bois, *Black Reconstruction in America,* 482.

54   **"an *essential* component in the counterrevolution":** Hogue, "The 1873 Battle of Colfax,"

54   **"The slave went free":** Du Bois, *Black Reconstruction in America,* 30.

Chapter Two: "The Day of Camouflage Is Past"

55   The title quotation is from W. E. B. Du Bois, "An Essay Toward a History of the Black Man in the Great War," in *W. E. B. Du Bois: A Reader,* ed. Lewis, 732–33.

57   **became so drunk he passed out and had to be carried away:** John Calhoun Fleming later told the FBI that he had breathed too many ether fumes. Gail William O'Brien, *The Color of Law: Race Violence and Justice in the Post World War II South* (Chapel Hill:

57   **for help paying the fine:** Blair and Morton sometimes helped rescue arrested blacks from bail "fee grabbers" if they considered mistreatment a factor in an arrest, but they did not assist "thieves, bootleggers, and whiskey drinkers." Ibid., 74.

57   **"Probably one hundred-fifty negroes":** Quoted in O'Brien, *The Color of Law,* 12.

58   **about forty-five miles north of town:** Unless otherwise noted, all the events on the evening of February 25 are described in O'Brien, *The Color of Law,* 12–13.

59   **Raymond Lockridge, told writer Juan Williams:** Juan Williams, *Thurgood Marshall, American Revolutionary* (New York: Three Rivers Press, 1998), 134–135.

59   **"Whites whose obituaries stated [they] died":** *Afro-American,* quoted in ibid. This idea that white deaths were covered up was not uncommon in black conversations about self-defense. Although whites' wanting to cover up deadly black armed responses is understandable, it is difficult to see how it would be possible to keep such deaths secret in small towns and rural communities.

59   **"not a single black-owned business":** "What Happened at Columbia," *Crisis,* April 1946,

60   **"militant" blacks "were moving on every front":** *Louisville Courier-Journal* editorial, quoted in Jason Morgan Ward, *Defending White Democracy: The Making of a Segregationist*

Movement and the Remaking of Racial Politics, 1936–1965 (Chapel Hill: University of North Carolina Press, 2011), 55.

60 **"The doors of the white man's party":** Smith, quoted in Ward, *Defending White Democracy,* 20.

62 **"Are we fighting this war":** Quoted in ibid., 40.

62 **"seeking to use the war emergency":** Broughton, quoted in Timothy B. Tyson, *Radio Free Dixie: Robert F. Williams and the Roots of Black Power* (Chapel Hill: University of North Carolina Press, 1999), 35.

62 **"There will be no social equality":** Eastland, quoted in Ward, *Defending White Democracy,* 81.

63 **for the American way of life:** It is worth noting here that some southern white veterans were changed positively by their war experience. In Columbia one of Billy Fleming's brothers, John Calhoun Fleming Jr., moved among the whites mobbed in the square encouraging them to go home. In fact, none of the elder Fleming's sons was on the square, not even Billy. O'Brien, *The Color of Law,* 131-132.

63 **"The white people of the South":** *Columbia Daily Herald* editorial, quoted in Chris Lamb, *Blackout: The Untold Story of Jackie Robinson's First Spring Training* (Lincoln: University of Nebraska Press, 2004), 11.

63 **"Negroes even in small communities":** Quoted in Herbert Shapiro, *White Violence and Black Response: From Reconstruction to Montgomery* (Amherst: University of Massachusetts Press, 1988), 363.

63 **"Before, Columbia was a hellhole":** Blair, quoted in Carl T. Rowan, *South of Freedom* (New York: Alfred A. Knopf, 1952), 43.

64 **"There won't be no more trouble":** Harlan, quoted in ibid., 48.

64 **a strong and sustained translation of war experience:** I do not mean to minimize the importance either of Reconstruction or of such late-nineteenth-century black leaders as Timothy "T." Thomas Fortune, Monroe Trotter, Ida B. Wells-Barnett, Mary Church Terrell, and others. They were, as historian Shawn Leigh Alexander so appropriately titled his book about them and their work before the NAACP existed, an Army of Lions. They are, unfortunately, dimly remembered today, although many were significant well into the twentieth century. Indeed, freedom, as the old movement song goes, has always been "a constant struggle" and phrases—such as "civil rights era"—that suggest the freedom struggle was confined to the 1950s and '60s are inadequate descriptors that misstate black history. But I use "sustained" here to emphasize that a continuum of civil rights or black freedom rights struggle and change stretched from World War I to World War II. It eclipsed the political impact of Reconstruction and directly shaped the decades of the 1950s and '60s.

66 **"Negroes are organizing all over the state":** Quoted in Cameron McWhirter, *Red Summer: The Summer of 1919 and the Awakening of Black America* (New York: St. Martin's Griffin, 2012), 165.

66 **"No colored maid in the kitchen":** Rebecca Sharpless, *Cooking in Other Women's Kitchens: Domestic Workers in the South, 1865–1960* (Chapel Hill: University of North Carolina Press, 2010), 85.

66   **The FBI actually began a formal investigation:** Bryant Simon, "Fearing Eleanor: Racial Anxieties and Wartime Rumors in the American South, 1940–1945," in *Labor in the Modern South,* ed. Glenn T. Eskew (Atlanta: University of Georgia Press, 2001), 84.

67   **"The increasing number of negroes":** *Secret Information Concerning Black American Troops,* quoted in *Crisis,* in a section called "Documents of the War," May 16–17, 1919.

67   **"was never another country":** Glenda Elizabeth Gilmore, *Defying Dixie: The Radical Roots of Civil Rights, 1919–1950* (New York: W. W. Norton, 2008), 17.

68   **"The forces of hell in this country":** W. E. B. Du Bois, "An Open Letter to Woodrow Wilson" *Crisis,* March 1913, in *W. E. B. Du Bois: A Reader,* ed. David Levering Lewis (New York: Henry Holt, 1995), 445–447.

68   **"the nadir":** The term "nadir" was originally used by historian Rayford W. Logan in *The Betrayal of the Negro: From Rutherford B. Hayes to Woodrow Wilson* (New York: Da Capo Press 1997), 52–53.

68   **"Race is greater than law":** John Sharp Williams, quoted in Lee E. Williams and Lee E. Williams II, *Anatomy of Four Race Riots: Racial Conflict in Knoxville, Elaine (Arkansas), Tulsa, and Chicago, 1919–1921* (Jackson: University Press of Mississippi, 2008), appendix A, 103.

69   **"We turned out the lights early":** Walter White, *A Man Called White* (New York: Viking, 1948), 10–11.

70   **"If a white mob":** Du Bois, quoted in Raymond Wolters, *Du Bois and His Rivals* (Columbia and London: University of Missouri Press, 2002), 75.

71   **fewest lynchings of anyplace in the state:** According to historian W. Fitzhugh Brundage: "When attempted lynchings receive careful scholarly scrutiny, it is likely that the portrait of southern blacks as sullen, powerless victims of mob violence will need serious revision. After most lynchings blacks well understood that vigorous protest would be suppressed brutally by whites. But prior to threatened lynchings aroused blacks were often inventive and vocal opponents of mob violence." Brundage, "The Darien 'Insurrection' of 1899: Black Protest During the Nadir of Race Relations," *Georgia Historical Quarterly* 74, no. 2 (Summer 1990): 234–253.

72   **"No organization like ours":** Du Bois letter to Spingarn, quoted in McWhirter, *Red Summer,* 27.

73   **They, too, were new Negroes:** The song "Lift Every Voice and Sing," known as the "Negro national anthem," was written as a poem by James Weldon Johnson and put to music by his brother, Rosamond, first sung in 1900 by schoolchildren welcoming Booker T. Washington to the Stanton School in Jacksonville, Florida, is a primary example of shifting black attitudes as the twentieth century began. Any verse can be picked out as a vivid illustration. The second of three verses reads:

Stony the road we trod, bitter the chastening rod,
Felt in the days when hope unborn had died;
Yet with a steady beat, have not our weary feet
Come to the place for which our fathers sighed

73   **"making the South safe for Negroes":** In Christopher S. Parker, *Fighting for Democracy: Black Veterans and the Struggle Against White Supremacy in the Postwar South* (Princeton: Princeton University Press, 2009), 33.

73   **"would rather fight to make Georgia safe for democracy"**: In ibid., 34.

74   **"a nigger jumping over the yard"**: Sparks, quoted in Judith N. McArthur and Harold L. Smith, *Texas Through Women's Eyes: The Twentieth-Century Experience* (Austin: University of Texas Press, 2010), 58.

74   **to wait at a nearby call box:** Ibid.

75   **was on its way to attack them:** C. Calvin Smith, "The Houston Riot Revisited," *Houston Review* 13 (1991): 91–92; see also Robert V. Haynes, "The Houston Mutiny and Riot of 1917," 418–439.

76   **"It was not a cold-blooded slaughter of innocents"**: Martha Gruening, "Houston, an N.A.A.C.P. Investigation," *Crisis,* November 1917, 18.

76   **"The negroes, dressed in their regular uniforms"**: "13 Negro Soldiers Hanged for Rioting," *New York Times,* December 12, 1917.

76   **"Thirteen young strong men"**: Du Bois, quoted in Patricia Sullivan, *Lift Every Voice: The NAACP and the Making of the Civil Rights Movement* (New York: New Press, 2009), 71.

77   **"were fighting for France"**: Colson, quoted in Chad Louis Williams, *Torchbearers of Democracy: African American Soldiers in the World War I Era* (Chapel Hill: University of North Carolina Press, 1976), 306.

77   **"There is not a black soldier but who is glad he went"**: Du Bois, "An Essay Toward a History of the Black Man in the Great War," 732–733.

78   **the writer and political activist Hubert Harrison:** The brilliant Hubert Harrison may be the most ignored of the early-twentieth-century black intellectuals. His newspaper, the *Voice,* was the first to emerge as part of the New Negro movement. The Liberty League's program "emphasized internationalism, political independence, and class and race consciousness." Jeffrey B. Perry, *Hubert Harrison: The Voice of Harlem Radicalism, 1883–1918* (New York: Columbia University Press, 2008), 5.

78   **"If white men are to kill unoffending Negroes"**: "Race Radicalism," in *A Hubert Harrison Reader,* ed. Jeffry B. Perry (Middletown, CT: Wesleyan University Press, 2001), 95.

78   **"Negroes can stop lynching in the South"**: "How to Stop Lynching. By the Editors of the *Messenger,*" in *African American Political Thought,* ed. Marcus D. Pohlmann, 6 vols. (New York: Taylor and Francis, 2003), 1: 212–217.

78   **"Each black soldier"**: William Colson, "The Immediate Function of the Black Veteran," *Messenger,* December 1919, 19–20.

79   **"an organization of soldiers, for soldiers, by soldiers"**: Chad Louis Williams, *Torchbearers of Democracy: African American Soldiers in the World War I Era* (Chapel Hill: University of North Carolina Press, 2010), 273.

80   **"I made up my mind"**: Houston, quoted in Gerald Astor, *The Right to Fight: A History of African Americans in the Military* (Cambridge, MA: Da Capo Press, 2001), 112.

80   **"poisoned with political and social equality stuff"**: Robert L. Fleegler, "Theodore G. Bilbo and the Decline of Public Racism, 1938–1947," *Journal of Mississippi History,* Spring 2006: 13.

81   **"The Nazi philosophy crystallizes"**: White, quoted in Gilmore, *Defying Dixie,* 346.

81 **"The fight against Hitlerism":** Quoted in Leon F. Litwack, *How Free Is Free? The Long Death of Jim Crow* (Cambridge, MA: Harvard University Press, 2009), 56.

81 **"So far as the colored peoples of the earth are concerned":** George Schuyler, *Pittsburg Courier,* September 9, 1939.

81 **"This is no fight merely to wear a uniform":** *Crisis* editorial, December 1940, quoted in Stephen Tuck, *We Ain't What We Ought to Be: The Black Freedom Struggle from Emancipation to Obama* (repr. ed.; Cambridge, MA: Belknap Press, 2011), 218.

82 **"We were in war":** Excerpt from transcript of *The Black Press: Soldiers Without Swords,* produced/directed by Stanley Nelson, 1988, www.pbs.org/blackpress/film/.

82 **"We, all of us":** Randolph, quoted in Gilmore, *Defying Dixie,* 361.

Chapter Three: "Fighting for What We Didn't Have"

83 The title quotation is from Neil R. McMillen, *Remaking Dixie: The Impact of World War II on the American South* (Jackson: University Press of Mississippi, 1997), 107.

83 **"Like almost half the whites in Mississippi":** Charles Evers and Andrew Szanton, *Have No Fear: A Black Man's Fight for Respect in America* (New York: John Wiley and Sons, 1997), 60.

83 **"Medgar and I had always wanted to vote":** Ibid., 59.

84 **"We ignored all the nigger baiting":** Ibid., 30.

84 **"You see these two little niggers":** Ibid., 31.

84 **"The best way to keep a nigger from the polls":** Myrlie Evers-Williams, *For Us the Living,* with William Peters (New York: Doubleday, 1967), 26.

85 **"rednecks . . . holding shotguns, rifles, and pistols":** Evers and Szanton, *Have No Fear,* 61.

85 **"I meant to die fighting for Negro rights":** Ibid., 63.

85 **"We'll get them next time":** Ibid., 67.

85 **the whites stopped following them:** John Dittmer, *Local People: The Struggle for Civil Rights in Mississippi* (Urbana and Chicago: University of Illinois Press, 1995), 1–2.

86 **"Fighting World War II woke up a lot of us":** Evers and Szanton, *Have No Fear,* 55.

86 **"For a long time I had the idea":** Amzie Moore, interview by Prudence Arndt for Blackside, 1979, *Eyes on the Prize,* PBS documentary series, Henry Hampton Collection, Washington University Film and Media Archive, Washington University Digital Gateway Texts, St. Louis, Missouri.

87 **"I'd been hungry in my life":** Moore, quoted in Howell Raines, *My Soul Is Rested: Movement Days in the Deep South Remembered* (New York: G. P. Putnam's Sons, 1977), 233–234.

88 **"Amzie was the only one I met on that trip":** Bob Moses, interview with author, April 25, 2013.

88   **"Only mass action":** Clayborne Carson, *In Struggle: SNCC and the Black Awakening of the 1960s* (Cambridge, MA: Harvard University Press, 1981), 27.

88   **especially Freedom Rides:** The Freedom Rides have been so romanticized as challenges to segregation that their greatest significance remains underappreciated: penetration by the Freedom Movement into the rural bastions of white supremacy of the Deep South. Although the rides changed little with regard to segregation in the little towns and hamlets the buses passed through, and despite the bombing of the Freedom Rider bus in Anniston, Alabama, they proved that organized civil rights struggle could be brought into these areas, which had seemed forbidden for so long. The resulting political tremors reached all the way to Washington, D.C.

89   **willing to compromise with southern bigots in order to achieve their political goals:** The response of the Kennedys to every major protest was to ask activists to agree to a "cooling off" period. In a May 24, 1963, meeting at Robert Kennedy's New York City apartment arranged by author James Baldwin, CORE activist Jerome Smith and Kennedy got into a heated argument. A number of prominent African Americans were present, including Harry Belafonte, playwright Lorraine Hansberry, psychologist Kenneth Clark, and singer Lena Horne. Afterward, Kennedy said of the group, "They seemed possessed," and he ordered the FBI to increase surveillance on Baldwin and the other participants. See Arthur M. Schlesinger, *Robert Kennedy and His Times* (New York: First Mariner Books, 1978), 333–334; also Evan Thomas, *Robert Kennedy: His Life* (New York: Simon and Shuster, 2007), 243–245.

90   **Marcus Garvey's UNIA:** There were fifty-six UNIA chapters in Mississippi during the 1920s; thirty-five of them were in the Delta. See Akinyele Omowale Umoja, *We Will Shoot Back: Armed Resistance in the Mississippi Freedom Movement* (New York: New York University Press, 2013), 18–20.

91   **honorably discharged four months later:** John Vernon, "Jim Crow, Meet Lieutenant Robinson: A 1944 Court-Martial," *Prologue* 40, no. 1 (Spring 2008), www.archives.gov/publications/prologue/2008/spring/robinson.html.

92   **rather than in organized political actions:** A notable exception took place in Birmingham, Alabama, after the war when members of the Southern Negro Youth Congress (SNYC) worked with veterans for voter rights. On February 1, 1946, one hundred black veterans converged on the Jefferson County courthouse demanding the right to vote. And in Georgia, black veterans founded the Georgia Veterans League, which had about three hundred members in four chapters.

92   **"The only thing you can say":** Christopher S. Parker, *Fighting for Democracy: Black Veterans and the Struggle Against White Supremacy in the Postwar South* (Princeton: Princeton University Press, 2009), 193; Parker, interview with author, November 7, 2012.

92   **Once, after Myrlie exclaimed, "He's disappeared again!":** Myrlie Evers, interview with author, July 26, 2012.

93   **"southern white folks didn't mess with a few intransigent black people":** Faith S. Holsaert, "Resistance U," in *Hands on the Freedom Plow: Personal Accounts by Women in SNCC*, ed. Faith S. Holsaert et al. (Urbana: University of Illinois Press, 2010), 189.

94   **he never bothered her children again:** Chana Kai Lee, *For Freedom's Sake: The Life of Fannie Lou Hamer* (Urbana: University of Illinois Press, 1999), 11.

94   **"You don't have no black children":** Townsend, quoted in ibid., 12.

95   **"the quintessential 'outraged mother'":** Ibid., 10.

95   **"You better not go around that counter":** Evers and Szanton, *Have No Fear,* 1–2.

95   **"Don't ever let anybody beat you":** Michael Vinson Williams, *Medgar Evers: Mississippi Martyr* (Fayetteville: University of Arkansas Press, 2011), 26–27.

95   **"He didn't smell like fear":** Evers and Szanton, *Have No Fear,* 15.

96   **"That was one of the stories Medgar shared with me":** Myrlie Evers, interview with author, July 26, 2012.

97   **"a little piece of legal crawlspace":** Bob Moses, interview with author, April 25, 2013.

98   **"at least a splinter on my shoulder":** McKaine, quoted in John Egerton, *Speak Now Against the Day: The Generation Before the Civil Rights Movement in the South* (New York: Alfred A. Knopf, 1994), 227.

98   **Henry thought it was "a fortunate thing":** Aaron Henry, *Aaron Henry: The Fire Ever Burning,* with Constance Curry (Jackson: University Press of Mississippi, 2000), 58.

99   **"Three years in the army":** Ibid., 58–63.

99   **"sensed undercurrents rising to the surface":** Ibid., 63.

99   **blacks would never vote in Mississippi:** Gail Williams O'Brien, *The Color of Law: Race Violence and Justice in the Post World War II South* (Chapel Hill: University of North Carolina Press, 1999), 92.

99   **accomplished by bloodshed if necessary:** Nan Elizabeth Woodruff, *American Congo: The African American Freedom Struggle in the Delta* (Cambridge, MA: Harvard University Press, 2009), 214; note that this book gives the Mississippi newspaper editor's name as "E. D. Schneider."

100   **"Actually I believe they were waiting to see":** Henry, *Aaron Henry,* 65.

100–101   **the Soviet Union could point to conditions in the United States:** This is a fascinating dilemma of U.S. diplomacy in the early years of the 1960s. Diplomats from newly independent African nations were routinely denied service in restaurants and prevented from using restrooms when driving between their Washington, D.C., embassies and the United Nations in New York. There was discrimination in housing, as well, particularly in the Washington neighborhoods catering to diplomats. President Kennedy established a special protocol section of the State Department to address this embarrassment, but it made no headway until southern struggle forced the 1964 Civil Rights Act. Kennedy himself was fairly dismissive of the travel problems of African diplomats, saying at one point that instead of driving, they should fly to New York as he always did. Charles E. Cobb Jr., *On the Road to Freedom: A Guided Tour of the Civil Rights Trail* (Chapel Hill, NC: Algonquin Books, 2008), 41.

101   **"I shall make no appeals based on prejudice or passion":** Stennis, quoted in Jason Morgan Ward, *Defending White Democracy: The Making of a Segregationist Move-*

ment and the Remaking of Racial Politics, 1936–1965 (Chapel Hill: University of North Carolina Press, 2011), 107.

103   **be opened to voters of all races:** Until the mid-1940s, political parties established all the rules governing participation in their elections and could therefore exclude members of any group they chose, including blacks. In 1944, however, the Supreme Court declared such rules unconstitutional.

104   **"DO YOU WANT Negroes beside you":** William A. Link, *Righteous Warrior: Jesse Helms and the Rise of Modern Conservatism* (New York: St. Martin's Press, 2008), 38.

104   **The "essence of the liberal position in Georgia in 1946":** Laura Wexler, *Fire in a Canebrake: The Last Mass Lynching in America* (New York: Scribner, 2003), 53.

105   **"far outstripped":** Ulysses Lee, *The Employment of Negro Troops* (Washington, DC: U.S. Army Center of Military History, 2000).

105   **61 percent of black soldiers:** Jennifer E. Brooks, *Defining the Peace: World War II Veterans: Race, and the Remaking of Southern Political Tradition* (Chapel Hill: University of North Carolina Press, 2004), 17.

106   **"We didn't push anything in that time":** Neil R. McMillen, *Remaking Dixie: The Impact of World War II on the American South* (Oxford: University Press of Mississippi, 1997), 106.

106   **"Since I lost a portion of my body":** Brooks, *Defining the Peace,* 19.

109   **"That was one of the first incidents":** Robert F. Williams, *Negroes with Guns* (Detroit: Wayne State University Press, 1998), xviii.

110   **"We ended up with a chapter that was unique":** Ibid., 14.

111   **"We shot it out with the Klan":** Ibid., 19.

111   **"a great and successful leader of our race":** Robert Williams, *Liberation,* September 1959, quoted in Clayborne Carson, senior ed., *The Papers of Martin Luther King,* vol. 5 (Berkeley: University of California Press, 2005), 17.

112   **"mislead Negroes into the belief":** Martin Luther King Jr., *Liberation,* October 1959.

112   **"When the Negro uses force":** King, quoted in Timothy B. Tyson, *Radio Free Dixie: Robert Williams and the Roots of Black Power* (Chapel Hill: University of North Carolina Press, 1999), 215.

113   **"the Lancelot of Monroe":** Tyson, *Radio Free Dixie,* 152.

Chapter Four: "I Wasn't Being Non-Nonviolent"

114   The title quotation is from Hartman Turnbow, quoted in Akinyele Omowale Umoja, *We Will Shoot Back: Armed Resistance in the Mississippi Freedom Movement* (New York: New York University Press, 2013), 75.

116   **"One of the things I felt in Mississippi":** Bob Moses, "This Transformation of People," interview with Charles Payne, in *Debating the Civil Rights Movement, 1945–1968,* ed.

Steven F. Lawson and Charles Payne, 2nd ed. (New York: Rowman and Littlefield), 175–176.

116 **This concern affected priorities:** Because movement organizers were identified as "Freedom Riders" and "nonviolents," there was frequently pressure from young people to launch sit-ins and other direct actions.

117 **"It isn't [done] by getting people":** Ibid., 176.

117 **"You killed my husband!":** Charles M. Payne, *I've Got the Light of Freedom: The Organizing Tradition and the Mississippi Freedom Struggle* (Berkeley: University of California Press, 1995), 124.

118 **"They were afraid of us":** Charles McLaurin, interview with author, March 23, 2012.

118 **"We thought you all was gonna be in the river":** Ibid.

118 **"The basic first step was earning the right":** Bob Moses, interview with author, April 25, 2013.

119 **"It's all dangerous":** Ibid.

119 **"The first obstacle to remove":** Sherrod, quoted in James Forman, *The Making of Black Revolutionaries* (Seattle: University of Washington Press, 1997), 249.

120 **"We wear the mask that grins and lies":** Paul Lawrence Dunbar, "We Wear the Mask," in *Dark Symphony: Negro Literature in America,* ed. James A. Emanuel and Theodore L. Gross (New York: Free Press, 1968), 41.

120 **"Resistance assumed the guise":** W. Fitzhugh Brundage, "The Roar on the Other Side of Silence: Black Resistance and White Violence in the American South, 1880–1940," in *Under Sentence of Death: Lynching in the South,* ed. W. Fitzhugh Brundage (Chapel Hill: University of North Carolina Press, 1997), 274.

121 **relationships in southern culture:** I may have felt this more than Mac and Landy because I was the only one of us in Ruleville without a Mississippi accent.

121 **"To battle institutions":** Lawrence Guyot, comment to author in Greenwood, Mississippi, 1963.

121 **"closed society":** From the title of James W. Silver's important 1964 book *Mississippi: The Closed Society.*

122 **"Joe McDonald had never looked a white man in his face":** McLaurin, interview with author, March 23, 2012.

123 **"my little old ladies":** Charles McLaurin, comment to author, August 1962.

123 **"they made *me* a man":** Charles McLaurin, comment to author (after formal interview), March 23, 2012.

123 **a tremor in the middle of the iceberg:** The letter is well-known in the Freedom Movement. It can be found in its entirety in Forman, *The Making of Black Revolutionaries,* 233.

123 **"Spectacle lynching":** I first heard this term used by Emory University professor Carol Anderson in reference to the large mobs of men, women, and children who gathered to watch and participate in lynchings. Pending lynchings were often advertised in advance, and body parts were often sold or given away as souvenirs afterward.

123   **"Nighttime marauders had learned":** Payne, *I've Got the Light of Freedom,* 204.

124   **"I keep a shotgun":** Mrs. Hamer, quoted in Kay Mills, *This Little Light of Mine: The Life of Fannie Lou Hamer* (Lexington: University Press of Kentucky, 2007), 48.

124   **"You had to turn off the highway":** Hollis Watkins, interview with author, May 31, 2012.

125   **"[to protect] us":** David T. Beito and Linda Royster Beito, "Blacks, Gun Cultures, and Gun Control: T. R. M. Howard, Armed Self-Defense, and the Struggle for Civil Rights in Mississippi," www.saf.org/journal/17/blacks.pdf.

126   **"You don't even have to put it in terms of race":** Hodding Carter III, interview with author, August 26, 2012.

126   **In November 1965, the Ku Klux Klan contacted Deputy Sheriff Earl Fisher:** Lance Hill, *The Deacons for Defense: Armed Resistance and the Civil Rights Movement* (Chapel Hill: University of North Carolina Press, 2004), 244–245.

126   **"Almost all of the planter-farmer types":** Hodding Carter III, interview with author, August 26, 2012.

127   **"There was a great deal of contact":** Ibid.

128   **illustration of this hypocrisy and resistance:** Quoted in Emilye Crosby, *A Little Taste of Freedom: The Black Freedom Struggle in Claiborne County, Mississippi* (Chapel Hill: University of North Carolina Press, 2005), 114.

129   **"We must be willing to kill":** Williams, quoted in Timothy B. Tyson, *Radio Free Dixie: Robert F. Williams and the Roots of Black Power* (Chapel Hill: University of North Carolina Press, 1999), 149.

131   **"Don't Buy Gas Where You Can't Use the Restroom":** It is worth noting that this was not a demand for desegregation, but a demand to have restrooms for blacks at white-owned gas stations. It would be interesting to know to what degree putting on the RCNL bumper sticker endangered drivers and how many actually traveled with it on their vehicle. But I have found no report on this.

131   **"recently sent a direct message":** Howard, quoted in David T. Beito and Linda Royster Beito, *Black Maverick: T. R. M. Howard's Fight for Civil Rights and Economic Power* (Champaign: University of Illinois Press, 2009), 107.

132   **"take the gun from its secret hiding place":** Pittsburg Courier, quoted in ibid., 103.

132   **"scared as hell most of the time":** Simeon Booker, interview with author, July 1, 2013.

132   **"Demonstrating that he bore no resentment":** Simeon Booker, *Shocking the Conscience: A Reporter's Account of the Civil Rights Movement,* with Carol McCabe Booker (Jackson: University Press of Mississippi, 2013), 66. The judge had ordered black reporters to sit at a card table, separate from the white reporters.

132   **"a long gun, a shotgun or a rifle":** Beito and Beito, *Black Maverick,* 120.

134   **"pursuing the agenda of the Klan":** Payne, *I've Got the Light of Freedom,* 34.

134   **"concerned and patriotic citizens to stand together":** Susan M. Weill, "Mississippi's History of Segregation and White Power," in *The Press and Race: Mississippi Journalists*

Confront the Movement, ed. David R. Davies (Jackson: University Press of Mississippi, 2001), 22.

134 **25,000 dues-paying members in the state:** John Dittmer, *Local People: The Struggle for Civil Rights in Mississippi* (Urbana and Chicago: University of Illinois Press, 1995), 45–46.

134 **"Published as a public service by the Citizens' Council of Yazoo City":** Myrlie Evers-Williams, *For Us the Living,* print-on-demand ed. (New York: Doubleday, 1996), 164.

134 **"These people are the agitators and troublemakers":** *Clarksdale Press Register,* quoted in *Aaron Henry: The Fire Ever Burning,* with Constance Curry (Jackson: University Press of Mississippi, 2000), 92.

134 **"Whites looked at the petition list":** Ibid., 93.

135 **"I had weapons in my house":** Stringer, quoted in Dittmer, *Local People,* 47.

135 **"Negro Leader Dies in Odd Accident":** *Jackson Clarion-Ledger,* quoted in ibid., 54.

135 **"was afraid to go to the polls":** *Aaron Henry,* 97.

136 **"My wife and I and thousands of Mississippians":** Courts, quoted in *Aaron Henry,* 97.

136 **"I feel I can do more alive":** Howard, quoted in Booker, *Shocking the Conscience,* 94.

137 **"Kenyatta, Medgar felt instinctively":** Myrlie Evers-Williams, interview with author, July 26, 2012.

137 **"Why not really cross the line?":** Quoted in Michael Vinson Williams, *Medgar Evers: Mississippi Martyr* (Fayetteville: University of Arkansas Press, 2011), 32.

137 **"We bought some bullets":** Evers, quoted in ibid.

137 **"Part of him realized that nothing could be solved by violence but more violence":** Myrlie Evers-Williams, interview with author, July 26, 2012.

137 **"It didn't take much reading of the bible":** Medgar Evers, "Why I Live in Mississippi," interview by Francis Mitchell, *Ebony,* November 1958, 65.

137 **"How's the little Mau Mau?":** Myrlie Evers-Williams, interview with author, July 26, 2012.

138 **"I wasn't being non-nonviolent":** Turnbow, quoted in Umoja, *We Will Shoot Back,* 75.

138 **"They come tellin' me":** Turnbow, quoted in Howell Raines, *My Soul Is Rested: Movement Days in the Deep South Remembered* (New York: G. P. Putnam's Sons, 1977), 265.

139 **"My daddy made sure we knew how to handle a gun":** Hollis Watkins, interview with author, May 31, 2012.

140 **"I was living with Dave Howard and his wife":** Ibid.

141 **"Black people had organized enclaves":** Bob Moses, interview with author, April 25, 2013.

142 **"I felt that you're in your house":** Cooper, quoted in Simon Wendt, *The Spirit and the Shotgun: Armed Resistance and the Struggle for Civil Rights* (Gainesville: University of Florida Press, 2010), 107.

142 **And out in the rural, when Mrs. Laura McGhee:** Payne, *I've Got the Light of Freedom,* 209.

145 **"If there is no struggle, there is no progress":** Frederick Douglass, "An Address on West India Emancipation (August 3, 1857), quoted in Waldo E. Martin Jr., *The Mind of Frederick Douglass* (Chapel Hill: University of North Carolina Press, 1984), 175.

147 **"I ripped into him":** Brenda Travis spent six and a half months in the Oakley reform school. Her mother was fired from her job at McComb. Brenda Travis, interview with author, March 21, 2013.

147 **"Mrs. Cooper wouldn't have turned around":** King, quoted in Josh Gottheimer, ed., *Ripples of Hope: Great American Civil Rights Speeches* (New York: Basic Civitas Books, 2003), 263.

148 **"Most people do not see themselves":** Worth Long, interview with author, March 24, 2012.

Chapter Five: Which Cheek You Gonna Turn?

149 **"Pilgrimage of Friendship":** Quinton Dixie and Peter Eisenstadt, *Visions of a Better World: Howard Thurman's Pilgrimage to India and the Origins of African American Non- violence* (Boston: Beacon Press, 2011), 65.

150 **"It may be through Negroes":** Gandhi, quoted in ibid., 12.

150 **Thurman was an important influence on him:** Dixie and Eisenstadt write in *Visions of a Better World,* "King was quoting Thurman in his sermons even before the latter arrived in Boston" (192). Thurman's slim 1949 book, *Jesus and the Disinherited,* an early rendering of Liberation Theology, had enormous influence on King and many black ministers of his generation. However, there are few references to Thurman in King's writing.

150 **"a cadre of black and white pacifists":** Nishani Frazier, "How CORE Began," (chapter one), from the manuscript of an untitled book to be published by the University of Arkansas Press.

150 **Charles Hamilton Houston, then dean of Howard University's law school, took a ferry:** Patricia Sullivan, *Lift Every Voice: The NAACP and the Making of the Civil Rights Movement* (New York: New Press, 2009), 213.

150 **Howard University student Kenneth Clark:** Henry Louis Gates and Evelyn Brooks Higginbotham, eds., *African American Lives* (New York: Oxford University Press, 2004), 170.

150 **sitting in the whites-only section of a bus:** Victoria Boynton and Jo Malin, eds., *Encyclopedia of Women's Autobiography: K–Z,* (Westport, CT: Greenwood Press, 2005), 416–417; Cheryl Mullenbach, *Double Victory: How African American Women Broke Race and Gender Barriers to Help Win World War II* (Chicago: Chicago Review Press, 2013), 55.

151 **"his courage and his commitment to freedom":** Parks, quoted in Timothy B. Tyson, *Radio Free Dixie: Robert F. Williams and the Roots of Black Power* (Chapel Hill: University of North Carolina Press, 1999), 307.

152 **"We cannot rely on the law":** Williams, quoted in James Forman, *The Making of Black Revolutionaries* (Seattle: University of Washington Press, 1997), 176; also Tyson, *Radio Free Dixie,* 149.

153 **"That's what I said and that's what I am going to tell them":** Phone call between Williams and Wilkins, in Tyson, *Radio Free Dixie,* 150–151.

153 **"Nonviolent workshops are springing up throughout black communities":** Williams, quoted in Christopher B. Strain, *Pure Fire, Self-Defense as Activism in the Civil Rights Era* (Athens: University of Georgia Press, 2005), 64. In a revealingly angry passage from an unpublished and undated manuscript cited by Strain here, while exiled Williams wrote, "There is an air that approximates latent racism and white chauvinism about these nonviolent moralists who cannot stand the thought of oppressed Afro-Americans defending themselves . . . [while they] are being raped, maimed, legally framed, murdered, starved, and driven into exile. What is more brutal? What is more violent?" 65.

155 **the historically black women's college just a few blocks away from A&T:** Bennett College president Willa Player is one of the great examples of the changing times. At the peak of the Greensboro protests, as many as 40 percent of Bennett students—known as the "Bennett belles"—were under arrest. Ms. Player backed them fully; she visited with them every day and arranged for professors to hold classes for them. "Willa Player, 94, Pioneer Black Educator Dies," *New York Times,* August 20, 2008.

155 **"Who do you think you are?" one of the whites yelled:** William H. Chafe, *Civilities and Civil Rights: Greensboro, North Carolina, and the Black Struggle for Freedom* (Oxford, New York, Toronto, and Melbourne: Oxford University Press, 1981), 85.

155 **"McNeil said, 'Well, we ought to have something like a boycott'":** Ezell Blair, transcript of a taped conversation among Ezell Blair, Stokely Carmichael, Jean Wheeler, and Lucy Thornton, with Robert Penn Warren, at Howard University, March 4, 1964, 1–2, in Robert Penn Warren's website Who Speaks for the Negro, www.whospeaks.library.vanderbilt. edu/interview/ezell-blair-stokely-carmichael-lucy-thornton-and-jean-wheeler.

156 **"police came from everywhere":** Rodney L. Hurst Sr., interview with author, November 18, 2013; also Hurst, *It Was Never About a Hot Dog and a Coke!* (Livermore, CA: WingSpan Press, 2008), 77.

157 **"the philosophical or religious ideal of nonviolence":** SNCC founding document, in *The 1960s: A Documentary Reader,* ed. Brian Ward (Malden MA: Wiley-Blackwell, 2010), 69–70.

157 **"We knew we wanted to be students":** Lonnie C. King, interview with author, February 11, 2013.

157 **"there really wasn't that much debate about it":** Charles McDew, interview with author, January 31, 2013

158 **"In Atlanta we accepted [nonviolence] as a tactic":** Lonnie King, interview with author, February 11, 2013.

158 **Acceptance of nonviolence as a way of life":** Charles "Chuck" McDew, interview with author, March 23, 2012.

158 **"When they arrested us they published our addresses":** Lonnie King, interview with author, February 11, 2013.

158 **"Charles Johnson, a Korean War veteran, told me this later":** Ibid.

159 **"I'd only heard about it because I read about [Martin Luther King] in newspapers":** Charles Sherrod, interview with author, October 30, 2012.

160 **"The only thing that ever caused me to question my nonviolence":** Ibid.

160 **were influenced more by the example of their fellow students:** Reverend King must be given a great deal of credit for students' interest in nonviolent direct action. It was the Montgomery, Alabama, bus boycott and his articulation of it that put nonviolence in the national media and thus into student consciousness.

160 **"And Lonnie said to me, 'Why don't we do this here?'":** Julian Bond, interview with author, October 12, 2012.

161 **Only seven other students were enrolled:** Julian Bond provided me with an official class list.

161 **"I took the gun home":** Annie Pearl Avery, "There Are No Cowards in My Family," in *Hands on the Freedom Plow: Personal Accounts by Women in SNCC,* ed. Faith S. Holsaert et al. (Urbana: University of Illinois Press, 2010), 455, 457.

162 **"The civil rights movement was about civil rights":** Ivanhoe Donaldson, interview with author, April 23, 2013.

162 **"inconsequential and fleeting":** Stokely Carmichael, *Ready for Revolution: The Life and Struggles of Stokely Carmichael (Kwame Ture),* with Ekwueme Michael Thelwell (New York: Scribner, 2003), 139.

162 **"that made a believer out of me. Instantly":** Ibid. Readers may wonder why. Stokely told me years ago that it was the image of young people—people his own age—engaged in struggle that captured him. Until he saw the sit-ins on television and read about them in the newspapers, civil rights struggles seemed to be something that grown-ups did.

162 **"I remember my first reaction":** Courtland Cox, interview with author, January 6, 2013.

163 **"The Negro race, like all races":** W. E. B. Du Bois, "The Talented Tenth," in *The Negro Problem: A Series of Articles by Representative American Negroes of Today,* ed. Booker T. Washington, facsimile reprint of the original 1903 book published by James Pott (Whitefish, MT: Kessinger Publishing, 2008), 33.

163 **their intellectual and political energy was evident:** So far, five "SNCC people" have been recipients of MacArthur Fellowship Genius Grants: Bob Moses, Bernice Johnson Reagon, Unita Blackwell, Maria Varela, and Marian Wright Edelman.

164 **"There will be no more discussion of protest":** This event was described to me in conversation with David Dennis, then a high school student on the campus along with Hubert "Rap" Brown. (Black universities often had schools on their campuses in those days.) Dennis would later become the CORE field director for Mississippi.

165 **"I was nervous about being under the leadership of any adult":** Lonnie King, interview with author, February 11, 2013.

165   **"Not long after we began sitting-in":** Ibid.

166   **"My daddy was a World War II veteran":** Ibid.

166   **dissolved the student government because of civil rights protests:** John Dittmer, *Local People: The Struggle for Civil Rights in Mississippi* (Urbana and Chicago: University of Illinois Press, 1995), 116.

166   **"I understood why adults favored gradualism":** Lonnie King, interview with author, February 11, 2013.

166   **"We had the confidence of a Mack truck":** McCain, quoted in Chafe, *Civilities and Civil Rights,* 83.

167   **"Something happened to me":** Anne Moody, *The Coming of Age in Mississippi* (New York: Dial Press, 1968), 235.

167   **"There was a clarity about everything":** Johnson, quoted in Emilye Crosby, "The Politics of Movement History," in *Civil Rights History from the Ground Up: Local Struggles, a National Movement,* ed. Emilye Crosby (Athens and London: University of Georgia Press, 2011), 19.

167   **a voter-registration wing and a direct-action wing:** Nashville, Tennessee, student leader Diane Nash headed the direct-action wing, and Charlotte, North Carolina, student protest leader Charles Jones headed the voter-registration wing.

168   **"was like a stop on the Underground Railroad":** Peggy Trotter Dammond Preacely, "Standing Tall," in *Hands on the Freedom Plow,* ed. Holsaert et al., 168.

169   **"[Mama Dolly] had this big shotgun":** Charles Sherrod, interview with author, October 30, 2012.

169   **"When we slept at night":** Preacely, "Standing Tall," 170.

170   **young black people emerged to help him:** In rural Chisholm Mission, about twenty miles from McComb, Hollis Watkins was told that Martin Luther King had come to McComb and traveled there to meet him. He was directed to Moses and asked him if he was Reverend King. Moses told him no and explained that he was in town to work on voter registration. He asked Hollis and his friend Curtis Hayes, who had accompanied him to McComb, if they would be willing to help. Both said yes. Charles E. Cobb Jr., *On the Road to Freedom: A Guided Tour of the Civil Rights Trail* (Chapel Hill, NC: Algonquin Books, 2008), 283–284.

170   **a local nonviolent organization:** The organization was the Pike County Nonviolent Movement. Hollis was president; Curtis was vice president.

171   **"I've been expecting you":** Robert P. Moses and Charles E. Cobb Jr., *Radical Equations: Civil Rights from Mississippi to the Algebra Project* (Boston: Beacon Press, 2001), 49.

171   **"as you went to bed":** McDew, quoted in Akinyele Omowale Umoja, *We Will Shoot Back: Armed Resistance in the Mississippi Freedom Movement* (New York and London: New York University Press, 2013), 60.

171   **almost everyone in Amite County seemed to know it was there:** Charles M. Payne, *I've Got the Light of Freedom: The Organizing Tradition and the Mississippi Freedom Struggle,* with a new preface (Berkeley: University of California Press, 2007), 114.

172   **"In the mythology of the Movement":** Jack Newfield, "From Liberty in Miss. to Justice in D.C.," *Village Voice*, December 2, 1965.

172   **"Farmers came over and were very anxious to try and register":** Moses, quoted in Dittmer, *Local People*, 105.

172   **It quickly became apparent just how dangerous those places were:** Dittmer, *Local People*, 108.

172   **Britt later reported to SNCC:** Forman, *The Making of Black Revolutionaries*, 230.

173   **"Can we really keep doing this?":** Moses and Cobb, *Radical Equations*, 51.

173   **sit-ins were not why they had invited them to McComb:** Sit-ins were not why Moses had come to McComb, either. The student protests caught Moses, McDew, and others working on voter registration by surprise. McDew was in McComb at the time for Moses's voter-registration effort. He commented that when he was confronted with the fact of student protest, "I thought about Gandhi when he saw his people massed for protest. 'There go our people,' he said. 'We have to hurry and catch up with them.'" Moses and Cobb, *Radical Equations*, 53.

173   **"had, to put it mildly, got our feet wet":** Moses, quoted in Taylor Branch, *The King Years: Historic Moments in the Civil Rights Movement* (New York: Simon and Shuster, 2013), 44.

174   **"I had become part of something else":** Moses and Cobb, *Radical Equations*, 56.

174   **"If you went into Mississippi":** Robinson, quoted in Seth Cagin and Philip Dray, *We Are Not Afraid: The Story of Goodman, Schwerner, and Chaney and the Civil Rights Campaign for Mississippi* (New York: Avalon Publishing Group, 2006), 145.

175   **to be staffed largely by SNCC and CORE field secretaries:** This effort was funded by the newly created Voter Education Project (VEP) based in Atlanta and funded with money from the Taconic Foundation. The COFO proposal for funding submitted in February 1962 was not approved until August. And although only $14,000 was granted for Mississippi, it enabled SNCC and CORE field secretaries to work on subsistence salaries for a year.

175   **Moses and SNCC targeted the Delta:** The Delta was also the real center of white power in the state.

175   **"My position":** Bob Moses, interview with author, April 25, 2013.

177   **"Steptoe and other people [in Amite County] chided me a lot":** Ibid.

177   **"Daddy wanted to put a gun in the car":** Eldridge W. Steptoe Jr., transcript of interview with Jimmy Dykes for the University of Southern Mississippi Oral History Project, November 14, 1995, 10, University of Southern Mississippi Oral History Collections, Hattiesburg.

177   **"I asked a local man to fire on anyone":** Peacock, quoted in Mary King, *Freedom Song: A Personal Story of the 1960s Civil Rights Movement* (New York: William Morrow, 1987), 311–312.

178   **Both sides argued their positions passionately:** The quotations in this paragraph from the discussion about nonviolence come from King, *Freedom Song*, 314.

179   **"Don't you see?":** Guyot, quoted in Taylor Branch *Pillar of Fire: America in the King Years, 1963–65* (New York: Touchstone Edition, 1999), 331.

179   **"At a mass meeting two nights after the last shooting":** Harris, quoted in Mary King, *Freedom Song,* 312.

180   **"My instructions were that nobody was to have guns":** Charles Sherrod, interview with author, October 30, 2012.

180   **in the rifles sight of an angry young black man:** Shirley Miller Sherrod, interview with author, October 30, 2012.

181   **"Mrs. Brewer asked me what did SNCC mean":** Block, quoted in Umoja, *We Will Shoot Back,* 83.

181   **"spilling gas everywhere":** Block, quoted in ibid., 111.

182   **"When I saw Red had a rifle":** Bernard Lafayette, interview with author, March 1, 2013.

183   **"Things happened so fast":** Sales, quoted in Cobb, *On the Road to Freedom,* 243.

183   **began purchasing large quantities of ammunition and some weapons:** Hasan Kwame Jeffries, *Bloody Lowndes: Civil Rights and Black Power in Alabama's Black Belt* (New York and London: New York University Press, 2009), 102–103.

183   **"Wal, in this county":** Strickland, quoted in Carmichael, *Ready for Revolution,* 458.

183   **"and Stokely wasn't inside the house":** Ivanhoe Donaldson, comment to author.

184   **"I got three guns from Mr. Steptoe":** Chuck McDew, interview with author, March 23, 2012.

184   **"there really wasn't any lengthy discussion":** Ibid.

185   **"The fire chief said the bomb was meant for us":** Dorie Ladner, interview with author, May 30, 2013.

185   **"I didn't think about white people and violence":** Ibid.

186   **"I am not a violent person":** Ibid.

Chapter Six: Standing Our Ground

187   **recalls being in the courtroom of the county courthouse:** David Dennis, interview with author, March 9, 2013.

188   **"There are only two bad sons of bitches":** Noble, quoted in ibid.

188   **"Every white man in that town":** Mateo Suarez, "An Oral History with Matt Suarez," interview with Harriet Tanzman, October 25, 2003, Civil Rights Documentation Project, University of Sothern Mississippi, Hattiesburg, www.usm.edu/crdp/html/transcripts/manuscript-suarez_matt.shtml.

189   **"was always fearless":** Mamie Chinn, interview with author, October 30, 2012.

189   **"He was raised to believe":** Clarence Chinn, interview with author, October 30, 2012.

189 **"Nowhere was there a pamphlet"**: Emily Stoper, "The Student Nonviolent Coordinating Committee: Rise and Fall of a Redemptive Organization," *Journal of Black Studies* 8, no. 1 (September 1977): 16.

189 **"meet the anger of any individual or group"**: Lance Hill, *The Deacons for Defense: Armed Resistance and the Civil Rights Movement* (Chapel Hill: University of North Carolina Press, 2004), 20.

190 **"[Chinn] believed we were doing the right thing"**: Mateo Suarez, interview with author, June 26, 2012. Although C. O. Chinn is celebrated in Canton today as "father" of the civil rights movement, it must be noted that he lost virtually everything he owned because of his movement commitment. He also served several years in jail.

190 **"Whenever we have a meeting"**: Dave Dennis, interview with author, March 9, 2013.

192 **"Don't stop for anything and, if forced to stop, shoot"**: James Farmer, *Lay Bare the Heart: An Autobiography of the Civil Rights Movement* (New York: Arbor House, 1985), 252.

192 **"[Education] was needed to cement the relation"**: Greta de Jong, *A Different Day: African American Struggles for Justice in Rural Louisiana, 1900–1970* (Chapel Hill: University of North Carolina Press, 2002), 189.

192 **"I value my life even more"**: Carter, quoted in Bob Adelman, "Birth of a Voter," CORE reprint, www.crmvet.org/info/63_core_adelman_voter.pdf; first published as "Birth of a Voter: Louisiana Parish Registers 1st Negro in 61 Years," *Ebony*, February 1964, 88–98, www.books.google.com/books?id=zjhihJmXoMcC&pg=PA88&source=gbs_toc_r&cad=2#v=onepage&q&f=false.

193 **"a nickel's worth of red beans"**: Long, quoted in Adam Fairclough, *Race and Democracy: The Civil Rights Struggle in Louisiana, 1915–1972* (Athens: University of Georgia Press, 1999), 44.

194 **"but most people nevertheless lived in abject poverty"**: "The town was little more than an appendage to a sawmill—crude shacks storing the human machinery of industry," writes historian Lance Hill, executive director of the Southern Institute for Education and Research. Hill, *The Deacons for Defense*, 12.

196 **their "freedom house"—their living quarters and operational headquarters**: Sometimes CORE and SNCC organizers stayed with families, and sometimes, as was the case in Jonesboro, they were given or rented houses from which they operated. These houses were known as "freedom houses" and were often targets of attack because they were generally unarmed.

196 **"was unbelievably supportive"**: Fred Brooks, interview with author, June 30, 2013.

197 **"What happened," Brooks related**: Ibid.

197 **"If we had a picket line"**: Ibid.

197 **"Many of these guys were older people! Old people!"**: Ibid.

198 **had, in fact, been born in Natchez, Mississippi**: Fairclough, *Race and Democracy*, 341.

198 **had studied engineering at Tulane University in New Orleans**: Charles Marsh, *The Last Days: A Son's Story of Sin and Segregation at the Dawn of a New South* (New York: Basic Books 2001), 36.

198   **"The concept that we are going to go South":** Adam Fairclough, *Race and Democracy,* 341.

198   **"They were looking for some black policemen to do their dirty work":** Thomas, quoted in Hill, *The Deacons for Defense,* 32.

199   **an armed escort for Moore and Lesser as they drove back to Monroe later that night:** Ibid., 34–35.

199   **The police chief also ordered two of the protesters' mothers arrested:** Ibid., 36–37.

199   **"there was going to be some killing going on":** Thomas, quoted in ibid., 37–38.

200   **Jackson's wife had opened fire on them:** Ibid., 40.

201   **"I got out of the car and realized that I was surrounded":** Fenton, quoted in ibid., 43.

201   **"Fenton was the one":** Fred Brooks, interview with author, June 30, 2013.

202   **"I hope that they will become a civic organization":** Fenton, quoted in Fred Powledge, "Armed Negroes Make Jonesboro Unusual Town," *New York Times,* February 21, 1965.

202   **"We were telling [CORE's national leadership]":** Dave Dennis, interview with author, June 24, 2013.

202   **"The Deacons have the effect":** Haley, quoted in Roy Reed, "Armed Negro Unit Spreads in South," *New York Times,* June 6, 1965.

204   **"I think it's best to discuss the controllable things":** Moses, quoted in Mary King, *Freedom Song: A Personal Story of the 1960s Civil Rights Movement* (New York: William Morrow, 1987), 318.

205   **"CORE nonviolence—never a way of life, but only a strategy—ended":** James Farmer, introduction to Inge Powell Bell, *CORE and the Strategy of Nonviolence* (New York: Random House, 1968), v; see also Simon Wendt, *The Spirit and the Shotgun: Armed Resistance and the Struggle for Civil Rights* (Gainesville: University Press of Florida, 2010), 69.

205   **"four tiers of membership in the Jonesboro Deacons":** Hill, *The Deacons for Defense,* 54.

206   **forming a women's auxiliary—"Deaconettes":** Christopher B. Strain, *Pure Fire: Self-Defense as Activism in the Civil Rights Era* (Athens: University of Georgia Press, 2005), 111.

206   **"A number of these men were church-going folk":** Dave Dennis to author, June 23, 2012.

206   **"Let's call ourselves the Deacons":** Frederick Douglass Kirkpatrick, Pete Seeger, and Jeanne Humphries, *Ballads of Black America,* 1972, Smithsonian Folkways, Archive Smithsonian Center for Folklife and Cultural Heritage, Washington, DC, sound recording.

207   **On March 8 students organized a boycott of the high school:** United Press International, March 29, 1965.

207   **"Men, take firing positions":** Christopher S. Parker, *Fighting for Democracy: Black Veterans and the Struggle Against White Supremacy in the Postwar South* (Princeton: Princeton University Press, 2009), 3; see also Fred Brooks, interview with author, June 30, 2013.

207   **into other parts of Louisiana, and then into a few other parts of the South:** How large or wide this expansion was remains unclear. It was certainly not to the fifty-five chapters later claimed by the Deacons.

208   **an entirely new segment of the black population in the South:** In the urban North, the Black Panther Party for Self-Defense (formed in Oakland, California, in October 1966) had a similar effect, as did the NAACP branch organized in Monroe, North Carolina, by Robert Williams, although that branch was not organized for the specific purpose of self-defense, as the Deacons were.

208   **"no redeeming touch of grace, beauty, or elegance":** Howell Raines, *My Soul Is Rested: Movement Days in the Deep South Remembered* (New York: G. P. Putnam's Sons, 1977), 416.

208   **"segregated from cradle to coffin":** Quoted in Fairclough, *Race and Democracy,* 348.

209   **"tagged as integrationists":** Strain, *Pure Fire,* 101.

209   **legislation aimed at destroying the NAACP:** These laws required that the names and addresses of all NAACP members and officers be revealed to the state government and required the organization to file an annual affidavit that none of their officers or of any out-of-state parent corporation (such as the national NAACP in New York) was affiliated with any communist, communist-front, or subversive organization, as defined by the U.S. House Un-American Activities Committee (HUAC). When the NAACP refused to file the affidavit, the state attorney general obtained an injunction barring it from "doing any business or acting as a corporation in Louisiana." See "Louisiana Moves to Oust N.A.A.C.P.," *New York Times,* March 2, 1956.

210   **"We have better things to do":** Quoted in Fairclough, *Race and Democracy,* 354.

210   **"My husband could never go out":** Valeria Hicks, quoted in Paul Pederson, "Deacons Prevented Violence Against Black Struggle in '60s," *Militant* 76, no. 11 (March 19, 2012); also see Hill, *The Deacons for Defense,* 92–93.

211   **"Up to that point I embraced nonviolence":** Miller, quoted in Hill, *The Deacons for Defense,* 96–98.

210   **the Klan attack never took place:** "I knew the men he wanted me to call because the names had already been placed on the wall by the telephone for times and situations we knew would soon come," says Hicks's daughter Barbara Hicks Collins. "My father had to prepare his children for the times." E-mail to author, January 27, 2014.

211   **Charles Sims, an insurance salesman and a legendary brawler:** "I've been in jail 27 times," Sims told an interviewer: "Three cases of speeding, about twenty cases of battery." Quoted in Philip Ardery, "Charles Sims, Silhouette," *Harvard Crimson,* December 10, 1965, www.thecrimson.com/article/1965/12/10/charles-sims-pif-youre-white-and/.

212   **"It takes violent blacks to combat these violent whites":** Thomas, quoted in Fairclough, *Race and Democracy,* 357–358.

212   **"We must obey the law":** Cutrer, quoted in Strain, *Pure Fire,* 102.

213   **"CORE is nonviolent," Farmer said later:** Farmer, quoted in ibid., 103.

213   **"CORE had projects throughout this part of Louisiana":** Dave Dennis, interview with author, March 9, 2013.

213   **"They were telling me how dangerous it was":** Mateo Suarez, interview with author, June 23, 2012.

213   **"were the forerunners of the Deacons for Defense":** James Forman, *The Making of Black Revolutionaries* (Seattle: University of Washington Press, 1997), 149.

214   **"aggressive violence":** Hamilton Bims, quoted in Hill, *The Deacons for Defense,* 162.

214   **"I'm gonna kill me a nigger tonight":** Thomas A. Parker, ed., *Violence in the U.S.,* vol. 1, *1956–67* (New York: Facts on File, 1974), 69.

215   **"between witnessing change or experiencing destruction":** Richardson, Geltson, and Citizens' Council spokesman, all quoted in "Gloria Richardson: Lady General of Civil Rights," *Ebony,* July 1964, 23–31.

215   **kidnapping of local movement leader Dr. Robert Hayling:** Dr. Hayling and the others were rescued because Reverend Irvin Cheney, a white minister who had slipped into the Klan rally, called the Florida Highway Patrol. By the time the police arrived, Hayling and his fellow activists had been beaten and were stacked like firewood in preparation for being doused with gasoline and burned alive.

215   **"This was about the roughest city we've had":** Cotton, quoted in Guy and Candie Carawan, eds. *Sing for Freedom: The Story of the Civil Rights Movement Through Its Songs* (Montgomery, AL: NewSouth Books, 2007), 115.

216   **"I and the others have armed":** Hayling, quoted in Taylor Branch, *Pillar of Fire: America in the King Years, 1963–65* (New York: Touchstone Edition, 1997), 111.

217   **"I'm tired":** Herzfeld, quoted in Wendt, *The Spirit and the Shotgun,* 48.

218   **His wife, LaPelzia Rogers, stood in sharp contrast:** Ibid., 52.

219   **"At that time, I wasn't a civil rights man":** Quoted in ibid., 54.

220   **"If we're going to do this thing, let's do it right":** Quoted in Harold A. Nelson, "The Defenders," *Social Problems* 15, no. 2 (Autumn 1967): 131. This study, the only one I have found on the Tuscaloosa group, is cited in Simon Wendt's *The Spirit and the Shotgun,* 57, and that reference is what led me to it. The study is unusual because Nelson uses pseudonyms; most of his sources demanded anonymity (128–129). Thus, Nelson calls Mallisham's unnamed group "The Defenders," Mallisham is called "William Smith," Tuscaloosa is called "Southville," and TCAC is called the Southville Action Organization (SAO). In any case, Nelson's study was published by a refereed journal.

220   **"The organization functions in a semi-secret manner":** Nelson, "The Defenders," 131–134.

221   **"As soon as [Mallisham] is informed of an incident":** Ibid., 138.

223   **"I'm here to see that the struggle remains nonviolent":** Quoted in Wendt, *The Spirit and the Shotgun,* 60.

224   **"violence-cannot-be-allowed-to-stop-the-movement reflex":** Stokely Carmichael, *Ready for Revolution: The Life and Struggles of Stokely Carmichael (Kwame Ture),* with Ekwueme Michael Thelwell (New York: Scribner, 2003), 449.

225   **"It was obvious to me from the beginning":** Cleveland Sellers, *The River of No Return:*

The Autobiography of a Black Militant and the Life and Death of SNCC, with Robert Terrell (Jackson: University Press of Mississippi, 1990), 162.

225   **"We did not want the march to lose its militancy":** Stokely Carmichael, comment to author, 1997.

226   **"Tactically and strategically the Deacons knew they couldn't maintain their usual posture":** Watkins, quoted in Akinyele Omowale Umoja, *We Will Shoot Back: Armed Resistance in the Mississippi Freedom Movement* (New York and London: New York University Press, 2013), 158.

Epilogue: "The King of Love Is Dead"

227   The title quotation is from Gene Taylor's song *"Why? (The King of Love Is Dead),"* which can be heard at www.npr.org/2008/04/06/89418339/why-remembering-nina-simones-tribute-to-the-rev-martin-luther-king-jr. Taylor, singer Nina Simone's bass player, wrote this song in reaction to hearing that Martin Luther King had been assassinated.

227   **"can mean in the end only black death":** *Crisis*, August–September 1984, 58.

227   **"unfortunate":** *The Martin Luther King, Jr. Companion: Quotations from the Speeches, Essays, and Books of Martin Luther King, Jr.*, selected by Coretta Scott King (New York: St. Martin's Press, 1993), 78.

227   **"betrayed the movement":** Lawson, www.breachofpeace.com/blog/?paged=4.

228   **"We are all, let us face it, Mississippians":** Quoted in Peniel E. Joseph, *Waiting 'til the Midnight Hour: A Narrative History of Black Power in America* (New York: Henry Holt and Company, 2006), 146.

229   **"Are our [Negroes] to be presented with freedom and a dagger?":** Jefferson to Adams, January 22, 1821, in "Quotations on Slavery and Emancipation," Jefferson Monticello website, www.monticello.org/site/jefferson/quotations-slavery-and-emancipation.

229   **"The movement's no place for guns":** Seamons, quoted in Taylor Branch, *At Canaan's Edge: America in the King Years, 1965–68* (New York: Simon and Shuster, 2006), 483.

230   **"We been head-lifted and upstarted":** Ruby Doris Smith Robinson, press conference, May 23, 1966, quoted in Taylor Branch, *At Canaan's Edge*, 469. Her words are a play on "uplift" and the then new Head Start antipoverty program.

231   **enough additional participants to create a white majority:** A few days later, one of these whites stopped by the NAACP leader's drugstore and told him, "I'm sure glad y'all went there to the voting place," Henry recalled in his autobiography. "They never let us get involved before, but when y'all showed up, they called us and let us have something to say at last." Aaron Henry, *Aaron Henry: The Fire Ever Burning*, with Constance Curry (Jackson: University Press of Mississippi, 2000), 172.

232   **"We didn't come all this way":** Kay Mills, *This Little Light of Mine: The Life of Fannie Lou Hamer* (Lexington: University Press of Kentucky, 2007), 5.

232   **"We were trying":** Bob Moses, quoted in Robert P. Moses and Charles E. Cobb Jr., *Rad-*

ical Equations: Civil Rights from Mississippi to the Algebra Project (Boston: Beacon Press, 2001), 82.

232   **"The national Democratic Party's rejection of the MFDP":** Cleveland Sellers, *The River of No Return: The Autobiography of a Black Militant and the Life and Death of SNCC,* with Robert Terrell (Jackson: University Press of Mississippi, 1990), 111.

233   **Alabama law required political parties to have a visual symbol:** The symbol of Alabama's Democratic Party was a white rooster, usually displayed with the slogan "White supremacy for the right." Stokely sometimes called the party "the white cock party."

233   **"The black panther . . . said":** Hulett, quoted in Stokely Carmichael, *Ready for Revolution: The Life and Struggles of Stokely Carmichael [Kwame Ture],* with Ekwueme Michael Thelwell (New York: Scribner, 2003), 464.

234   **"There ain't no Negro in Alabama":** *Hosea* Williams, quoted in Hasan Kwame Jeffries, *Bloody Lowndes: Civil Rights and Black Power in Alabama's Black Belt* (New York: New York University Press, 2009), 167.

234   **"We just told folks to pull the lever":** Courtland Cox, interview with author, January 6, 2013.

234   **"What you have in this country":** Carmichael, quoted in Jeffries, *Bloody Lowndes,* 170.

236   **"Mrs. Hamer is no longer relevant":** Clayborne Carson, *In Struggle: SNCC and the Black Awakening of the 1960s* (Cambridge, MA: Harvard University Press, 2001), 240.

237   **"We were all tired":** Cleveland Sellers, interview with author in 1997 for *Emerge* magazine article, "From Stokely Carmichael to Kwame Ture," republished in *Callaloo* 34, no. 1 (Winter 2011): 89–97.

Afterword: Understanding History

239   **"I tried to aim my gun":** Walter White, *A Man Called White* (New York: Viking, 1948), 10–11.

240   **"full retaliation from the black community":** Clayborne Carson, *In Struggle: SNCC and the Black Awakening of the 1960s* (Cambridge, MA: Harvard University Press, 2001), 254.

243   **"The same low-income young people of color":** James Forman Jr., "Racial Critiques of Mass Incarceration: Beyond the New Jim Crow," *New York University Law Review* 87, no. 1 (February 2012).

243   **"There are many inner-city communities where individuals work":** Maria Varela, e-mail to author, August 17, 2013.

244   **"We are a very violent culture":** Ivanhoe Donaldson, interview with author, August 15, 2013.

244   **"It would certainly be a lot nicer":** Thomas Sowell, "Egyptian Mirages," *Real Clear Politics,* August 20, 2013, www.realclearpolitics.com/articles/2013/08/20/reality_versus_mirages_in_egypt_119642.html.

245   **"It's still always about the mission":** Ivanhoe Donaldson, interview with author, August 15, 2013.

245   **"SNCC was very rare":** Ibid.

246   **"In order for us as poor and oppressed people":** Ella Baker, quoted in Robert P. Moses and Charles E. Cobb Jr., *Radical Equations: Civil Rights from Mississippi to the Algebra Project* (Boston: Beacon Books, 2001), 3.

247   **"Rosa sat down":** Julian Bond, comment to author.

247   **"When I read about the Albany Movement":** Emilye Crosby, "The Politics of Movement History," in *Civil Rights History from the Ground Up: Local Struggles, a National Movement,* ed. Emilye Crosby (Athens: University of Georgia Press, 2011), 19.

247   **"The mistake I made there":** Martin Luther King Jr., interview by Alex Haley, *Playboy,* January 1965, as republished in: *A Testament of Hope: The Essential Writings of Martin Luther King, Jr.,* ed. James M. Washington (San Francisco: HarperSanFrancisco, 1991), 344.

248   **"gave me the power to challenge *any* line":** Quoted in Crosby, "The Politics of Movement History," 9.

248   **"What did we win?":** Searles, quoted in Pete Seeger and Bob Reiser, *Everybody Says Freedom: A History of the Civil Rights Movement in Songs and Pictures* (New York: W. W. Norton, 2009), 81.

250   **"In the practice of guerilla history":** Staughton Lynd, *Doing History from the Bottom Up: On E. P. Thompson, Howard Zinn, and Rebuilding the Labor Movement from Below* (Chicago: Haymarket Books, forthcoming), preface.

INDEX